with love, to John,)
Marion

To John Evans

with every good wish

Margaret H Harris

# ONE OF THE PRESIDENTS' MEN

# ONE OF THE PRESIDENTS' MEN

## TWENTY YEARS WITH EISENHOWER AND NIXON

MAURICE H. STANS

BRASSEY'S
Washington • London

**Library of Congress Cataloging-in-Publication Data**

Stans, Maurice H., 1908–
    One of the presidents' men: twenty years with Eisenhower and
Nixon/Maurice H. Stans.
        p.   cm.
    Includes index.
    ISBN 1-57488-032-2
    1. Stans, Maurice H., 1908–   .  2. Cabinet officers—United
States—Biography.   I. Title.
E840.8.S65A3   1995
330'.092—dc20                                                95–11351

10 9 8 7 6 5 4 3 2 1

Printed in the United States of America.

*To Kathleen, my beloved companion
for fifty-one years, who shared with me the
satisfactions and disappointments recorded in this
book with calm and confidence.*

# Contents

# Acknowledgments

To Arden Kendall, Mary Elia, Sharon Gregory, and Kit-Bacon Gressitt, who presided excellently over the mechanical and technical aspects of producing the manuscript for this book.

To Robert Smalley, my former speechwriter, whose review of the first draft of this manuscript was invaluable in shaping it.

# Foreword

A generation hence, those writing honest accounts of the cold war will emphasize the presidencies of Dwight David Eisenhower and Richard Nixon. An important link between those epochal eras was Maurice H. Stans, who served Eisenhower as director of the Bureau of Budget and Nixon as secretary of commerce. His new memoir, apart from being a fascinating account of an inspiring American life, contains vital information about our times that no fair historian can afford to neglect.

The two presidents shared much in common but nothing as abiding as their high regard for Maury Stans. The day after winning the 1968 election, when Nixon called on Eisenhower in his suite at Walter Reed, the former president made only two specific requests of the president-elect. One was to name Stans to an important Cabinet post. Stans, said the general, "is one of the ablest and finest men I have known in government." President Nixon, in turn, considered Stans to be one of the most decent and dedicated members of his own administration, where among many other accomplishments he blazed new trails in encouraging minority capitalism, an issue that would become a lifelong preoccupation. In his first book, *The Terrors of Justice*, he described the witch-hunt to which he was subjected during the latter days of the Nixon administration. He and many others were viciously harassed for no other reason than that they had been loyal supporters and friends of the president. Previously unknown but now revealed in *One of the Presidents' Men* is that Stans received similar treatment in the early 1960s at the hands of the Democrats as a result, in large part, of his equally loyal service to President Eisenhower as one of our country's fiercest and most effective watchdogs of the public purse.

The reader who thinks fiscal prudence was easier in the late 1950s than now need only consult the second volume of Eisenhower's presidential memoir, in which he details with admiration the ends to which budget chief Stans went to force those *inside* the administration into lowering their expectations. "With determination and dedication that amazed as much as it delighted me," Eisenhower wrote, "[Stans] deluged the Cabinet and—when possible—the public with statistics that made truly fearsome ogres of the gaudily garbed promises of the spenders."

Such tactics earned Stans the ire of many a hungry bureaucrat but also the distinction of being the last author of a balanced federal budget. In 1961, he proudly bore this badge of honor into private life. Going to work in California as a banker, he remained active, much to the delight of his new colleagues, as a respected commentator and a savvy but evenhanded adviser to Republican critics of the Kennedy administration's own spending plans. He also assisted former vice president Nixon in his campaign for governor of California. For these efforts, he was nearly ruined. Detailed here for the first time is the successful campaign waged at the highest levels of the Kennedy administration to punish Stans for his political activities. The White House, the Justice Department, and even the Central Intelligence Agency used their full authority to pressure a member of his corporation's board of directors to tell him to resign. Stans bowed to the pressure, which included trumped-up and ultimately discredited inferences of wrongdoing that he documented in careful accounts of the meetings and conversations he had at the time. Painstakingly reconstructed now and told with the author's characteristic dispassion, the story is fascinating and chilling.

During the 1970s, Stans survived "the terrors of justice" as he had survived the trials of politics in the sixties. Anyone who knows him, as both our families do, knows that he prevailed because of a strength of character anchored deep within him and nurtured from his earliest days by those who loved him best. As is true of so many notable men, the most important time in his life was his childhood, because it was then that the influences of family, community, school, and church were strongest. Those early years are lovingly described in this memoir. Thus one of this important book's lessons is that those who enter the tumult of public life should be fortified by the blessings of a strong family.

As high school valedictorian in Shakopee, Minnesota, three quarters of a century ago, Maury Stans told his classmates: "Let us hold fast the great truth that without unspotted purity of public faith, without sacred principle, fidelity, and honor, no mere forms of government, no machinery of laws, can give dignity to human society." One could imagine the same words being spoken by Dwight Eisenhower of Abilene and Richard Nixon of Yorba Linda. Maury Stans's legacy is a triumph of will, principle, and character.

David Eisenhower
Julie Nixon Eisenhower
Berwyn, Pennsylvania
March 1995

# Introduction

This book recounts the life of a young man from a small town in Minnesota who was educated in a parochial elementary school and public high school. With Horatio Alger–type ambitions and a fertile mind, and on the advice of teachers and friends, he decides to leave home for Chicago to secure an education to qualify himself for the world of business, and then reaches his goal by building up a large national accounting firm in twenty-five years while personally receiving all the major honors of his profession.

He is a man who had no ties to a political party, with a total lifetime contribution of ten dollars for political purposes (but is a regular voter), with no friends or contacts in Washington, and with no knowledge of Potomac fever, who turns his attention to that city as a point of curiosity and volunteers to serve on a committee of experts for two months, and parlays that assignment through two others into a presidential appointment to a Cabinet-rank position within five years.

This is the story of his adventures in Washington and its orbit of interest as he encountered its powers, its bounties, and its controversies.

# CHAPTER ONE

# Growing Up in a Fast-Changing Era

To many millions of impoverished people in Europe in the last half of the nineteenth century, America was the Promised Land. In country after country they saved and pooled their pittances to send a relative, friend, or neighbor ahead to check out the stories of golden opportunity on the farms and in the burgeoning cities. They waited breathlessly for each letter that told of experiences in the new land, while suffering at home from erratic harvests, dictatorships, wars, and uncontrollable disease. When word filtered back of great expanses, fertile plains, and unlimited freedom, those who could do so sold their small farms, their few cattle, and whatever they could not carry to get the price of tickets for the family to cross the Atlantic on crowded, often stinking, ships.

In 1865, that process brought Hubert Nyssen, a young single man of twenty-one from Boijen, a hamlet near Dilsen in the Limburg province of Belgium, to Baltimore and shortly thereafter to Shakopee, Minnesota. In June 1881, similar circumstances brought forty-three-year-old Hendrik Stans of Opgrimby, twelve miles from Stokkem, with his wife and six children to a destination in Chaska, Minnesota, only four miles from Shakopee, and that is how my two grandfathers, unknown to each other in Belgium, met in the New World; and that

1

is how the stage was set for the son of one and the daughter of the other to be educated in the local elementary schools, to meet at a country barn dance, to be married in 1904, and to become my parents in 1908.

When Mathilda Nyssen, twenty-three, became the wife of J. Hubert Stans, twenty-seven, on June 7, 1904, they set up housekeeping in a rented two-room wing of a small brick house a block from the center of Shakopee. The town, which had a population of less than two thousand, was about twenty crow miles or thirty road miles from central Minneapolis and equally distant from St. Paul, the state capital. It was idyllically located in a fertile valley on the south bank of the Minnesota River, a stream navigable by shallow freight and passenger ships going to and from the Mississippi, about twenty miles away.

In the back room of that small house I was born early on March 23, 1908, just after midnight. My arrival was duly noted in the local *Scott County Argus*, not because it was an augury of significance, but because all such demographic information was of interest in a small town. Although our family was still relatively new to the community, Dad had become a noticeable part of the local scene as the director of the Shakopee Cadet Band.

After Dad finished the eighth grade in the local school, he went to work at heavy labor in the local brickyard. It was the only phase of his life he ever openly resented, and he manifested his feelings on a few occasions over the years by jealously ridiculing the "high school clerks," his more successful contemporaries. He was nevertheless able and ambitious. By the time he was eighteen he had become a highly accomplished musician, largely self-taught, and had been elected director of the Chaska Sodality Band, an unusual organization whose membership of twenty included the five Stans brothers and six brothers of the Ess family, all excellent musicians. Their talents became legendary, and the band became reputed for a quality of music not matched short of the Twin Cities.

Dad played every instrument in the band with dexterity, but his specialty was the cornet, that era's version of the trumpet. I will never forget seeing him directing the band with a baton in his right hand and playing a triple-tongue solo part while holding and fingering the cornet in his left. He must have been very proficient, because at one time in his younger days he was offered the position of first trumpet in the Minneapolis Symphony Orchestra but turned it down in favor of small-town life.

After he left the brickyard at about twenty, Dad learned house painting, which included paperhanging and general interior patching as well, and moved to Shakopee to avoid competing in Chaska with his brothers. The twenty-five cents an hour that his account books show as his charge was the going rate, but it was pretty meager, even at the price levels of the early 1900s, to support a family soon grown to four by the addition of my sister, Lauretta, since the winter weather conditions limited his working year to about seven outdoor months. And there were not always jobs to be done, as the townsmen were mostly frugal types who did much of their own painting and papering in spare hours. It was to add to his irregular income that he had established the Shakopee Cadet Band in 1902, as its director, while continuing the same relationship with the Chaska band.

But it turned out that the combination of part-time painter and part-time musician produced an income barely adequate to provide for his family. And in the cycles when times were hard, the charge account at the John Berens grocery sometimes sustained us for periods as long as a year. When the account got too high, Berens found some painting or paperhanging to be done in the store or at his home to keep the credit in bounds.

Despite our limited circumstances, though, we were never conscious of poverty even though we realized we had to do without a lot of the conveniences our neighbors enjoyed. There was always the confident expectation of better days.

In 1908, while awaiting my arrival, Dad decided it was time to build a home for his family-to-be. He bought a lot across the street and paid his total savings of $1,000 to a builder to go as far as that would take him in the construction. It was enough to provide a basement and foundation and the shell of a two-story wooden frame structure. Uncle Bill Hentges, a traveling plasterer once married to one of Dad's sisters (she had died in her thirties) came from time to time to do some plastering, and Dad added the interior woodwork by his own hand, but the two didn't get around to finishing the upstairs quarters for about fifteen years.

There were four small rooms on the first floor: a kitchen, a dining room, a living room, and a bedroom where Mother and Dad slept. The upstairs in its unfinished state was a high-ceilinged attic large enough to be made someday into four bedrooms. From the time we left our cribs and the downstairs warmth, my sister, Lauretta, who arrived when I was fifteen months old, slept in one open wing and I in another. Without ceilings, walls or insulation, we were at the mercy of Minnesota's wide-ranging elements. In the winter when it was below zero outside it was below zero inside, and we slept in bulky featherbeds under heavy quilts, with our heads under some of the covers. When it got much below zero we were allowed to pick up our bedding and bring it to the living room and sleep on the floor. If we stuck it out upstairs we would jump out of bed in the morning, grab our clothes, and dress in the kitchen. In summer, the temperature upstairs sometimes got above 100 degrees in the day-time and cooled very little at night. On such occasions we were allowed to move to our screened front porch and sleep in the humid outdoor air.

Dad's resources were never enough to afford the cost of connect-ing the house to the local water system or sewage outlet, so we had neither convenience. Soft water for washing came through the hand pump connected to a ten-foot-deep cistern under the kitchen that collected rainwater from the eaves and downspouts. Hard water for drinking and cooking had to be carried by pail from a neighbor's deep-well pump. The pail had to be refilled every day, sometimes more than once, as did the hot-water reservoir within the kitchen range. In winter we had to be sure to wear gloves so our hands didn't freeze to the iron pump handle. Toilet facilities were in a typi-cal wooden two-holer in the backyard, and needless to say it was zero inside there, too, when it was zero outside. The second-latest Sears Roebuck catalog was its only fixture, except for the Kendall Oil poster on the wall picturing a pretty girl with blond hair. I don't remember ever spending more than an absolute minimum of time there.

Our family's economic situation was made bearable by the fact that both my father and mother came from backgrounds in which frugality was a way of life. Under the relatively simple conditions of those early years of the century, we did without many of the conve-niences that we knew the more affluent had.

To build the larder, mother always kept a flock of about thirty or forty chickens in a coop inside a small fenced-in area in the back-yard. They were expected to produce enough eggs to supply our wants, and if a hen got noticeably lazy she ended up as a guest at a Sunday dinner. Besides giving the flock the table leftovers and some purchased grain, we crushed the shells of the eggs we ate and fed them back to the hens to provide calcium for more eggshells.

I entered the first grade in St. Mark's school at six and a half. There were no nursery schools or kindergartens in those days, and the rules prevented me from starting my education until the school year that began after my sixth birthday. From the beginning, the subjects all came easily, and I never had difficulty with any studies. In those days, German was taught along with English at St. Mark's, and I learned it too with ease, but when World War I came, the anti-German attitudes in the country regrettably forced our school and many others to give up teaching that language.

Whatever the subject, competition stimulated me and I was always at the head of the class. As a result, after a year in first grade, I finished the second and third in one year and the fourth and fifth in another, putting me two years ahead of schedule. I breezed through the sixth grade and won a medal for having the highest average of anyone in the entire school. What happened then was one of the distressing events in my life, one that annoyed me much more in later years than it did at the time. The nuns decided that I was too precocious and that it would be dangerous for me to associate with children so much older, and they convinced my parents that I should remain in the sixth grade for another year.

I never forgave those responsible. The year was a total bore, I knew all the lessons by heart, and obviously I was an irritation to my classmates who were struggling along with the daily assignments and all the homework.

After I finished as valedictorian of my graduating class of seventeen at St. Mark's ("Safe on First, Now Score" was the title of my address), I entered the public Shakopee High School and again had no difficulty with the classwork. My four-year average was above 95 and I was again valedictorian. I bravely chose "The Constitution in the Making" as my topic, and after extolling at length the virtues of that document and the courage of its makers, ended up the peroration with this appeal that it be preserved for the long future by the conscious dedication of all Americans to its moral aims: "Let us hold fast the great truth that without unspotted purity of public faith, without sacred principle, fidelity, and honor, no mere forms of government, no machinery of laws, can give dignity to human society." What I wrote and spoke with some eloquence at that time was sincere and deliberate. It became the design of a compass for my own subsequent career, wherever it might take me.

Though my academic achievements were noteworthy, when it came to athletics, I was a total dud. Too skinny and too light in weight, and always associating with students one to three years older, I never really qualified for any organized sports team. At one point I was elected manager of an independent baseball nine called the Shakopee Juniors, averaging about thirteen in age. My title did not mean that I had anything to do with directing the players, but only that I had the job of raising enough money to keep the team in baseballs and to finance its transportation to a few out-of-town contests. We did that by an occasional raffle. In return, I was allowed to work out with the players, and in the last game of that career was permitted to bat as a pinch hitter. I hit a blooper over the first baseman's head and ran safely on to third. As official scorer, I properly gave myself a three-base hit and saw to it that in the team's published final statistics for the year I appeared at the top of the batting with a neat 1.000 average.

One year, I believe it was 1924, a barnstorming pilot landed a rickety plane near the fairgrounds to take up passengers, one at a time, for five dollars for a five-minute ride. I dug into my savings to pay for the thrill of my first trip into the air, seeing for the first time the expansive beauty of the Minnesota River valley. I also took the trouble to remember that the pilot was named Lindbergh, whose home in Little Falls was less than fifty miles away and whose move into the limelight was still three years off.

Because I was quite timid, I did not find many occasions for romance as I grew up. Even in Shakopee there were social strata, and I did not feel comfortable with the girls of the higher level. My dates were so few that I still remember them all. First was a Polish girl from Chaska whom I took to a hometown historical pageant in a borrowed car. Next was a girl from St. Paul who appeared in a Scottish dancing troupe at the Scott County Fair when I was sixteen and a member of the Shakopee band; she gave me her phone number and I arranged a date in St. Paul for the following week, but when I saw her without her Scotch plaid costume and she saw me without my braided band uniform we seemed to lose interest in each other. That was the end of that. Anyway, she turned out to be German, not Scottish, and there were plenty of German girls closer to home than St. Paul.

Whenever there were no group activities to interest me, or I found spare time because I would stay far enough ahead in class to avoid homework, I thought of things to do alone. Like almost every boy of the era, I delivered *The Saturday Evening Post* for a while. In another period I peddled a group of weeklies headed by the *Saturday Blade* and *Chicago Ledger*, published by W. D. Boyce of Chicago, founder of the Boy Scouts and Lone Scouts movements in the United States. I collected stamps. I bottled and sold horseradish from my mother's garden. I peddled lightbulbs. I earned twenty-five cents a week delivering a hot dinner every evening to a foreman at the stove factory from his home.

On one occasion when I was fourteen or fifteen I entered a contest to get subscribers to the *St. Paul Dispatch* and won a radio, one of the first in Shakopee. It was a crystal set, with a headphone. It changed my life, as radio changed the course of living for the world.

Youngsters of later generations who matter-of-factly turn on the television to watch *Sesame Street* or sports events cannot conceive of the breathtaking thrill of listening in on the primitive over-the-air broadcasts of sound in the early 1920s.

The first radios were simple devices. A cylindrical cardboard tube about three inches in diameter and six inches long, set between two square ends of wood, covered with windings of bright copper wire across which moved a finger of brass, was the tuning mechanism that adjusted the wavelength of the device to the desired stations. It had two wire projections, one connected to a hard rubber cylinder resembling a telephone earpiece, the other a light-gauge "cat's-whisker" leading to a small fixture holding a magical half-inch cube of a silvery-looking ore called a galena crystal. The galena was the miracle ingredient. By slowly moving the cat's-whisker across the cube, with unbelievable patience and intense listening, it was possible to strike tiny spots that brought sounds, sounds that electrified the ear with voices and music. Sometimes it took twenty minutes of delicate jiggling to locate the minute place that brought in the words clearly enough to be understood.

This was enchantment. One could sit in bug-eyed amazement to hear a scratchy voice say, "This is WLAG in Minneapolis. We will now play John Philip Sousa's march *Semper Fidelis*, performed by the United States Marine Band." Unbelievable! Friends given the opportunity to listen for the first time would yank off the earpiece and look around for a gramophone or telephone or some other deceptive source. There was none. The band's tooting and thumping was still coming through the earpiece. Somehow, without electrical connection or other generated power, by the magic created out of a bit of wire and a tiny piece of rock, music was caught moving through the air. Even in its earliest form, without imagining the next move into visual transmission by television, radio was easily the most exciting discovery of a lifetime.

It was a tenuous pleasure. If a heavy foot landed on the floor, or if the incoming music turned to dull conversation and the metal finger had to be moved along the wire to locate another station, the cat's-whisker would lose its delicate hold and the scratchy time-consuming search process had to be repeated. But in due course there would be a voice pleading "Figaro" or "Carmen" or giving baseball scores or telling of storms or tragedies—sound and fury that theretofore could be heard only by being on the spot.

What a convenience to have the world's pleasures and problems brought to one's living room, instantly and alive! I would sit for hours after school and into the evening, hypnotized, filling my head with radio's gift of facts, fiction and invisible harmony until my arm fell asleep from the effort of holding the device tight against my throbbing ear.

In time, as the technology advanced, I wanted a more sophisticated vacuum tube set, so I built one for myself after buying the SD-11 and 199 tubes, condensers, transformers, and rheostats in St. Paul. A friend, Harry Dressen, wanted one too, so I built one for him. We decided to go into the manufacturing business. He acquired some secondhand Edison phonograph cabinets, and with Bakelite panels that we fitted and inserted, we designed a dial system to operate the chassis units we assembled and installed. The total production of our venture was five sets, which we sold to friends at cost, and surprisingly they all worked for years after our factory in Harry's basement folded.

When I got to high school I would read a book a day from the school library, in the time between classes and at home. Occasionally I would get hold of a thrilling Nick Carter adventure. *The Saturday Evening Post* stories of primitive Asia and Africa by Roy Chapman Andrews and Carl Akeley entranced me, and I read them over and over. *Boys' Life* brought adventure, too, and I dreamed of the African safaris and Asian tiger hunts that I would take when I was older. Whenever possible, I read the stories of Horatio Alger and these made a convincing impression on me.

From reading, I learned about scouting, but there was no Boy Scout troop in town, so I became a Lone Scout, learning the principles of scouting by mail and taking, on the honor system, the tests for various degrees of advancement.

In Lone Scouting, one carried on a large amount of correspondence around the country with pen pals. I exchanged long letters, joined "tribes" by mail, contributed stories and articles to monthly tribe publications, and even attended Minnesota state conventions. After a lot of such participation I became Chieftain over a Midwest region of seven states. While I was somewhat secretive about these activities at the time, I have since come to believe that they were very valuable in building character and the understanding of others. I perhaps got every bit as much out of Lone Scouting as youngsters get out of being Boy Scouts today.

I did become a musician of sorts. Dad was doing quite a bit of teaching of local fellows on band instruments, at fifty cents for a half-hour lesson, and occasionally urged me to try out his cornet, but I resisted for several years because I didn't have enough wind to blow it. Then he had an opportunity to buy a secondhand clarinet for two dollars and I agreed to play that. It was in bad shape, with a long crack in the barrel that we filled with beeswax and wrapped with black tire tape to hold the thing together. Happily, the sound was not impaired, and in time I managed to do well enough to join him as a member of the Shakopee, Chaska, and Chanhassen bands. I allowed Dad to give me only one lesson, and from then on I practiced diligently on the finger exercises until I could play all the pieces that the bands had in their repertoires. By then I was fourteen. But I never really became good at it. I could play only by reading notes and did not have a musical ear, so I couldn't even handle "Home, Sweet Home" at the end of a concert without the sheet music before me on the stand. In this, I was something of a disappointment to Dad, who was a great improviser and could shift all around in the course of a melody and do sleights of hand in transposition of harmony and in impromptu variations on a theme.

Music gave me my first meaningful earning power, however, as I was paid two dollars for playing at each evening concert, and got five dollars for each afternoon-and-evening's work during the three-day county fair in the fall. My previous earnings hadn't allowed for any savings. One summer I earned a nickel a day for helping the milkman deliver milk over his morning route, but I had to be very careful not to forfeit my pay, because the milk was delivered from a tank on the wagon to the customer's pot or pan by way of an unsteady quart measure, and spilling wasn't tolerated.

When I was around twelve there were a few times when I earned ten cents an hour for weeding onions or picking fruit. Once I had my first lesson in the law of contracts when I was one of a small group of boys chosen by a farmer to harvest strawberries at ten cents an hour on his farm five miles from town. He picked us up in town with his truck and drove to the farm early in the morning, but at the end of the day when he paid us we learned that we had to walk all the way home. He said he hadn't promised to bring us back. I didn't know about legal terms, but I resolved right there that never again would I make a deal without knowing what I was getting into, from beginning to end.

As often happens to us, one other casual youthful experience created an indelible memory and exercised a strong influence on my life. One day, when I was twelve, my father bought for me a $1,000 insurance policy on my life. Being an avid reader, I sat down and devoured the entire text of fine print until I came to a paragraph that read somewhat like this: Upon the payment of premiums to age ninety-six, no further premiums shall be payable and the face amount of the policy will be payable to the beneficiary. I stopped at that point and fixed in my mind a fanciful thought that I could and would live to collect that $1,000. Not surprisingly, that thought came back frequently as the decades went by, and I seriously believe it has played a subconscious part in extending my life.

There were wonderful advantages in going to Shakopee High School when I did. The school was small and the freshman class had only about twenty-five students, some of whom had come from St. Mark's and some from the public elementary school; this dwindled to thirteen by the time we were graduated as seniors. The quality of the teaching was high, and with small classes we received a personalized education that could not have come from a larger institution. Each teacher knew the pupils well and worked to develop them to the fullest. The superintendent of the school, for example, taught both sociology and economics to five of us seated around a table in the library, where we talked informally but intently, and really got to understand these subjects. When I made the excellent decision to take all the commercial subjects available to me, I was fortunate to be taught bookkeeping, shorthand, and typewriting by Viola Neveaux, an attractive and able young woman who not only nurtured the skills that later financed my way in college, but also was one of the people who played a major role in aiming my career.

Many persons seemed to take an interest in me as I progressed through school and I was grateful for all their helping hands. But there were three to whom I could never extinguish my obligation for guidance at the time that counted most in fixing my goals.

Viola Neveaux, the teacher of commercial subjects, was the first. She stimulated me to do my very best in my commercial classes and saw to it that I went far beyond the work requirements of the courses. She encouraged me to enter the regional high school typing contest, where I won first place. I let her down in the ensuing state contest, though, where I was one of 5 boys against 110 girls, and under that obvious pressure the best I could do was come in about fiftieth in total standing, although first among the boys. She and other teachers encouraged me to compete in the state high school spelling contest where I ended a creditable fifth among one hundred, and a "discussion-type" public speaking contest, where contestants were required to talk extemporaneously on surprise topics such as "Child Labor" or "Compulsory Arbitration." I again won in the region but failed to match the sophisticated competition from the major cities in the state event. These were contests that our school had never before entered.

Her finest help to me, though, came in our talks about planning a career. Miss Neveaux was convinced that I had the makings of a certified public accountant and that I should get the college background to qualify. There were no family resources to pay for a regular degree course, but she countered that I could take selected subjects in night classes and work in an office during the day. To my small-town mind at that point, an accountant was just a man who counted money and kept books in a bank, but she patiently pointed out the choices available in business, finance, and government if I qualified as a professional, and sold me on her idea. It was not easy to overcome the doubts and fears of a seventeen-year-old who had never been more than thirty miles from home and convince him that he should pack up and venture alone as far as Chicago, 450 miles distant. That was necessary because at that time neither the University of Minnesota nor the Minnesota colleges had the night classes I needed. With the help of an educational counseling service offered by *Redbook* magazine, I settled on Northwestern University.

The next person who had a hand in all this was a former superintendent of Shakopee High, O. W. Herr. Although he had moved elsewhere a year earlier, he thought enough of me to write to my father in my senior year, urging that I be given a college education, notwithstanding the financial obstacles. He said confidently in his letter that "the thing Maurice can do better than anyone I know is to become a business manager, to run some large concern. He would shine in any profession." To Dad, my leaving home was a big loss as it deprived him of a potential partner in the house-painting business,

but the letter had the intended effect and he proudly gave his blessing to my departure.

The third person to help to fix my goals was "Curly" Feldman,
and I know he talked to me from the heart. Then in his fifties, his
own life a failure, he was a good-enough friend of our family to
want something better for me. He had been a farm worker and then
a small-time farmer, but he had never been able to pull his affairs
together and was back at itinerant labor. He was a fellow member of
the Chaska and Shakopee bands and one night in the summer after
my high school graduation we walked home from a concert and sat
on our front steps to chat. I told him some of my fears about leaving
home and speculated about what I might do if I stayed in Shakopee.
He cut me off quickly with some blunt advice: "Son," he said, "are
you going to stay here all your life, waste your brains, and become a
bum like me, or are you going to get out and make something of
yourself? If you don't go, I'll give you a good boot in the ass every
time I see you." With that, he reached in his pocket, pulled out his
purse, emptied it, and said seriously, "All I've got in the world is
three dollars and fifty cents, but I'm giving it to you to help you get
going, so you don't make the same mistakes I did." Curly was not a
bum, but a great person with a generous heart and meager education
whom life had not treated well. I never forgot his offer even though
I didn't take his money.

Of such fine passing deeds lives are formed. I was not unthankful
at the time and did express my appreciation to these three people
who had done so much for me, but not until later years did the real
impact of their wonderful encouragement and confidence take on its
full dimension. They are all gone now, but I have continued to try to
repay all three by helping youngsters in the indecisive stage who are
willing to listen to my suggestions for their careers.

All of this added the finishing touches to seventeen and a half
peaceful years in Shakopee, and on September 15, 1925, I left
alone on the afternoon bus for St. Paul and the overnight train to
Chicago to seek adventure and fortune. Corny as those words are,
they were exactly what was in my mind as I kissed my parents
good-bye and set out boldly with a saxophone in one hand and a
suitcase containing the rest of my worldly possessions in the other.
I also had that $251.00 in the bank. In my pocket was a character
letter "to whom it may concern" from my most recent school
superintendent, E. J. Sweeney, attesting to my "exemplary habits
and qualities for leadership" and ending with the words, "He will

make good in anything he undertakes. He can be depended upon to do his best." Fully armed with unlimited confidence, I no longer had qualms about what might be ahead.

I never returned to Shakopee to live, but I went back at least once or twice a year to see my parents and friends. And my mind flitted there often as I reflected on my home life, my family, and the motivations that took me away. Not that anything in my experience was highly unusual or unique, but the coincidences of good fortune in birth, location, and education gave me the best of all possible reasons for making life meaningful and creative after I left.

Looking back later at my youth over the wide gulf of more than seven decades, I am shocked at the degree of independence and self-assurance I carried within me. I was not willing to accept help or advice from my parents on any subject. They accepted my displays of unaccountable disdain for their advice, apparently comforting themselves with pride over my scholastic achievements. Not once would I allow either of them to see my homework, and not once did I go to them with a question about something I didn't understand. When I began to play the clarinet, it was not out of respect for my father's wishes that I follow him as a musician, but simply because I saw it as a way to earn money.

Much of this intellectual arrogance probably came as a counter to my physical limitations. I never forgot an incident when, at about eight, I tried to help Dad unload a heavy object from a wagon. His assistant nudged me aside, with the remark, "You're too weak in the poop." Resenting this, I took determined physical exercises for some weeks, trying to emulate the body-building achievements of the then advertised Charles Atlas, but it was useless. Weak in the poop I would continue to be, so I would show everyone I could outdo them in other ways. Leadership in academics became a passion, and I took on every challenge I could find.

However normal or abnormal this may have been, I long since came to regret the burden of understanding that my independent attitude placed on my parents. I simply went my own conceited way, without consulting them or explaining to them, and there must have been many times when my abrasive manner of brush-off pained them. Not until I was over twenty-five and tempered by years of living away from home did I come to regret that behavior and to show a decent respect, a full appreciation for the burdens they had borne in rearing me.

Without doubt, Dad was a person of considerable ambition in his younger days, who never found the opening that would develop his abilities. But he took pleasure in simple things, like infrequent card games of five hundred or schafskopf, or just walking with Mother a few blocks to a corner saloon and spending a chummy evening hour or so with neighbors over a couple of glasses of beer.

In middle age he began to slow down, with an undefined ailment that wiped out his energy, and not until I took him to the Mayo Clinic in Rochester when he was about sixty did we learn that he was a victim of polycythemia vera, a debilitating blood disease marked by a massive overproduction of red cells. Blood-letting from time to time relieved his discomfort and prolonged his life, but today's treatments had not yet been developed and he gradually weakened and passed away at sixty-nine. He was alert to the end and reconciled to leaving, and his last words to me were a calm "What must be must be!" With that, he called for his most prized possession, the silver cornet that he had imported in 1899, and asked me to give it to my son Steve. I could not keep my composure, but he did.

His passing was my first such experience, and it was traumatic. Suddenly, I became aware of the narrow line between life and death, when from one hour to another a living, talking person becomes a cold, still, decaying corpse. In our house in Shakopee, when I had slept as a child in that barren upstairs attic, I could hear at night the vibrations of his baritone voice talking to Mother on the first floor, although I could not decipher their conversations. In those last few days of his life, when I was home with him, I could once more hear them talking, after I had gone to bed in that same upstairs, his voice still resonant and strong. The familiar sound returning from my younger days gave me assurance and peace. Then one night the haunting voice was gone, and all was still. The realization suddenly came upon me, as I lay between the covers with my wife, Kathleen, at my side, that I would never hear it again. That was what death meant, and for the first time in my life I felt it and resented it. For the first time I knew the pain of an irretrievable loss and, in my agony, turned and embraced Kathleen as my shoulders shook with grief and sobbing, and the tears came in waves.

Dad lived a clean, moral life. I never heard of his doing wrong to anyone, or speaking ill of anyone (although he never had much respect for politicians at any level), and he was a devoted husband and father. All this constituted a proud legacy for me, but what brought home his fine character more than anything else was to hear his older brother say on the day of his funeral, "Hubert never said a profane word in his life." I had not thought of that before, but it was true.

Mother was a placid person, never ruffled or excited. If I inherited a sense of ambition from my father, I should have acquired a calm bearing from her, but it didn't show up until I became well along in years. She was a warm person, always solicitous, defending us when necessary, praising us when we gave her a reason. Nothing ever fazed her and she lived on for six years after Dad died, in the comfort of her neighbors and friends and pride in her family, now including grandchildren, until a recurrence of abdominal cancer took her away at seventy-one.

Her passing was a deeply felt blow to me, not only in the realization that both parents were now gone, but particularly in the fact that I knew I would never again share in her quiet calm and affection.

I could not have been blessed with two better parents. Each gave to me characteristics that formed my life in a way that made it possible for me to do what they never had the chance to do. From them I acquired, consciously but without deliberation, a religious morality, a belief in work, faith in idealism, an urge to excel, a trust in people, a powerful ambition, and a confidence in life's rewards. I'm glad I realized my debt to them while they were alive and was able to show my appreciation and affection in meaningful ways.

There is much to be said for the advantages of growing up in a small town, certainly in my era. The pleasures were simple, but they were plentiful. The social system was stratified but informal, and most people knew and respected one another. Although we were certainly not well-off, we were not made conscious of poverty. Education was personalized. Nature was close at hand. Triumphs and tragedies were shared with neighbors, and a helping hand was always around.

But I was impelled to leave it, and seventeen was the correct age for that. Opportunity elsewhere was unlimited and inertia was an evil to be avoided by one with a sense of purpose. Despite its advantages there was a dangerous quality in small-town life for the eager: except for the few who became successful merchants, professional men, or elected officials, the promise was scant, and too often the hopeless ruts of ordinary labors led to middle-age frustration, excessive drinking, and an early demise. I could see that by observing people I knew. And my ambitions were extraordinarily strong. It was not in any sense that I rebelled against having been deprived of anything; it was more an inborn matter of wanting to compete and to achieve, somehow to excel.

I'm not at all embarrassed to admit even now that Horatio Alger played a large role in giving me the conviction that anything was achievable if I worked hard and lived cleanly. I read several times every one of his books that I could get my hands on. While I never got to marry the boss's daughter, as his heroes usually did, I did find that dedication to work paid off and that honesty avoided a lot of problems. This prescription influenced millions of Americans as it did me, and thereby played a large part in the nation's economic and social development. In an age when greats like Henry Ford, Thomas Edison, Harvey Firestone, and the Wright brothers were living role models, it was not hard to accept this philosophy.

# CHAPTER TWO

# Suffering the Great Depression

$O$n the morning in September 1925 when I arrived in the Northwestern Railroad station, tired and dirty after an all-night coach ride, I checked my luggage, washed up, and set out on foot. For the moment, I had no destination in mind; I just wanted to look, to see the heart of the big city, to feel its vibrations and sense its vitality.

I walked up Michigan Avenue all the way to Lincoln Park, and then sat down on a bench to gather my impressions and make some plans. I knew that none of the people in these moving mobs was going to help me find a place to live, or to work, and that it was up to me to sort out such matters. So I selected the order of events. I would go to Northwestern's downtown school and register, then I would find a place to live, and then I would see about a job. Only a person of sublime confidence would pick that sequence.

Northwestern's shabby downtown building at State and Lake deflated my dreams, until I learned that a new campus was being built on Chicago Avenue near Lake Michigan and the school would be moved there in less than a year. I registered for evening classes in accounting, commercial law, and business English. By selecting the specific subjects in this way, I would necessarily miss the cultural advantages of foreign languages, social studies, and liberal arts, but I would get directly to the topics I needed to master for my CPA examination in a few years. I stuck to this plan from then on.

My education arranged, I picked up my suitcase and saxophone and got directions for a streetcar to Kedzie Avenue, where I got off and walked to 3117 West Monroe. Someone back home had given me the name of Leo Madigan as a person to see about a place to live. Leo turned out to be a drifter type, a door-to-door salesman of children's photographs, pots and pans, and various types of come-on and coupon merchandising. But he was a happy-go-lucky and good-hearted Irishman with a pleasant wife, and to make ends meet they had taken in a few roomers. I arrived at a time when there "just happened to be" a vacancy, so I solved this problem by moving right in at eleven dollars a week for a room and breakfasts, with dinners thrown in on the evenings I didn't go to school. I paid two weeks in advance (Leo was in one of his recurring financial emergencies and I was a godsend to him), and this, plus the $75 I had paid at Northwestern, depleted my capital to $154. But I was still wealthy and had no fear.

The next day the Northwestern University employment office evaluated me and decided I should be a bookkeeper or stenographer, whichever came first. In a day or so I came upon Harry Levi & Company, importers of sausage casings, and was hired as a stenographer at thirty dollars a week. I was set. I could cover my expenses and save money too.

I promptly learned that there were some drawbacks to the work. The company imported sheep intestines and similar items from Turkey and the Middle East for sale to sausage makers. Since there was no inspection process at the source, all the goods had to be unpacked, rewashed, inspected, and repacked. This was done in a large workroom behind the office and the horrible odors that resulted came right through to my desk. It took a while to become used to that, especially when I found that the smell went along in my clothes onto the streetcars, into the classrooms, and all the way home. I tried keeping extra garments in lockers along the way so I could change clothes frequently, but never really licked this problem until a year later when the company moved to a larger building near the stockyards in which the office was insulated from the workroom odors.

The first location on West Lake Street was bad for another reason. There were no places to eat nearby except on Madison Street three blocks away, and that was the center of Skid Row. The prices were cheap; a bowl of bean soup was five cents, and coffee and two doughnuts cost another nickel, and these were digestible; but when I ventured into poorly disguised stews and hashes I almost permanently ruined my digestive system. I have not been able to eat spicy foods since.

The work was a tough challenge at first. Harry Levi was a fine, gentle old man who was very understanding of my inexperience and helped me whenever he could. With him were two Goldberg brothers, Milton and Jim, who were the company's main salesmen, and they almost destroyed me—but not intentionally. Their dictation was ungrammatical, rapid-fire, profane, and obscene, and I realized right away that I could never put it all on paper. However, the dictation at two hundred words a minute, punctuated by irrelevancies, was only their way of letting off steam, and I found that if I managed to get their principal meaning into a letter, sans profanity and vulgarity, that was all they expected. Although there were some dissatisfactions with my work at the beginning, and I overheard conversations indicating that my future was in doubt, I managed to hang on until I learned the personalities and the trade lingo. From then on I got along quite well. They were all distressed a few years later when I moved on.

On this job I got an initiation into business practices, and what I learned took me some years to outgrow. Ethics in the sausage casing business were not very high. Goods rejected by a customer were shipped right back in the same tierce with a few sound layers put on top. Rotting and unsalable casings were mixed in with good ones, and workmen in customer plants were bribed to let shoddy stuff pass inspection. This was all done in such an unabashed way that I took it to be common in business generally. When I wondered about it out loud one day, I was solidly told that it was none of a stenographer's business to ask such questions. Milton Goldberg's philosophy of ethics, as he expressed it, was "What are friends for if you can't screw them once in a while?" I took this all as part of my education but fortunately learned quickly enough in life that not all business was done that way. I never knew how ethical Levi's competitors were. Anyway, Levi's is gone now, and the animal casing business has long ago given way to synthetics. I have no surviving apprehension about cleanliness or ethics when I eat a hot dog.

One other thing I learned at Levi's also stayed with me. I became enamored of a pretty Polish girl in the back workroom and one day made a date with her to go to the movies. When the office manager heard about it the next day he told me in no uncertain terms that the company rule was to "keep your pecker out of the payroll." In my näiveté, anything else had not occurred to me, but I nevertheless tucked the message in the back of my mind for future guidance.

I stayed on for two and a half years and did well enough to get pay raises that brought me to $175 a month, meanwhile continuing my schoolwork three nights a week. It was a hard grind, because I also had to study at least another three nights and part of the weekends. The streetcar rides from the office near the stockyards to the new McKinlock campus at Lake Michigan and from there back to the West Side boardinghouse were so long and slow, requiring changing cars at least once on each trip, that I usually got home late and exhausted. The folks at the boardinghouse were poker fanatics, and I was constantly being tempted by them to get into a penny-ante game; on free nights or weekends I sometimes did play because I usually managed to win a dollar or so to help with my budget.

After seven semesters and twenty-one courses at Northwestern, I had been through all the basic accounting and commercial law subjects, and had learned some cost accounting, income taxes, economics, business English, business mathematics and related subjects. I felt I was ready.

By answering a newspaper ad, I got to Alexander Grant & Company, a small CPA firm, took a written examination, and was hired. It was a shock to find that the starting rate for junior accountants was only $125 a month, which meant that I had to take a 30 percent drop in income. But that did not deter me from my objective, as I knew I had to start at the bottom. Eventually I spent more than twenty-five years with A G & Co., most of them at the top as executive partner, and when I withdrew in 1954 to go into government it had grown to a size far beyond our expectations.

My accounting career began casually enough when I was assigned to spend a month as office boy rearranging the filed and unfiled papers in the vault. But soon it moved fast. I had worked as a junior accountant on only one assignment when the firm was engaged to audit a group of about twenty laundries and dry-cleaning plants in Illinois and Iowa that were to make up a new consolidation to be known as Mid-Continent Laundries. With only about eight auditors on the entire staff the firm was undermanned, but it resolved the problem by promoting me overnight to senior accountant, and I left Chicago all alone with some expense money and a briefcase of blank paper to make audits of four plants in Waterloo, Ames, and

Oskaloosa, Iowa, in a period of four weeks. It was a risk for the firm to send out anyone as inexperienced as I was on an important mission, but the clients' employees I met were unacquainted with auditors and my greenness didn't show through. In any event, I completed the work on schedule and with success, even uncovering an embezzlement at one plant in Ames where the manager was stealing regularly from his partner and both were cheating on Uncle Sam's share. My audit papers and figures withstood the regular office review, and I became a qualified veteran by the time I was twenty.

Alexander Grant, the founder of the firm, made a lasting impression on me by teaching me early in life a fundamental rule of human relationships. He was one of the most able and personable individuals I ever met, with a keen mind and a quiet charm. A potential business genius who died in 1938 before he was forty, his hopes for fame and success were dashed as were those of millions of Americans by the calamitous conditions of the Great Depression.

The incident with him that most impressed itself on me involved an ordinary business meeting with an ordinary person on an ordinary subject. I don't remember any of it. I do remember the conversation that followed. I made broad conclusive remarks of disparagement to Grant about the person because of the ineptness with which he had handled a series of business affairs. Grant took me to task, pointing out some of the man's successes, his interest in the welfare of others, and his generosity, all of which I had to concede. He then said simply, "Every man ought to be judged on his net. There is some good in every bad person, and some bad in every good person, and the one should be subtracted from the other in reaching a judgment." His use of an accounting term in this context was apt, and it taught me a memorable lesson.

The three years in Chicago followed my scenario. I lived frugally, worked diligently, and studied hard. I acquired business experience and a considerable knowledge of human character. I completed the major part of the education I needed to write the CPA examination, and I had a good background of diversified experience in auditing in a very short time.

There was little beyond routine in my other activities in Chicago. After a year I left Madigan's boardinghouse and moved in with other friends under a similar arrangement. For a short interval I shared a room with an artist acquaintance, but he unveiled homosexual ideas that didn't appeal to me and I quickly found another lodging.

It didn't seem that I was ever truly lonesome for my old home and family or that I found it difficult to make the transition from small-town life to the big city. Once a year I took a vacation trip by train back to Shakopee, and the first two of these trips were at county fair time so I could join the band again for a few days.

Despite my sojourn in Iowa I completed my school program for the remainder of the year at Northwestern and won an award for the highest average of any three-year student in the School of Commerce. It was a scholarship for the fourth year, but unfortunately I never got to use it. Alexander Grant & Company's practice included a considerable number of investigations for insurance companies, including Lloyds of London, of claims filed by policyholders for fire, robbery, and similar losses. The most intricate type of such claims was for business interruption, wherein a policyholder was entitled to be reimbursed for the profits he would have made if the catastrophe had not occurred. Such claims were naturally an intriguing invitation to the optimism of the policyholder, especially in those days when forecasts and budgets were seldom a part of business planning. It was our job as auditors to bring suddenly inflated expectations back down to proper relationship with historical reality; I enjoyed this kind of work.

Anyway, the Grant firm was given such an assignment on a big alcohol refinery in Philadelphia early in September 1928, and I was asked to give up my classes for the next semester to go there to assist in the audit. This was a new adventure and I agreed. When the particular case was concluded, the manager of Grant's one-man New York office, Milo Hopkins, invited me to join him there as his principal assistant, and again I accepted. In New York I could continue my part-time education, and I did so for a few more years in night classes at Columbia. Wasn't this the way Horatio Alger was supposed to work out my future?

I arrived in New York in January 1929, in time to lose my savings in the October stock market tumble, and to see the economy enter the horrendous era of the Great Depression. Living through the depths of the depression was a lasting and frightening experience. Our accounting business fell apart as clients went under or, if they stayed alive, couldn't pay their bills. There were months in which there was no money to pay our salaries, and we had to save every nickel, in the office and at home.

Even so, we did better than most people. Anyone who did not live through that period can't possibly know the mood of despair and hopelessness that engulfed those who were out of work and helpless. Unemployment in New York was as much as 30 percent; many of those working were on part-time or reduced pay, and the apple seller on the street corner was the sign of the times. Investments became worthless, fortunes were wiped out, poverty multiplied, and there were no meaningful government mechanisms to help cushion the blow for businesses or for individuals. It was probably the nation's worst hour.

One facet of the misfortunes of others saved the day for us and our little accounting office. The four people there in 1931 would not have been able to carry on had it not been for a large surge in insurance claims, especially among jewelers and garment manufacturers, that required investigations and audits. Without doubt, the pressures of creditors induced many merchants to create fires or simulate burglaries in order to sell unsalable inventories to the insurance companies, or to claim excessive values even in legitimate losses. For three years I spent practically all my time on this type of work, and the experiences were enormously educational. Each claim was a multiple question mark: Was the event real or staged? Did the goods exist? What were they worth? What is a diamond bracelet with a $3,000 price tag worth if there are no buyers for it and it can be reproduced for much less? What is a warehouse of piece goods worth if there are no buyers for the dresses into which they can be made? And so on.

There were dozens of claims that were padded or overpriced 50 percent or more, in one way or another. It was my job to ferret out such discrepancies, and I took to it enthusiastically. It was the most difficult and most exhilarating auditing work one could do, and without being unfair, I took each case as a distinct battle of wits. Nothing I ever did sharpened my mind more than these insurance loss assignments. And again, I learned a lot about the temptations and frailties of human nature.

One Friday afternoon I was working in the office of a manufacturer of jewelry on an upper floor on Canal Street, checking the books on articles suspiciously priced after a holdup. After I left for the day, to return Monday and finish the job, I reached in my overcoat pocket when I was a few blocks away and discovered a jewel case with a magnificent diamond bracelet worth at least several thousand dollars. I was not willing to risk my career for a bribe, so I retraced my steps to return it, but when I got back, the jeweler's office was already closed. Then a frightening thought came through. Was this an attempt to frame me, by setting me up for a charge of theft so I might be blackmailed into approving the entire claim? In total fright I waited out the elevator and rushed down the street looking for a telephone. In my fear, I reasoned that the only security lay in telling the insurance company about my predicament before something happened. After endless minutes I got through to an official who was working late and gave him the story. On Monday morning, to save embarrassment, I handed the case and bracelet to the jeweler and merely said that someone must have put it in my pocket by mistake. I never did learn what the plot was, but he accepted without argument my 60 percent reduction in his claim.

I had several offers of jobs that sounded pretty good from insurance companies in those days, but I stuck to my objective and turned them down. By 1931 my technical education was adequate for me to take the examination for the CPA certificate. I was encouraged in this by my employers, who promised me a partnership if I qualified to become a member of the American Institute of Accountants. After studying the educational and experience requirements of several states' jurisdictions that licensed certified public accountants, I found that by taking the separate CPA examinations of New York and Ohio and the membership examination of the American Institute of Accountants, it would be possible for me to qualify fully in each of these three jurisdictions because of the manner in which their experience credits were interwoven. I did exactly that, taking all three examinations in the space of a few months and passing them all.

Presented with this fait accompli, the firm announced at once that I had been admitted to partnership. Under the conditions of 1931 this meant merely that my responsibilities had increased, but not my income.

My housing experiences were adventurous, too. For a year or so I lived at the Prospect Park YMCA in Brooklyn; next, for about a year, with three young men from Illinois in an apartment on Eleventh Street in Greenwich Village; then for a year as a roomer with a married couple in an apartment on Twenty-Third Street in Manhattan; and finally with the same couple in an apartment in Montclair, New Jersey. Through these moves, and the many rambling walks I took on weekends, I saw and smelled and felt a lot of life of the metropolis. On foot, I covered Broadway from end to end, the Bowery and Chinatown, Hester Street and the lower East side, Brooklyn and the Bronx. I read Jacob Riis's *How the Other*

*Half Lives* and knew from what I could see that his descriptions of poverty and deprivation were not exaggerated.

Life in a YMCA was more than interesting, and there was always something going on. I became the handball champion of the fifth floor, only to lose out for the club championship ignominiously by a disastrous 21–2 to a fellow on the fourth. I attended lectures and political speeches and once was impressed by hearing Fiorello La Guardia, then a leading political figure in New York City and later its mayor. I fended off several homosexual advances. And there were a lot of bull sessions, long talks about politics and careers and girls and sex, and many things in general. Out of one of those meetings came a compact among four of us who had not yet had a sexual experience. The deal was that the first one who had the opportunity would not only take it, whatever the circumstances, but would make very precise notes and report back to the others.

I was the winner. On an audit assignment in Plattsburgh, in upstate New York, I met a charming redhead who was in college there. We had dinner and then drove to a park on the bank of Lake Champlain. The setting, the moonlight, and nature's instincts took over, and before the evening had passed I had lost my innocence. I was not wholly truthful or thorough in my account later to my friends at the Y, mostly because I wanted to keep the occasion and the feeling wholly mine. I still remember every detail, sixty-five years later, and often have wished I could tell Louise again how considerate, sweet, and lovely I thought her to be on that evening. Unfortunately, my work took me back to New York the next day and we never met again.

I was too busy for several years after reaching New York to be looking for serious romance, and I had still not shed my uncomfortable feelings in the presence of the opposite sex. Despite one success, I didn't seem to know the right approach, and I felt myself very much a country hick in the big city. It took a long while to outgrow that.

Early in 1931 the firm's work took me again to upstate New York, this time for about two months to work on an investigation of contract costs at a company in Herkimer. I found life there exceedingly lonesome; that company's policy did not permit me to associate after hours with its employees, and I knew no one else within hundreds of miles. Then there came a day when a gold inlay fell out of one of my teeth and I had to get a dentist to recement it. His receptionist was a young, attractive girl of my age, just what I was looking for, but the dentist ushered me in and out so efficiently that I had no time to get acquainted with her. Being determined not to miss such a lovely prospect, and not even knowing her name, I considered the various approaches I might take but none seemed practical. I couldn't just barge in the office and ask for a date, and I didn't think I would fare any better by waiting outside the door at closing time. After some cogitation, I hit on a solution. That night I maneuvered with a pin for an hour to dislodge the inlay again so I could legitimately go back to the dentist. It worked. By arriving thirty minutes ahead of the appointed time, I managed to get into enough conversation to invite her to dinner, and she accepted. The dentist was bewildered at the failure of the filling to stay in and mumbled something about "poor cement these days." Catherine was a delightful person and we became good friends, but, as in the usual summer resort romance, we lost track of each other soon after my assignment ended and I had to return to New York.

But love did come, as it does to all struggling storybook characters. Somehow I recognized it from the start, but I almost lost the girl by ineptitude.

Late in 1931, the treasurer of one of our client companies invited me to his home on Staten Island for dinner and a game of bridge. The fourth was his wife's sister, tall and lanky, attractive, with a vivacious personality, and a Powers model who had been educated at Hunter College in Manhattan. She made me feel at ease through the evening, and when I was driven to the ferry back to Manhattan and we separated, I was bold enough to squeeze her hand and ask if I could call her for a date. She was agreeable.

Eleven weeks later I phoned her, as though no time had intervened. I had been in the middle of an intensive review course for the CPA examinations and had given that all my attention. There just was no time to devote to anything but the studies I needed to carry out my life plans. She was a very popular person, always sought for dates, and the idea of being set aside for so long intrigued her so much that when I did phone she was willing to take another look at me.

Whatever the chemistry is that makes romance bloom, it was present when Kathleen and I were together, although our meetings were not always smooth. She was hesitant about committing herself to marriage, and held out long after I was sure she was destined to be my life partner.

On one sometimes touchy subject, she gave me no concerns. Coming from a modest background, her expectations were modest.

When I asked her what she wanted a husband to achieve in life, she thought he should someday be earning $500 a month and should have $30,000 saved to assure security for old age for both. In 1932 these amounts were not exactly insignificant, but they did seem to be mini-targets for my lofty ambitions.

We saw each other often and spent an increasing amount of time together in 1931 and 1932, at parties, movies, the theater, playing tennis, and with members of her family. I worked up a considerable degree of conviction about marriage and was in the process of breaking down her reluctance to the idea when fate intervened and almost destroyed the romance entirely.

Early 1933 was the worst of times and it brought Alexander Grant & Company to the rocks. The firm had been started in 1924 by Grant, then a brilliant young CPA of twenty-five whose ambitions exceeded his rate of progress within the accounting firm of Ernst & Ernst, so he had resigned to establish his own practice. He achieved a reasonable degree of success and by 1929 had four partners, offices in Chicago and New York, and about a dozen employees. The depression years cut his clientele considerably, but being a man who dared difficulty, he undertook in addition to try to save a floundering stove manufacturer from bankruptcy. In the course of that undertaking, he invested all his money and much of his time in acquiring control of the company. The desperate situation, in the face of the declining economic trend, bore down heavily on his personal attention to the accounting practice. In the face of all this, his Chicago partners withdrew from the firm early in 1933 and took their clients with them, leaving very little behind with which to continue. There were then two partners in New York, Milo Hopkins and I, and we anguished over the probable dissolution of the firm and our own fates in that event.

At this juncture, Grant suggested that I move to Chicago and pick up the pieces there as managing partner, leaving Hopkins in charge in New York. This desperation plan didn't seem quite like the kind of opportunity Horatio Alger would offer, but after some deliberation and hesitancy I agreed to go. Kathleen encouraged the decision, on the grounds that a period of separation would give us time to ensure we were meant for each other. Optimistic as usual, I promised to return for her as soon as I got everything straightened out in Chicago.

Not until after I arrived there on March 1, 1933, did I find out how desperate things were for the country and for our practice. I didn't realize it then, but March was to become the very month that the nation's banks were closed by presidential order, to be opened one by one only if and after examiners found them worthy. Unemployment reached its worst.

Grant and I reviewed the remains of the client list and concluded that the total annual income we could count on for sure was only about $5,000. I scanned the suite of ten offices and asked what the rent was. "It's $585 a month," Grant said, "but don't worry about that. We're not paying it."

That was true enough, and it was not unusual. Office buildings with continually declining tenancies, often 50 percent vacant, had no choice but to permit indigent tenants to stay on and accumulate unpaid rent in the hope that some of them, someday, would recover and pay up.

That was the base from which I started there, and the going was grim. New clients were hard to find and old ones had difficulty in paying. But there were possibilities of work here, too, as in New York, in connection with insurance claim audits, and I spent most of my time for some years on such assignments. I acquired considerably more expertise and an enhanced reputation in insurance circles as a result of this activity, and wrote articles and gave a number of lectures on the subject of detecting and settling falsified claims.

My salary was sixty dollars a week, but like the rent, it just remained unpaid when there was no money in the bank. These were not exactly ideal conditions in which to get married, with my savings less than a thousand dollars and with current income indefinite.

But true love is supposed to find a way, and it did. Grant and his wife drove to New York in the early summer of the year and, sensing my loneliness, prevailed upon Kathleen to ride back with them as a houseguest. Not knowing about this in advance, I had arranged to have my troublesome tonsils removed on credit by a friendly but clumsy doctor. When Kathleen arrived in Chicago, I was in the hospital, literally quite speechless. After I recovered a few days later we drove with the Grants to their summer home in Madison, Wisconsin; there, one evening in Lover's Lane on the shore of Lake Mendota, I proposed and she accepted. The wedding was set for early September in New York. She did not have to clear this with her family; I found out later that they had been rooting for me against the competition for a long time.

A week before the wedding I bought a brand-new red Plymouth coupe with a rumble seat for a toughly negotiated price of $620 plus

$35 for a radio, payable $175 down and $40 a month for twelve months, without interest. Not being able to finance the cost of a suitable diamond, I convinced Kathleen that I would get her a much better one if she were willing to be patient until my income grew. I did buy her a gold wedding band, engraved inside with our initials, from a friendly wholesale jeweler for exactly two dollars.* I set out at once to drive to New York, with just enough money left for the wedding and honeymoon. After the ceremony and family breakfast on September 7, 1933, we headed north through New England to Canada and westward to Minnesota.

My father and mother, who had not met Kathleen, could not afford to attend the wedding, so we spent several days with them when we reached Shakopee. Our Chaska relatives initiated Kathleen with a noisy shivaree of pots and pans and other noisemakers, and the Shakopee band came and played a few numbers. Then Mother left with us for the drive to Chicago, her first trip outside of Minnesota, and a visit to the tiny three-room apartment I had selected for our home. It was a tribute to Kathleen that everything went smoothly under these confined conditions. She had been welcomed enthusiastically by every member of the Stans family, and that spirit of affection gave us both added courage to face the inevitable hazards of living in those serious times.

---

*This was a good investment, as the cost averaged out to about four cents a year of our married life. Kathleen had to wait almost ten years, however, before she received a diamond ring worthy of her.

# CHAPTER THREE

# Challenging the Ways of Accounting

The election of Franklin D. Roosevelt in 1932 had offered a germ of hope for the national economy, but the country had to go through the frantic consequences of bank closings, bankruptcies, and massive unemployment, the National Recovery Administration (NRA) and other political nostrums, and suffer many tremors and hasty remedies. Finally the approach of a world war brought a recovery.

After our marriage in September 1933, Kathleen worked for several years as a model at Marshall Field's store in order to augment my irregular income. By 1935, despite continuing sluggish conditions, the accounting business began to improve and my salary was paid regularly.

Alexander Grant died in 1938, still working desperately to save the stove manufacturer; more fairly stated, he died trying to save the jobs and security of its three hundred employees when few people had the means to buy its products.

Hopkins, my partner in New York, had a tempting offer to become a vice president of the Hanover Bank there in 1940 and withdrew from the accounting firm, leaving me as its sole owner. I agreed to his departure with the condition that he arrange with the bank to stay on as chairman of the stove company until after the end of the forthcoming war. This meant that I had to find a new partner in New York and then balance my time between holding the stove business together and building an accounting firm in both Chicago and New York. For several years I worked a regular fifteen-hour day and seven-day week, and was away from home almost two thirds of the time. But somehow the economic crisis lessened and gradual upward momentum began to help carry everything along.

We sold the stove company in 1945, for the benefit of the widow of Alexander Grant. Meanwhile, I found capable new accounting partners in both cities, and set out for new worlds to conquer. My personal clientele in Bloomington, Illinois, and La Crosse, Wisconsin, grew to the point that we established an office in each place to service them. A series of insurance claim audits in Los Angeles took me there frequently enough to set up an office and give it a start under a partner transferred from Chicago. A client in Phoenix introduced me to a CPA in that city, and I succeeded in getting him to merge his office into our firm. The same happened in Cincinnati and Washington and Honolulu and Roanoke and elsewhere, and we joined the pattern of rapid expansion being set by the eight large national accounting firms. We resisted offers of merger into several bigger partnerships, determined to grow the hard way on our own. I traveled widely from one city to another, dealing with client relations and the firm's progress. The time was right for aggressive growth, and with the help of its cadre of young partners, Alexander Grant & Company continued to expand spectacularly.

In 1934 times had been so bad that Kathleen and I had no vacation, but in 1935 we spent several weeks with another young couple at a resort near Ely in northern Minnesota. It was a lovely spot, but our fishing fun was constantly being interrupted by long-distance calls from the office and daily bundles of mail needing attention. We had little real relaxation on the trip, and I was determined that that would not happen again. A vacation together was one custom that Kathleen and I adopted early in our marriage; it not only refreshed us from time to time from the stresses of my work but also gave our personal relationship periodic occasions to renew and strengthen. To enhance those benefits we also adopted the scheme of taking our annual vacations outside the United States. This provided us with opportunities for the uncommon adventures we both enjoyed.

Although Kathleen was a city gal who had never before held a wriggling fish in her hands, she became an ardent fisherwoman on that first trip and was more than willing to do it often. So the next summer we scheduled a fishing vacation in western Ontario at a small remote fishing camp that could be reached only by driving to the northern end of the roads and portaging by canoe for a day through a chain of five lakes. It was primeval country, untouched by man's civilization, and the fishing was unbelievably good. At McDonald's Lodge, we caught—and put back into the water—muskies, northern pike, wall-eyed pike, and lake trout each day until we were completely exhausted.

After a week of that, I hired an Indian guide and set off on a canoe trip into an unmapped area, just to explore, leaving Kathleen in camp with the McDonalds. On the third day out, my guide spotted another Indian paddling vigorously across the lake to catch up with us. He had spent three days in the chase, and he proudly handed me a telegram from the nearest railroad terminal more than fifty miles away by water. It was from my office in Chicago: *Please telephone urgently before Thursday.* I read it twice and then slowly and deliberately tore it into small bits, with a broad smile. It was now Saturday and the crisis, whatever it was, was past. The poor bewildered Indian messenger never understood what madness could cause the white man to pay so little attention to something that was supposed to be so important.

The emergency had been handled in the meantime, of course, and my point had been made. From then on I was never interrupted on my holidays. But once having started the practice of distant vacations we continued it, and in the next twenty years took foreign holidays. There were foreign trips and tours in Europe, Mexico, Bermuda, and Asia. Then we discovered Africa.

Despite the long hours and frequent travel connected with my business, there was time in these Chicago days to think of building a family. When nature failed to come through with children, we adopted a baby boy from St. Vincent's Orphanage in Chicago; he was followed a year later by a baby sister from the same orphanage. On December 7, 1941, we completed negotiations to buy a fine, sturdy, French Provincial house in Kenilworth. The price was $28,500, my salary was barely $100 a week, and the war that was sure to follow threatened all sense of security. But we went ahead with the purchase, and a year later had the courage to adopt twins, a boy and a girl, from The Cradle in Evanston.

These four children, Steven, Maureen, Theodore, and Terrell, completed our family plans and gave us a merry time. Their personalities and characteristics differed over quite a range, and there were frequent problems of health and behavior. Kathleen knew instinctively how to cope with each concern as it came along, and in the custom of the decades of the 1940s and 1950s, she bore the brunt of their rearing. She was a magnificent mother and made up fully for my extended absences during the years when I was trying so hard to build a business. Each child in his or her own way developed into a fine citizen, and we mixed pride and pleasure in them with gratitude for our own good fortune in finding them. The accident of birth being what it is, in that character cannot be foreplanned, we never felt a loss in not having children born to us.

Bringing them up was far from a smooth affair. Their problems included such widely different behavior and adjustment difficulties as minor police incidents, educational setbacks, hyperkinesis, temporarily impaired eyesight, psychological disturbances, and the later trauma of one's early divorce. Fortunately, their passage through the teen years predated the drug culture and the era of college upheaval. Eventually, all our concerns were ironed out, each child married happily and settled down, in time adding nine grandchildren and three great-grandchildren to our succession.

Through the years there were business experiences that were especially gratifying, and one or two of them were landmarks in my personal education. For example, the seven years I spent as a part-time officer of Alexander Grant's small stove factory after he died seemed to involve every conceivable type of business difficulty. There were continuing concerns with design and engineering, sales, production, pricing, capital expenditures, budgeting, and finance. In an operation of $2 million to $3 million a year, it gave me an invaluable insight into the special problems of small businesses and an appreciation of those of a company of any size. In addition, there were the human interests of internal politics, competition among employees, and labor relations. The plant workers were members of one of the oldest unions in the country, the Iron Molders and Foundry Workers Union, and we succeeded during World War II in working out differences between management and labor without strife. With three hundred employees it was not possible to know every one personally, but it was at least possible for them to know us, and both Hopkins and I worked hard to cultivate an amicable relationship. We attended each annual picnic and played baseball with the foundrymen and sheet metal workers and enamelers. On one occasion, when I had taken a vacation in Canada and shot a moose, we had a moose-and-beer picnic for the entire plant upon my return. The feelings of respect must have been reciprocated, because in 1943 I was invited to a meeting of the local and was inducted an honorary member of the IMFWU. I have retained my card ever since, with real satisfaction, even though I could never make a mold or pour a casting.

Another experience that worked out well was with Illinois Wesleyan University. In the late thirties this fine old institution was running out of money at a rate that threatened its closing in a year or so. As its auditor, I saw its plight. With losses of $150,000 a year, a poorly invested endowment of only $2 million, and a low-paid faculty, there was not much hope of survival. The chairman of the Board of Trustees, Ned Dolan, had become a good friend and we discussed the dilemma on several occasions. Endowment income could not be increased because most of the money was invested in farms that were not salable while farm product prices were low. I proposed that the school recognize its desperation and chance some of its assets on investments that could be heavily leveraged, using small down payments and huge debt, with the objective of an annual return of 30 percent to 50 percent on their actual equities. The board placed a limited amount of capital from the endowment fund at my disposal, and I invested it accordingly.

A typical transaction involved the purchase of a wire spring company for $750,000, of which 5 percent was paid down and the balance was to be due over ten years, with low interest. If the business prospered, the school got a high return. If it failed, the loss was bearable. Within two or three years, I put the school into about twenty such ventures with a total cash investment of around $600,000. Not one was a loser. A few broke even, and some had to be renegotiated, but enough were successful to provide income to cover the college's operating losses and build its capital funds. The improving economy made these years right for such financial adventuring, and it perhaps could never be repeated; but the operation while it lasted earned perhaps $5 million for the university. While it may be an exaggeration to say that this program saved Wesleyan, the income certainly made its survival in that troubled era a much more likely outcome. The president of the school reported in 1954, for example, that in that year alone the income from these investments reduced what would have been a deficit of $520,000 to a mere $20,000.

During this Chicago period, in 1937, Kathleen and I decided to create the Stans Foundation, a nonprofit corporation that would be a family fund for charitable purposes, making it possible to share with others some of the good fortune we confidently expected to enjoy. In the early years, we placed in it some low-cost securities that we hoped would grow in value, and they did. Some small further contributions brought our total investment to about $150,000. Increases in values of securities and real estate in its portfolio vaulted the assets of the foundation to about $5 million by 1990, by which time over $3 million more had been distributed as grants to selected charities. We received no personal benefits from all this beyond the satisfaction of giving to worthy causes and the personal gratification of having built a successful investment program for the foundation.

Besides regular annual amounts to churches, colleges, and health causes, the foundation stimulated and supported two specific large projects. One was the Nature Museum of York County (later the Museum of York County), South Carolina, to which it made contributions to help build the Stans African Halls, a natural history display of African artifacts and animals. Largely as the result of our gifts in money and exhibit specimens, the Halls' two buildings soon will house in simulated natural backgrounds the largest display of fully restored African animals, in number of varieties, anywhere in the world, and will be an important educational medium for thousands of children each year.

The Stans Foundation's other major interest has been the Minnesota Valley restoration project known as Murphy's Landing, a historical collection of original buildings that reconstructs a Minnesota village of one hundred years ago, located just outside my hometown of Shakopee. Our total contributions to this venture and to the Stans African Halls have each amounted to well over $1 million.

Accountancy had undoubtedly turned out to be the right career for me to build on. From the beginning I was fascinated with the capabilities of numbers. Herding them into orderly and balanced arrays to serve management and fiscal purposes came naturally and easily. Public accounting is essentially the challenge of testing the accuracy of data compiled by others. This became more interesting the more the assignment departed from the routine, as it did in my early days in examining embezzlement, fire, and robbery insurance claims. Later, the same sense of fiscal analysis took me into a considerable level of activity in planning business combinations and mergers, or developing personal investment programs and estate plans for clients. Instinctively, from the day I left home at seventeen, I kept a full set of accounts of my personal income and expenditures and my personal net worth throughout my life.

Twice in the early 1940s I had the temerity to testify before the Senate Finance Committee in Washington on tax matters. In 1943, I presented arguments on behalf of several clients for the repeal of what was known as the "second windfall provision" of the income tax law. Originally designed to put a confiscatory tax on business windfall earnings resulting from the war, it had been written in a way that caused unintended inequities, some of which I was able to demonstrate from actual case histories. The second time was in 1945 when, as an official of the stove manufacturer, I appealed for the elimination of the "luxury" excise tax that then applied to stoves and ranges, which I contended were unquestionably home necessities and not luxuries.

In both cases my efforts were successful, and I was given to believe that my testimony had been a main factor in the outcome. There was something very exhilarating in these two experiences. Although I began testifying in trepidation and awe, I found courage in the obvious desire of the committee members to learn what the facts were and then deal with them objectively. The first two senators I met were Walter George of Georgia and Robert Taft of Ohio, and I was captivated by their informality and their interest and knowledge of the subjects and, of course, was pleased to have them endorse the views I presented.

From 1941 through 1955, I gave a large share of my time to work in and for the accounting profession, holding leadership positions in several state and national organizations and writing and speaking frequently.

One amusing incident happened in Illinois while I was chairman of a public relations committee of the Illinois Society of CPAs. I conceived the idea that we ought to do more to impress the leading politicians about the special talents of CPAs, so with the help of other members I arranged for presentations to be made by meeting, letter, or phone to the city, county, and state leaders of the Republican and Democratic parties. We asked specifically that CPAs be considered more often in the future for appointment to positions involving accounting or financial skills. We received no promises but got one response that showed how the political mind sometimes works. Some months later there was a vacancy in the office of coroner and a certified public accountant was appointed to the post! Word had obviously gone around among the politicos that something should be done for those accountants, and this was the first thing that came along.

In my professional practice and in my readings of original corporate financial reports and their excerpted versions in the daily press, I came to feel that professional accounting techniques had not advanced adequately in the fifty years since the profession had originally acquired its footing in the United States. As a respected cadre of professionals skilled in the processes of testing the accuracy and dependability of representations made to owners and creditors as to their periodic earnings and financial strength, the more I looked into the matter as an individual and as a member of the American Institute of Accountants Committee on Accounting Procedure, the more I became convinced that continued inadequacy in serving this purpose would lead the profession into a corner from which the only escape would be government regulation. I conceived of the issue as being one of social responsibility that should instead be attacked by the profession as a whole, which meant that it would be delinquent if it did not seek to fulfill that responsibility. The obvious penalties of inattention were bound to be government control of the standards and processes of the accounting function when it really ought to be self-regulation by the profession. In a number of speeches and articles, I made that point. Although the Securities Acts of 1933 and 1937 had specifically fixed certain accounting requirements to be met in financial statements filed with the Securities and Exchange Commission, there was still a vast gap of inadequate reporting.

Understandably there was no widespread human cry of support for these broad suggestions, but there was a considerable amount of discussion among the major accounting firms and banks and businessmen. A retired manager of the international firm of Price Waterhouse, highly respected in the profession, wrote a caustic reply disagreeing with much of what I had proposed, and I analyzed it carefully and responded. I received many suggestions from individual accountants and partners of large firms urging that I continue the protest. I proceeded to preach the same message over a period of several years until it took on the dimensions of a one-man crusade.

In 1947 I made some speeches on the social responsibility of accounting, with the theme that "those who deal with financial accounting should help to establish strength for the system by permitting no compromise with either independent truthfulness or with a vocation to serve the public interest." My full text was reprinted in the *Journal of Accountancy* in August 1948 under the editor's headnote summarizing the content as contending that "[g]enerally accepted accounting principles will have to improve if financial reporting is to measure up to the social responsibility accounting should assume. Work must be done on form of income statement; on codification of principles, on concepts of income, reserves, disclosure, terminology. By improving these factors accounting can help resolve social conflict."

Behind all this was the idea that, as a concomitant of the industrial revolution, accounting had become the language of business, and it was the duty of its professionals to see that it evolved as rapidly as possible into a vital tool of the economy it served. In performing that function it had not only to be honest in the hands of its artisans but also truthful in the images it conveyed. This was not possible unless there was greater uniformity in the meanings of terms and in the application of principles, so that the same set of facts in two situations would produce essentially the same result in a similar format. Such a goal could not be achieved until principles were enunciated authoritatively and codified for all to use, and until currently permissible variations in practice were narrowed.

If this were done, the representations of companies and their auditors as to earnings and other financial data could be unfailingly relied upon by all those interested, including investors, bankers, the general public, labor unions, legislators, and government agencies. This, in turn, would build a base for confidence in the system by eliminating misunderstandings of the wage-cost-price-profit-capital relationships and by correcting erroneous impressions as to the size of earnings, the impact of taxation, or the benefits received by owners. I contended that current accounting practices were inadequate for a real public understanding of the facts of business. I alleged that they lacked clarity, completeness, comparability, definition, limitation, and uniformity, and that they had just enough ambiguity, inaccuracy, inconsistency, noncomparability, and extremes of practice to create a tool of distortion and confusion for those who served adverse purposes through public unrest or distrust.

I then went to battle on some of the specifics of weaknesses in financial reporting by first focusing on the subject of reserves, and my article on this, following a number of speeches, appeared in the

*Journal of Accountancy* in March 1948. It was a common practice at that time for companies in good years to understate their earnings by creating "reserves for possible future losses" of one kind or another. These provisions were entirely arbitrary or at best subjective and not susceptible to any valid system of measurement. When bad years came along, reported earnings were then improved by transferring back some or all of the reserves. These patent attempts at equalization of profits distorted the historic facts and made comparisons between years and between companies meaningless.

I was so bold as to recite a number of specific companies that had engaged in this practice, and this brought down on me the wrath of some of their officers and their auditors. One that I especially quoted was a press story that read, "Harassed by strikes United States Steel Corporation was able to operate at a profit in the first half of 1946 only by lavishly dipping into reserves, it was reported yesterday." The company had reported net income of $24 million only after transferring $29 million from reserves set aside in earlier years. This was accounting by management whim, whereby profit could be whatever the company wanted it to be, and it was inexcusable. Many companies, in blunt terms, could hide profits when they were good and pad them when they were poor, and I contended that there was no social justification for such practices. They gave labor unions the weapon for claiming that corporations generally concealed and distorted their profits. My words were a bold attack on an inexcusable procedure, and with the strong consensus that followed, the institute promptly legislated the practice to an end.

I went on to urge CPAs to take an increased part in the workings of the political parties, to attend political meetings, and to interest themselves in the affairs of government at all levels; to support every proposition that would emphasize the value of better accounting and financial administration in government; and to enlist for service in government positions in the executive branch that could benefit from specialized accounting skills.

Accounting change did come, but it was painfully slow. The institute's Committee on Accounting Procedure was succeeded by an Accounting Principles Board with more weight, and that in turn was supplanted in time by a Financial Accounting Standards Board of accountants, businessmen, and government officials with still more power and influence. Over the years income statements have been improved, terms have been better defined, basic principles have been formalized and enunciated, and practices have been narrowed. Corporate financial statements are now much more reliable and comparable. Public accounting is recognized as having a responsibility to all segments of the society rather than merely to a select clientele.

Nevertheless, the complexity of these matters, difficulties with semantics, and the resistance to change within and without the profession conspired to reduce the process at times to a crawl. The long time occupied in achieving progress in the technical objectives, and the further steps remaining, regrettably prevented the achievement of the really important goals. I do believe that I was a leader in awakening the profession to a sense of responsibility, and that it did move forward with a deliberate speed that made it unnecessary for government to force it to do so.

Then on another front, one thing that could be done for the independent local CPA was to codify somehow the material he ought to know and observe. The larger firms had organized much of these data to suit their purposes, but it was closely held. Marquis Eaton, a brilliant and farseeing Texas CPA, agreed with me that what was needed was a CPA handbook that would give the small practitioner a statement of high standards (as applied in practice) in such a way as to make them readily accessible. It would "deal with all things that would help the accountant to run his own office, cut down his costs, reduce waste of time, and tighten his procedures." I agreed to prepare an outline of such a project, which I did with Eaton's endorsement, and presented it to the institute's executive committee in July 1950. It was endorsed enthusiastically, and as always happens, since I was the one who made the presentation, I became chairman of the committee to produce the product.

The final work contained 1,800 pages in two volumes and was well received. Tens of thousands of copies were sold in the course of time, before it eventually succumbed to new requirements and new presentations. Probably more than anything else, my work on the advancement of the professionalization of public accounting, in lieu of freehand judgment of practitioners, and the CPA Handbook influenced a grateful profession to honor me twice on the same day in September 1954 with the institute's annual gold medal for outstanding service and with election to the presidency of the institute. It was the only time the two honors were ever given simultaneously to an individual.

In my one-year term as president I traveled widely, making talks to professional and business groups in more than half the states, from Maine to Hawaii, attending for a week an Inter-American Conference on Accounting in São Paulo, Brazil, and participating in extensive negotiations with representatives of the American Bar Association on the matter of the rights of CPAs to engage in income tax practice. In between, in lieu of a vacation, I spent a month under a contract with our government's foreign aid program in a survey of the fiscal and accounting system of Thailand. Each of these covered stimulating new ground, each was intensely challenging, and each produced memorable incidents.

The controversy between the legal and accounting professions over income tax work in those days was intense, serious, and in a way critical to both. At the extremes, there were members of the bar who felt that the preparation and defense of income tax returns was the practice of law and that accountants should do none of it; and there were accountants who believed that all tax work, including the handling of cases in the tax court, was accounting work that lawyers were incapable of doing. In between were reasonable members of both professions who saw that both disciplines were essential. In an attempt to break the impasse, saner heads on both sides had caused a National Conference of Lawyers and Certified Public Accountants to be created in 1951. I was one of the CPA members. Negotiations continued for several years, punctuated with occasional bursts of state litigation despite the pleas of the conference to allow time for the problem to be worked out amicably.

When I became president of the AICPA, I set as one of my major goals the finding of a mutually satisfactory solution. We developed a proposal for cooperation between the professions, but the ABA rejected the document. The subject was finally resolved, on approximately the lines we had proposed, shortly after my term of office had expired.

All of these professional activities through the years, added to my responsibilities with Alexander Grant & Company and to the several companies that I served as a director, made life go by at a lightning pace. I was told by persons in a position to know that no earlier president of the institute had driven himself so hard. But that was only for one year. All my other years were just as busy. My sense of adventure in whatever I did was not to be denied, and I was willing to take on whatever tasks to which it led me.

No aspect of all those years with Alexander Grant & Company gave me more satisfaction than the success I had in picking people to work with me. It built my sense of pride to see them develop in capacity, take on increased burdens, and succeed in filling important niches in the firm and in the profession, to which they made many contributions. The ultimate payoff on all this was the continued success of the business after I left it later for other fields, and nothing pleased me more than to see its forward progress continue and accelerate.

At the beginning of 1953 when I was forty-five years old, I could look back at my experiences in public accounting and conclude that, with the help of many carefully selected partners and thousands of overtime hours that we had all contributed, our accounting firm had grown to a point where it was clearly in reach of our original objectives. We had enlarged its geographical spread from two cities to twenty, its number of partners from three to about eighty, and its employee roll to four hundred. Its name and reputation were well and favorably recognized in financial and business circles, and the latest exchanges of confidential information among our major competitors showed that we could accurately claim to be the ninth largest public accounting firm in the United States. With the profession generally divided in the public mind between a "Big 8" and "all others," it was clear what our next goal would be. But I did not wait to see all that happen. I had itchy feet, and in 1953 my footsteps aimed toward Washington.

It was at this juncture, coincidental with the election of Dwight D. Eisenhower to the presidency, that opportunity intervened, at first in a minor and unpromising way and then in a series of unexpected advances into the federal government. During the Eisenhower administration I attained a prominent Cabinet-level position in the forefront of the federal government's fiscal affairs, a fortuitous rate of progress seldom achieved by a person lacking government know-how or political acumen. Without realizing it, I was on my way to the highest and most dramatic moments of my life. Along that course I was also destined to encounter some of the most bizarre aspects of Washington's way of life.

CHAPTER FOUR

# Modernizing
# Benjamin Franklin

After Eisenhower's election in 1952 and shortly
before he took office in 1953, I learned that a group of certified
public accountants, some from the business world and some from
public accounting firms, was going to be formed by John Taber,
chairman of the House Appropriations Committee, to assist in the
committee's review of the federal budget for 1954. There had been
a precedent for this procedure in 1946, at the outset of the Eightieth
Congress, when the Republicans held control of the House for the
first time since 1930, and Taber had asked Ed Kracke, a partner in
the national accounting firm of Haskins and Sells, to get a number
of such accounting experts together for a similar reason. The group
had apparently turned out to be effective in finding potential savings
in the Truman budget for fiscal 1948, despite their limited firsthand
knowledge of government programs. Now, in 1953, the Republicans
had gained control of the House for the second time in more than
twenty years and Taber wanted a similar operation. This time it
could be even more effective because Eisenhower, who had campaigned on a promise of government economy, had assured Taber of
the cooperation of his entire Cabinet, a circumstance that had not
prevailed in 1946: his new director of the budget, Joe Dodge, a

43

tough Detroit banker, welcomed any help he could get in carrying out Eisenhower's directive to slice the spending proposals for fiscal 1954 that Truman had presented to Congress just before he left office.

I knew about the Kracke-led team that had explored the 1948 budget, so at the first feasible date after the 1952 election I volunteered my services to him if he were to be called on again. Taber had already asked him, he said, and he welcomed my offer. Ultimately, he put together about seventy-five CPAs and, with the guidance of the House Appropriations Committee staff, assigned them one by one to examine individual segments of the budget and make their recommendations for reductions. It was to be a six-week chore for each person; we were to be paid fifty dollars a working day for our services, this to include travel and living expenses.

On the day in February that I reported to the committee to begin work, the details of the budget for the Post Office Department were ready for review. The mail service was, or was supposed to be, a business-type function, and its scale of operations made it comparable to a major corporation. It had massive payrolls, transportation costs, and expenses of buildings and facilities, all adding up to almost $3 billion a year at that time. In addition to delivering mail, it conducted banking and money order activities, and the scope of its turnover had to be immense. Its financial transactions amounted to $10 billion a year. It looked like a good target for economy, and that was what I wanted. I was given a general briefing for a few hours on the federal budget processes and then, with the help of two young assistants from the General Accounting Office (GAO), set right to work.

The mystique of dealing in billions was intriguing. I tried to visualize a billion pieces of mail or a billion dollars and my imagination left me gasping. So did the idea of 520,000 employees working in 49,000 places (post offices, branches and terminals), or 400 million money orders a year, or 200 million insurance transactions annually. Magnitudes like those were far beyond the scope of my previous experience, and I knew I could not be effective unless I could adjust my mind to them. It would be useless to take a nickel-and-dime approach to budget-cutting in such a universe. It took a while, but eventually I bridged the gap and began to relish the reality that, with multipliers so large, a saving of a fraction of a cent in one repetitive operation could multiply into a budget reduction of millions of dollars.

At the end of six weeks I had learned a lot about the U.S. Postal Service and almost all of it was appalling. Coming from the outside world of efficient business, I found myself in a never-never land of government inefficiency, political patronage, meaningless record-keeping, and historically inept management. It was a world of frozen precedent, waste, and resistance to change.

An institution with an unparalleled tradition of service touching the lives of almost every family daily, our mail system had failed to take notice of the passage of the nineteenth century and the first half of the twentieth. With high quality personnel, many recruited in the depressed 1930s when post office work was treasured for its job security, the mail service was trying to carry on its unique and invaluable function, delivering billions of letters and parcels, without any of the tools considered essential to managing and operating a huge enterprise.

Without a treasurer or controller to match those managing the finances of a business operation, the Post Office had no accounting system for its executives to work with in exercising control over the colossus they had to run. Its books were elementary in form, having last been "modernized" in 1908, forty-five years earlier. In fact, only two years had elapsed since the department in late 1950 had acquired the right to keep its own books; until then every voucher for postal expenses had been examined, recorded, and filed by another agency of the federal government, in a bookkeeping plant in Asheville, North Carolina, far away from postal management. Financial statements were not available until more than a year after the period to which they related.

Mail was still being handled as it had been in the days when Benjamin Franklin was the first postmaster general under the Continental Congress, even though the volume had grown to fifty billion pieces a year. The Pony Express had been replaced by the railroad and the airplane, but the sorting and distributing of letters and magazines was still being done by individual reading of address-es and manual sorting into pigeonhole cases. On the average, each piece of mail passed through seven or more pairs of hands and eyes before it was delivered.

Worst of all, the Congress had a stranglehold on almost everything the Post Office management did. By law, Congress had retained exclusive authority to alter services, and by practice, it exercised a heavy hand over the hiring and firing of postmasters, supervisors, clerks, and carriers. There was not a single certified public accountant in the entire postal system, and only a couple of engineers. There was no program of innovative research, and none aimed directly at the unique needs of the department in handling and routing its billions of pieces of mail of all sizes. No new post office building had been built with government money for fifteen years. Mailboxes and trucks were still covered in drab green paint because the Navy had a large overstock of it after World War I and had given it to the Post Office, and no one had thought to change specifications after that supply was used up.

According to financial reports of the department, it was running at a loss of $700 million annually and headed for worse. Even that was a meaningless figure, because it had been loaded through the years with a long list of free services and subsidies for other government departments and for the public. Airline subsidies were being paid by the Post Office, and mail was being carried free for all government agencies and the Congress. On the other hand, the department received free benefits and services from other government units, principally the use of government-bought buildings. No one had ever put down on paper the dollars-and-cents effect of all these transactions on the postal deficit, or computed what the real loss was. Postage rates had not been changed in more than twenty years, and a letter was delivered anywhere in the country for three cents, despite large wage advances and other cost increases, principally because the Congress had never expressed a financial policy against which revenue needs could be documented. Postal box rents had not been increased for fifty years. Prices of stamped envelopes, despite much higher costs, had not been raised since 1947.

Consistent with this lack of attention to revenues, there was no organized program of cost reduction, and no application of engineering sciences to increasing the efficiency of mail pickup, transportation, and delivery. I did not exaggerate in calling the Post Office at this time "the most antiquated, antediluvian, obsolete, tradition-riddled institution in the government." Obviously a massive infusion of modern management principles, practices, and technology was long overdue.

Upon finishing my review of the department's budget and operations late in March, I wrote a report of over one hundred typed pages. It was not of much immediate help to the Appropriations Committee in budget-cutting, because it recommended reductions of only $22 million in a proposed budget of $2.8 billion, or less than 1 percent. But my work could be of real assistance to the postmaster general in appraising his problems, I thought, and could produce large benefits in the long run if it contained helpful, constructive suggestions as to how to manage his colossal department. My fundamental conclusion was that its budget had too long been nibbled at by marginal reductions that never got to the heart of the problem, and these narrow actions had really prevented progress.

The time had come for business methods to supplant the historic deference to paternalism and politics in the department. There were more than two hundred recommendations in my report, built around a four-year plan of fiscal modernization. The first was to put into an immediate research program the $22 million that would be saved by the budget cuts I had identified, and to continue thereafter to spend a suitable percentage of revenues each year in search of better ways of doing business. Next, I proposed a basic approach to long-range elimination of postal deficits in this formal language:

A definite, consistent and clear-cut method of segregating subsidies and free services from the regular budget of the department;

A permanent policy aimed at attaining break-even operations for the postal establishment as a whole;

The accomplishment of break-even operations through maximum reductions in unit costs of services rendered, achieved through the fullest use of managerial skills and services developed by private industry; and

Adjustments of postal charges from time to time to the extent required to secure amounts of revenue necessary to cover changes in cost levels.

There were impediments in the way of reaching these goals that would have to be dealt with, and I named the principal ones as (a) restrictions on freedom of management imposed by outmoded laws, (b) inadequate accounting and auditing procedures and controls, (c) excessive emphasis on career promotions and insufficient recognition of the need for skilled engineers and financial people, (d) unsatisfactory organization and inadequate staffs for research and development, controllership, employee training, and other phases of management engineering, and (e) general inertia and resistance to modernization.

However inadequate the U.S. Postal Service may sometimes seem
to be at the present time, and it will always have critics, it would
have fallen apart disastrously under the doubling of the number of
pieces of mail in the subsequent decades had Postmaster General
Arthur Summerfield in 1953 played the usual politics and not tackled the job of bringing the operation into the twentieth century.
With so many years of accumulated neglect, prompt major surgery
and renovation were essential. Unfortunately, the Congress took a
long time to act on many of the proposals, especially on those reducing its powers to wield influence over the department; it really did
not yield at all in many major respects until 1970 under President
Nixon when the Postal Service was transferred to a public corporation. If the Congress had adopted in 1953 the proposed policies,
without strings attached, the present postal corporation would have
been far better equipped to fulfill its responsibilities when it was
formed seventeen years later, and its forward movement since then
would have been accelerated.

When I delivered the report to the Appropriations Committee
staff, I knew full well that I had not produced the kind of document
I had been expected to develop, which would have been a simple list
of budget cuts. What I had done was to present a four-year plan of
modernization, and this was of little help to a one-year budget. But I
was overwhelmed with the belief that the best service I could perform for the committee in my six-week stint was to focus as much
attention as possible on the long-range necessities, and I was hopeful
that in doing so I would find a receptive ear somewhere in
Washington.

I did, sooner than I expected. After submitting the report, I spent
two informal days reviewing it with Appropriation Committee members and saying farewell and thanks to those who had worked with
me. On the second day, as I was about to return to Chicago, I
received a phone call from Summerfield.

"I've read your report," he began, and I thought I detected an
ominous note that may have meant I had given offense, "and I
would like to talk to you about it right away."

It was Summerfield's way of commanding action. I saw him in his
office a half hour later, and he came right to the point.

"I like your report and I want you to help me put it into operation. Will you come into the department as controller?"

Much as I was flattered, and tempting as the offer was, I couldn't
do that. I was head of a then national firm of CPAs and could not

neglect my responsibilities there. Summerfield and I discussed a number of alternatives and settled on a course that satisfied the desires of us both. I would select a qualified certified public accountant to be controller, and my accounting firm would contract with the department on a professional basis to assist in the development of a modern financial system. I would spend half of my time directing this work. In the same period, a firm of management engineers would be working with Deputy Postmaster General Charles Hook, Jr., in developing improvements in operational procedures other than financial.

This became the pattern of effort. The firm of Heller and Company worked for several years on the organizational structure and mail-handling processes of the department and was effective in producing notable results. As months went on and the various financial tasks on which I worked began to bring forth measurable gains, I gave more and more of my hours to them and actually spent about 80 percent of my days in the department for a year. At the end of twelve months, many of the goals in the financial reorganization had been realized. My firm's contract was renewed on a considerably smaller scale for a further period, and I gave less time to it thereafter. That was necessary in part because I had become president of the American Institute of Certified Public Accountants in September 1954 and had to devote more than a hundred days in the ensuing year to travel, meetings, and speeches in its behalf.

Then, late in the summer of 1955 Hook resigned as deputy postmaster general, the number two post in the department, and at his suggestion, Summerfield asked if I would succeed him. I took several days to reply. Such a move would require severing myself completely from the accounting firm I had been building up for twenty-two years, ever since I took over the head office in Chicago in 1933. My extensive absences in the preceding two and a half years, however, satisfied me that the firm was strong and successful enough to continue to grow even if I were no longer around. The idea of beginning a new career at the age of forty-seven was intriguing.

As a result of my business income and some favorable outside investments, particularly in real estate, I considered that I had achieved my early goal of becoming a millionaire. This meant that we could afford to live relatively well in Washington and continue to put our children through private schools and colleges although the salary of the deputy PMG was only $17,500 a year. I also gave up four directorships in important corporations, and in severing my affiliation with Alexander Grant & Company, also found it necessary to cancel out the balance of the term of its contract with the department. Since I had been earning well above $100,000 from the firm, this was a sacrifice in income of more than 80 percent; this statistic more than anything else measured my eagerness to take an important post in the federal government. I accepted, saying publicly, "My father was an immigrant; my mother's father was an immigrant. The country has been good to us and I believe we owe it a great deal more than merely paying taxes." I meant it.

By this time I knew Arthur Summerfield quite well. He was an unusual person, even beyond the dynamism that was his trademark. He was energetic, full of ideas, resourceful, and a man of immediate action. He was on every problem in minutes after it surfaced, with meetings, telephone calls, and every other usable means. Like many individuals who were products of poverty, he never recognized an obstacle as anything but a dare. A successful businessman and community leader in his hometown of Flint, and politically powerful in Michigan, he had entered the national scene as campaign chairman for Dwight Eisenhower in the successful election of 1952. His reward was the traditional political plum of postmaster general, the best-known recent holder of which had been that earlier master of political statesmanship, Jim Farley. According to common stories, Farley had used the office as a base for partisan patronage across the government, seeing scores of petitioners every day and rewarding party workers with appropriate plums.

To Summerfield, patronage was a messy game that he would deal in only for his own department, as a matter of political necessity; even that detracted from the time he wanted to devote to managing the mail service. He played the game, but he worked also to gradually reduce the areas for political appointment and to upgrade the standards for those he would accept even under that system.

The $700 million-a-year deficit Summerfield inherited was abhorrent to him. Equity demanded a transfer of this loss from the general taxpayers to the users of the mails, through increases in postal rates. It was not a popular idea, despite its logic, and he drove harder and harder for attention and support. Unable to succeed in 1953 when he was new to the office, Summerfield found that Congress would not act in 1954, because it was a year in which its members had to face the public in an election. In his frustration with delay, he sometimes made enemies where he needed friends. At one indiscreet moment he accused Senator Olin Johnston of having "cranberry juice in his veins." Since Johnston had the powers of the chairmanship of the Senate Committee on the Post Office, he made up his mind to frustrate Summerfield as long as possible. It wasn't until 1958 that Johnston allowed the overdue increase in the letter rate to four cents to be enacted, and by then it was already inadequate because wages and other costs had gone up fully as much in the meantime.

Meanwhile Summerfield was pushing ahead just as determinedly in research and mechanization, building utility-type post office buildings, instead of pillared and terraced public monuments, and filling them with new equipment as fast as it could be invented. He advanced patterns of mail transportation, reorganized employee pay structures and training, introduced new delivery equipment, developed employee relations and public relations programs, and carried through enthusiastically on the other recommendations of my original report and those of Heller and Company. Some of his ideas were way ahead of his time; he experimented with rocket mail in one flight on the east coast, and conducted tests of facsimile mail, in which written messages were sent as photos by wire and delivered in facsimile by letter carriers, an innovation soon overtaken by today's almost universal fax service by telephone.

Considering the low state of the art when he took over, and the inherent difficulties in making changes in government, Summerfield accomplished as much toward bringing the mail service up to date, and holding down costs, as any person in the country could have done. Unfortunately, in the glacial pace of Washington, all he could do in those few years was to start a course of movement after centuries of inertia.

Summerfield was a dedicated public servant with a one-track mind. He was also a fine human being, and could charm almost anyone with his warm personality and his stock of anecdotes. The passing janitor or letter carrier always got a friendly word from him. Without doubt he rated high with everyone in the service except those who opposed change, and there were many of them. He was the kind of man I wanted to work for. I was convinced that my ideas for the future of the department would fit in perfectly with his and was eager to begin my new responsibilities under my official title.

At this juncture I encountered an unfamiliar tactic by a political opponent so unnecessary, time-wasting, suspenseful, and fruitless that it astonished and then annoyed me to the point of recognizing it as one of Washington's unique experiences.

When my presidential nomination to be deputy postmaster general became subject to a required senatorial public hearing and a Senate vote on the nomination to express its duty to "advise and consent," I naively assumed that in my case this would be a mere formality, within which my business and professional record required nothing but a statement of past associations. It was not that way. Within a few days the chairman of the committee announced that my hearing would be preceded by an investigation of the contracts between my firm and the post office department to determine whether any improprieties existed in their origins or in the amounts of payment for services. Hearing that through the press, I gathered together all of the documents involved into a full briefcase of data that I assumed would answer all questions, and I arranged for the department's general counsel to communicate with the chairman of the committee and tell him that such records would be available for preliminary inspection at any time. No reply came and nothing happened for weeks at a time. I was left in continuing suspense as to what the investigation was covering and what it was learning. Several inquiries made directly and indirectly to the committee at the end of three months and six months respectively produced no response other than the "investigation is under way." At the end of nine months, the strain of uncertainty was so great that I decided an indirect approach was the only means left to me. So I contacted a friendly St. Louis banker and asked for his advice, since he was sure to know the congressman for his district. The cloud lifted immediately when the banker reported to me within a day that he had discussed the matter with the congressman and received a promise that the hearing would take place at once. It did, and the only question I was asked was by the chairman of the committee: "Mr. Stans, does this biography which you furnished to the committee correctly state your background?" I answered, "Yes," the chairman called for a vote, and at that instant I received unanimous approval. It was my first personal experience with the bizarre practices of political life in Washington. There had been no purpose whatever in the delay except a desire on the part of one congressman to irritate the postmaster general for his failure to make a clerical appointment requested by him.

I served for two years as deputy postmaster general, which means that altogether, as financial consultant to the postmaster general and as deputy PMG, I had spent almost four and a half years in the department.

During that time I had the satisfaction of seeing about 80 percent of my original recommendations for the service carried into effect. When I departed, I gave Summerfield a final report in which I listed the hundreds of improvements accomplished and those still to go. It also proposed a new series of actions to be carried out to further advance the objectives of better service and less cost. While the Post Office was far from being as efficient as it should be, it had come a long way in the four years since early 1953. In government, that was an astounding accomplishment.

To chronicle all the events of the years I spent in the postal reorganization would be to invite tedium, since much of it would be technical and almost all would involve detail. A recitation of some of the changes with due regard to brevity nonetheless gives a clear picture of how primitive the operations were and how simple it was to modernize them, despite internal opposition from traditionalists in the department.

One example of a simple change that should have been easily accomplished, but which encountered strong opposition from the Office of Chief Postal Inspector until Summerfield overruled him, was to streamline the money order system. The Postal Service sold 400 million money orders a year. It was losing money on every one, largely because of an unbelievably cumbersome procedure. To buy a money order the customer had to go to the post office, find an application blank, and fill in his name and address, the name and address of the payee, and the amount. He then took the completed application to the window and waited while the clerk copied the identical information on a money order form, and some of it again on several stubs. The customer got the money order and one stub, and the clerk kept a stub and the application. Studies showed that in addition to the time spent by the customer the clerk took an average of more than a minute to sell each money order.

We proposed eliminating the application blank and the recording of the names and addresses, so that all a purchaser need do would be to go to the window and say, "I want a money order for $7.92." The clerk would at once validate a blank form and a stub for that amount and give them to the purchaser, who would fill in the name of the payee as he would on his own check. That would save at least twenty seconds of issuing time in each transaction, which to the government would mean saving 130 million minutes, worth at the time about seven cents a minute, or a total of around $9 million a year. That seemed like something worth doing, but the Postal Inspection Service fought the change bitterly. It would make auditing very difficult, they said. And the clerk would have to be at the window anyway, so the minutes wouldn't be saved after all.

We contended in rebuttal that the auditing wouldn't be any more difficult than for a banking transaction, and that the capture of the time-saving was a normal responsibility of management in monitoring work efficiency. Upon the approval of the postmaster general, the shift was made quickly and smoothly, to the full satisfaction of the public and the postal clerks.

Another of the delightful reforms I worked out was bringing to an end the procedure derisively but accurately called "cigar box" accounting. It was literally true that in almost all post offices and stations in 1953 the window clerks kept apart the receipts from money orders, stamps, postal savings, and lock boxes by putting each in its own cigar box until the end of the day and then making a separate bank deposit and report from each box. We disbanded the whole procedure in one sweep by providing one cash box, with a simple daily report for each clerk that brought the totals together from the transaction records in a balanced accounting and a single deposit. This eliminated preparing and handling three fourths of the reports and saved more than $1 million a year.

An unbelievably outdated procedure in the Postal Service in 1953 was the method of handling the cash receipts at the end of each day. At closing time more than 38,000 post offices in the country bundled up their intake of money and sent it by registered mail to 56 large post offices, where it was all rehandled, recorded, merged, recounted, and banked. About one fifth of all the registered mail handled by the Postal Service went to perform this one in-house function. The simple solution was either for each post office to deposit its receipts in a local bank or to send them by regular mail to a "lock box" in a major city where a bank would pick them up and do the bookkeeping for the deposit. This gave the department the immediate use of its funds and also saved the money handling and the time and intricate paperwork. It made possible the direct elimination of more than six hundred unproductive jobs and an economy of more than $2.5 million.

Another of the postal services was the sale of envelopes bearing a printed return address. At that time, every order from a local post office anywhere in the United States was sent to Washington, where it was edited and recorded by a staff of sixteen people, then sent to the printing contractor in Dayton, Ohio, where postal employees recorded it again and followed its progress. We eliminated the Washington unit entirely, just by having the orders sent directly to Dayton, and then cut the work and personnel in Dayton because they were doing recordkeeping also being done by the printer. There was another problem, too. The payments to the printer for these envelopes were limited by an annual budget appropriation; if the public bought more envelopes than the available funds could pay for, the operation had to cease until a supplemental appropriation went through the Congress. We corrected this by getting the Congress to create a revolving fund to which all sales proceeds were credited so there was always enough money to pay for the envelopes purchased. And the postmaster general raised the price of printed envelopes for the first time in many years.

Still another simplification so obvious as to make one wonder how it could have been overlooked for so long related to employee fidelity bonds. Each employee of the Post Office was required to buy every year a personal bond costing ten dollars, to protect the department against theft or other fidelity losses. The department spent at least that much to record the bonds and police the system to see that everyone had complied. We arranged for a single blanket bond covering all employees at an annual premium equal to about one fifth of the sum of the premium on individual bonds. This new premium being much less than the previous expense of looking after the individual bonds, it was then paid by the department, and postal employees were relieved of the nuisance and cost burden entirely.

The expense of registered mail was high because the procedure required the witnessing and recording of each item every time it changed hands en route between mailer and addressee. To reduce the cost in those cases when the only function desired by the mailer was proof of mailing, we introduced certified mail for much less postage. It was one of the first service innovations since the invention of the airplane led to airmail.

We found many other elementary but previously ignored ways of saving bookkeeping work. Handwritten payrolls were mechanized; wage payments in cash were replaced by checks; one third of the forms in use were dispensed with; vast rooms filled with useless records going back fifty years or more were emptied and file space released; and so on. The comptroller general, who had assigned seven systems accountants to work with us, said in writing that it had been "a most exhilarating experience" to review the results that had been achieved, and extended his commendation. He called the program "a well-conceived plan for accounting improvement and an orderly method for its installation," and confirmed that five thousand positions had been eliminated in these functions alone.

The small fourth-class post office, which consisted usually of a window in a country store, was another anachronism. There once had been more than 30,000 of them, and their number was dwindling, but not as rapidly as their usefulness declined. There were still about 19,000 in 1953. Congressmen inevitably fought bitterly, regardless of merit, against the loss of patronage when an office was closed, and it was often said in the department that the only time to discontinue them was in the first three months after a new congressman was elected, before he knew what was going on. The only real beneficiary was the local postmaster, because in the main the farmers were better served by rural delivery service. It was not unusual for a fourth-class office to generate less than $500 a year in revenues and cost $2,000 to operate. In 1953 there were still 7,500 offices in that category. Summerfield worked hard to close them, and was partially successful, but the situation remained for a long time. In 1976, when the comptroller general recommended closing down 12,000 of the still existing third- and fourth-class offices at a saving of $100 million, the same congressional resistance rose to oppose it.

The physical appearance of a post office in 1953 was abominable. The customer was separated from the clerk by a ceiling-high wall or screen, broken only for a small cage window at which transactions took place. Neither reasons of security nor secrecy justified this structure, and it was costly. If banks could handle their money over counters, with merely a low screen or none at all, so could post offices. This change was eventually made along the lines we had recommended, and most post offices are now far more attractive and pleasant on both sides of the counter.

The room for experimentation and development of mechanical stamp vendors, coin changers, money order issuing machines, and similar devices was broad in 1953, when almost none was in use. Many of them were later engineered for postal purposes and placed in general service. We even promoted the sale of postage stamps in convenient rolls rather than flat sheets, and invented a round plastic holder from which they could be withdrawn by the user as needed. Gradual innovation and improvement has made possible "self-service" sections in post office lobbies and also independent self-service stations in shopping centers and business districts.

Examples like this well prove, it seems to me, the sleepy, unprogressive character of the Postal Service in 1953. They could be multiplied manyfold across the whole range of the service, with hundreds of illustrations of change, from simplifying daily reports by post offices to standardizing forms, and from eliminating railway mail cars to computerizing accounting. In six months' time the lag in production of financial statements of operations was reduced from more than twelve months to only three weeks. The mailboxes were changed to red, white, and blue colors. So were the mail trucks, and this cut their accident rates by a third because they were more visible. Most precedent-shattering of all, in 1956 the scratchy, ink-spitting post office pens were finally retired in favor of ballpoints, thereby eliminating one of the oldest jokes in America. Unfortunately, the ballpoint pens soon had to be chained down.

All in all, it was the kind of thing that constituted a systems expert's dream, and made the modernizing of the fiscal operations of the Post Office most gratifying.

While all this was going on, one distinctive type of experience that gave me serious concern as deputy postmaster general was exercising judgment in cases involving charges against postal employees. This period paralleled in part the era of McCarthyism, in which Communists were being sought out in "sensitive" posts all through government. An employee's past membership in a "subversive" organization characterized him as a potential security risk. Under a national security program introduced in 1947 by President Truman, the Congress had passed laws requiring such persons to be judged before they could continue to be employed; the Post Office, which was considered to be a sensitive agency, had an elaborate set of procedures to apply whenever a charge of subversive activity was made against an employee. As deputy postmaster general I exercised the final decision in any cases that were appealed by the individuals involved, and these troubled me immensely. It meant playing God with human lives. I felt sure that many persons who were victims of the depression of the 1930s could easily have toyed with "un-American" concepts for a time without at all having become dedicated Communists or wanting to overthrow our system.

For example, I remember one case of a widow whose deceased husband had attended some Communist meetings twenty years earlier. She had gone along a few times but never signed up. There was no reason to believe that she had Communist leanings or was a security risk, but because of those long-ago associations her job was in jeopardy. After deliberating the principles involved, I overruled the examiner's recommendation of dismissal and allowed her to remain. Unless the facts showed a long commitment of interest and activity in "subversive" organizations, I took a compassionate view that accepted the innocence of the accused and his or her suitability to hold the job. It was an unpleasant duty, and I worried much over the possibility of doing undue harm to people who were inadvertent victims of circumstance.

There were also a few instances of alleged homosexual behavior that came up on charges, and these were especially difficult when there was conflicting testimony about persons with otherwise exemplary records. In a few cases I ordered lie detector tests, but even this didn't resolve my doubts about guilt or innocence, or about the justice of stigmatizing a person for life because of some accusation. My sense of compassion in these matters caused me to be lenient in my decisions, sometimes to the irritation of personnel officials who had worked hard to demonstrate the guilt or unacceptability of the persons involved.

There was one inherited function of the Post Office that Summerfield did not alter, to my knowledge, and that was assisting the intelligence agencies of the government in mail surveillance. Both the CIA and the FBI had regular arrangements to intercept mail or monitor mail movements, principally directed at disrupting Communist propaganda or blocking pornography, but also at detecting other criminal actions. Such procedures were installed by the chief inspector of the Postal Service at the request of the intelligence agencies, who named the targets of the inquiries. The general responsibility for this intervention was assumed by the postmaster general, to whom periodic reports were given, and while I knew such activities were going on, I did not know their volume or frequency. On one occasion Summerfield mentioned to me that several million pieces of incoming Communist printed matter had been intercepted and destroyed. I also recall that the department had accumulated quite a roomful of confiscated pornographic material, consisting of printed matter, photos, films, and "sensual aids." Access to this room was limited to a few people, and this led to an inside story that the postal inspector in charge of the pornography inventory was enjoying his work too much: he was reported to be spending an extraordinary amount of time reviewing the evidence.

The forward-looking program begun during the eight-year term of Postmaster General Summerfield was the continental divide between the primitive methods of Franklin's day and the modern mail processes of today and tomorrow. I believe it was one of the outstanding management achievements of all time. I am proud to have been a part of that history-making effort. Even if it had not been a stepping-stone for me to more important government posts, I would consider my Post Office work well worth in satisfaction the physical and monetary sacrifice it exacted from me.

There were gratifying acknowledgments, too. *The Washington Post*, not usually given to praise of public servants, called my work as deputy postmaster general "a creditable performance." On a copy of the book *Financial Policy for the Post Office Department*, Summerfield wrote an inscription in his own hand that not only gave me credit for producing the volume but addressed it to me as "one of the most able and outstanding men with whom I have had the privilege to work." That praise was the highest reward I could have sought from him, and the promotion I next received from President Eisenhower was evidence that I had performed in the Post Office Department to his liking, too.

# CHAPTER FIVE

# The Balancing
# Act of 1960

$S$hortly before I had finished serving two years as deputy postmaster general, I was approached by Percival Brundage, director of the Bureau of the Budget, with the idea that he would like to ask President Eisenhower to nominate me to be his successor in that position. Brundage was a certified public accountant, a retired senior partner of Price Waterhouse, and he believed that the preparation of the budget of the United States could be done best by a person who had an accounting background. Despite this logic with which I completely agreed, Brundage had been the first CPA to hold that post and I would be the second. Earlier budget directors apparently had been mostly bankers or lawyers.

The position of director of the Bureau of the Budget held Cabinet rank, which would have been a considerable advance for me. As such it was very tempting, but I felt that I should get Kathleen's concurrence before replying. I told that to Brundage and said I would give him an answer the following day but felt that it would definitely be positive. He said he had already talked to the president about it, and the president was prepared to extend the invitation to me by telephone as soon as he was assured by Brundage that the answer would be favorable.

After Kathleen's quick acquiescence, I called Brundage to say that such an appointment would be very exciting to both of us and I would await the president's call. That afternoon, Eisenhower was on the telephone and extended the offer of the appointment. I told him that I would accept it with full confidence in my ability to carry it out in a manner that would be to his liking, but that there was one condition that I would like to impose. That idea seemed to startle him, but he quickly suggested that I go ahead, so I simply said, "Mr. President, I think it very important that I undertake the job with the full knowledge of your expectations for the budget in the present economic circumstances of the country, and the specific goals for the next budget to be prepared." He replied without hesitation and made it clear that the subject was currently very much on his mind.

When we met in his office a few weeks later with Brundage present, this is what he said: "I became president with the conviction that the budget should be balanced in every year and I have tried hard to accomplish that. Unfortunately we have had a couple of recessions that threw us into temporary deficits, but we have always been able to come back to a surplus. We are in a recession now and people are throwing many proposals at me to try to speed up the recovery by tax cuts, large capital projects, and other actions which I sincerely believe would merely make things worse. I would like to go out of office with the finances of the country in good shape, and there is only the budget of 1960 by which we could still do that. So, my answer to you is that I want to see that next budget in balance if it is at all possible."

My reply was, "Mr. President, I am not well acquainted with all of the details, but I believe we should try in every reasonable way to bring the budget back into balance, but I also believe that I can do that only if I have your strong support."

"You will have my total support against any appeal from your budget decisions so long as you can assure me that the security of the country is not at stake. Within that goal I would want to see that we would do for the people everything that is necessary, but we would not do what is merely desirable or what could be postponed."

"On that basis, Mr. President, I accept the responsibility." I knew it would be a monumental task, but I never lost confidence that it could be done. Up to this point my contacts with Eisenhower had been relatively few, limited mostly to the instances when I had attended Cabinet meetings or other ceremonies as an alternate for the postmaster general. For the next three years I would come to see him almost every working day, in which time I came to admire and respect him as a gifted person and a great American.

The Bureau of the Budget (the name and mission of which have been changed to the Office of Management and Budget) was the most powerful agency of the federal government, not in its own right but as a major arm of the president. By its budget decisions, made only after full study by qualified staff experts and careful review by the director, the bureau had almost life and death power over programs and projects. Its job in brief was to put into priority order, consistent with the president's broad agenda, the thousands of spending ideas advanced by all the agencies.

Only the bureau had the whole picture before it and could make the judgments that put first things first across the panorama of the government. Its recommendations carried strong weight with the president, but normally he still had to deal with appeals from dissatisfied departments or offices, all of whom presented their cases with eloquence and urgency. Once such an agency had been given the budget figure authorized by the bureau and tentatively approved by the president, it had that right of appeal, but it knew in advance that its chances of success in getting much more were usually not great. And once the amount appeared in the printed document sent to the Congress, it could not openly ask for more; it was bound to support the president's policies. Usually the agency could do little but pray that congressional cuts would not be too severe after House and Senate appropriations committees took their successive whacks at the figures.

Beyond its task of preparing the annual budget, a document of 1,100 pages in 1960, the bureau had other important duties. It was responsible for promoting the improvement of management, accounting, and statistics across the whole gamut of government agencies. It advised the president on whether he should sign or veto legislation passed by the Congress. It coordinated the legislative proposals of the various units to iron out differences between them and to see that the proposals were in accord with the president's overall program. It approved or rejected opinions on proposed laws before they could be expressed by an agency to the Congress, because the president could not allow public differences among his subordinates as to what his policies were (except in the few cases in which he might deliberately decide to air those differences).

All in all it was scarcely an exaggeration to say that the director of the bureau had more of the federal government in his hands than any other person in Washington.

To make a smooth transition from Brundage, I moved to the bureau on October 1, 1957, six months ahead of his departure, and served as his deputy in the preparation of the budget for fiscal 1959, which had to go to the Congress in January 1958.* Brundage had managed to put together two successive balanced budgets in 1956 and 1957, but he ran into trouble in the recession of 1958. By the time he left and I became director on March 15, 1958, it was evident that he had handed me a real hot potato.

I had foreseen some of this when I took the job. When I was sworn in I issued a statement saying, "I am accepting this new responsibility of Budget Director under no illusions. This is one of the most difficult budgetary times the country has ever had to face short of war. I am convinced, however, that the soundness of the American economy will soon allow our efforts to be directed again toward balanced budgets."

This characterization of the times was no exaggeration. The Soviet feat of orbiting sputnik not many months earlier had thrown a panic into American educational, scientific, and military circles. The Congress had been confronted with a myriad of proposed programs alleged to be necessary to reestablish our national superiority. Some of them were enacted in haste, more were under way. The president was considering an increase in the defense budget. A new civilian space agency was about to be launched. The specter of Soviet strength in space was being used by various interests and lobbyists to support all kinds of new spending ideas, especially for education and science. In addition, the 1958 recession had set in, threatening federal revenues and engendering a vast array of proposals to stimulate the economy. There were demands for a tax cut, for billions of dollars of new public works money, for enhanced unemployment insurance benefits, and a host of other welfare and related programs "to get things going again."

Secretary of the Treasury Robert B. Anderson was advising against tax reduction at the time, and he was backed by Secretary of Commerce Sinclair Weeks and Federal Reserve Board Chairman William McChesney Martin. The president had agreed with them, and was also refusing to go for any emergency public works spending because the money flow would take too long to crank up, and by then the emergency would be over.

---

*At this time the fiscal year of the government ended on June 30. Some years later it was changed to end on September 30.

Meanwhile, the immediate fiscal situation was building to a crisis. The planned 1958 budget surplus had evaporated and a deficit was certain. Fiscal 1959 was in worse shape; months before the year was to begin it was clear that Brundage's projected surplus of a half-billion dollars was going to become a deficit of large proportions. My job was cut out for me, and it wouldn't be easy.

I discussed this with Eisenhower briefly one day before a Cabinet meeting where it was clear that the trend of growing deficits was likely to continue. He made it certain without qualification that he still felt his was the right policy and he wanted to hold on to it as long as there was hope of finding a better way out.

"We'll be better off as a nation if we leave a greater share for the people to use as they will. There have been some setbacks, but by and large we've done pretty well. I want to continue the same policy, even though Congress will always give us trouble. I don't like people using this recession to clamor for tax cuts and more spending. It just seems that we can't get the public to see how dangerous such things can be," he added plaintively. "They ought to have more confidence that this economy will turn itself around."

Philosophically, his views gave me no difficulty, as I was by nature a fiscal conservative. Practically, I interpreted Eisenhower's desires to be to ride out the immediate situation with confidence, while resisting raids on the Treasury that would only make things worse in the long run. As it turned out, this line was successfully held, tax cuts and massive new public works projects were averted, and the economy began to recover on its own by the latter part of 1958. There had been some concessions: a $1.5 billion extra appropriation for defense; about $600 million for supplementary unemployment benefits; at least that much for a housing bill insisted upon by Congress; and some acceleration in ongoing public works projects, stockpile acquisitions, and government purchases. Beyond these items, current outlays had gone up heavily because of automatically increasing "economic stabilizer" payments such as unemployment insurance and welfare. It was too late to help the current budget. Fiscal 1958 ended up with a deficit of $2.8 billion. The full impact of the recession and sputnik hit the budget for 1959; with a drop of $6.1 billion in revenues from original expectations and a net increase of $6.3 billion through unbudgeted expenditures. I found that I had presided over the largest peacetime deficit in history up to that time, $12.4 billion.

However, the optimism about the strength of the economy turned out to be justified. As it recovered, the tax revenues improved and benefit payments began to ease. By the middle of 1958, when it was necessary to gear up to finalize the 1960 budget, I was optimistic enough to believe that it could be brought back into more respectable dimensions, but I did not yet see how we could make the quantum jump of producing a balance.

In the preliminary stages, I learned some frustrating things about the content of the federal budget. Most of the government's expenditures are "uncontrollable." Interest on the national debt must be paid as a matter of contract. Veterans' benefits and compensation are fixed by law, as are the pensions of retired government employees and the military. Fixed too is the pay of government civil and military employees, Social Security benefits, subsidies to farmers and shipowners, and many other items of outlay. Public works projects under way can't be abandoned or even suspended. All this meant that in large part the outlines of the budget for 1960 were drawn in legislation of previous years. There were some expenditures that could be postponed, some that could be pared, and some but not many that could be eliminated, but in the aggregate a budget director could work his will on only about 25 percent of the total requests before him, and that in a limited way.

In good times and bad also, there was constant pressure for the government to do more things, far beyond its ability to pay for them. Eisenhower said it this way to me one day: "I'm trying to hold down the cost of government, but these things keep coming to me in separate pieces, and they all look good at the time. But invariably they cost a lot more than anybody ever guessed and it's only when you see the real aggregate that you understand what's happening."

As we got into the early mechanics of the 1960 budget, I increased my meetings with Treasury Secretary Anderson. He had maintained his opposition all along to a tax cut and recession-induced public works spending, and was very anxious to know what could be done in the 1960 figures. Raymond J. Saulnier, Jr., the chairman of the President's Council of Economic Advisors, joined us and we formed an informal triumvirate for mutual support as we moved toward the budget decisions.

The first run of the spending requests of the government agencies added up to $85 billion. With the best revenue estimate from Treasury then at $75 billion, we were headed for a deficit of $10 billion. That could not be accepted. Close scrutiny at the margins found many items that could be pruned, deferred, or lopped off. But it did not seem that the reductions could be nearly enough to bring about a balance.

I reported this to Eisenhower one day in his office. He told me that he would be very disappointed to leave office without bringing the budget back into balance. The 1960 fiscal year was the only one left that would begin and end in his term. I replied that it was not impossible to bring about a balance for 1960, but to do so would require me to apply unusual austerity. He told me to see what I could work out along that line and said I would have his backing. From this point on, I was determined to present a picture with all expenditures met and a surplus, however small.

Just at the point at which I needed more reinforcement, it was supplied by Anderson. He returned from an International Monetary Conference in New Delhi on November 1, shocked at the reactions of other major countries. Foreign governments questioned over and over again whether the United States could or would get its financial house in order and doubted the soundness of the dollar. He felt that the only convincing sign we could give was a solvent financial policy. Anderson, Saulnier, and I discussed the question of whether a small deficit would be adequate evidence of our determination, and we came to the unanimous conclusion that psychologically it would not. There had to be some more turns of the screw. I went back again to the tables, and my weary staff continued to review all the amounts over and over again.

As the effort progressed, the three of us had several meetings with the president and I had quite a few with him alone. On November 3, I got his approval to a list of eighteen items that still had to be slashed to bring the spending below $80 billion. Gradually the bureau whittled the allowed expenditures down further to around $79 billion; meanwhile, Treasury projected that economic improvement justified an increase in its revenue estimate to $76 billion. That still left a potential $3 billion deficit, with not much leeway left.

The job was tougher than I had expected, for all the logical reasons. While some of the department heads saw the problem and cooperated willingly, others resisted with objections they thought valid: some programs just had to be expanded; built-in growth of uncontrollable benefit programs had to be recognized; many new needs had to be met; and there was no way to reduce present programs without undue loss of their momentum and objectives. My staff and I listened to all these arguments and went right on with our job of cutting the cloth to fit.

We kept a close hourly track of the figures as they evolved, but we had to go back to the drawing board more than once because the revenues and expenditures still did not come together. The Department of Defense had not finished reworking its amounts, and we weren't quite sure how they would come out, but we got signals that the minimum amount its officials considered acceptable was $41.75 billion. That was more than I could see possible in a balanced budget. Meanwhile, pressures to ease up began to grow from some of the Cabinet liberals, particularly Secretary of Labor James Mitchell and Secretary of Health, Education, and Welfare Arthur Flemming.

Apprised of these developments, on November 6, Eisenhower called an executive session of the Cabinet and laid down the law. All budget allowances, including those already tentatively approved, were going to be given another hard look, he said. He wanted a balanced budget and I had assured him that I would produce it, with his backing. He called for drastic reductions and said, "We're going to take hold of the bush, thorns and all. I'm tired of being liberal with other people's money." He followed up this lecture with a memo to the heads of all departments and agencies that contained even stronger language. He asked each to live within the amount that would be allocated by the Bureau of the Budget, ". . . appealing to me only when you feel that to keep within such amount will impair the security or welfare of the country."

No director of the federal budget had ever had such a strong mandate. I set to work to keep my promise, and in doing so my staff and I had to deal patiently with one appeal after another to get everyone to realize that I was being fair within the amounts available. In this process I coined a phrase that the *Reader's Digest* later printed as Stans's Law: "Good budgeting is the uniform distribution of dissatisfaction." This expresses a truism that applies with equal aptness at home, in business, or in government, because there is never enough to satisfy all desires. I had to convince the head of each department and agency that he was getting his reasonable share, even though it may have been far below what he considered essential.* In this process, I was sure we were helping the nation, not harming it, even though it meant that some programs just had to be reduced, some held level when they were expected to grow, and no new ones could be started. The "no new starts" policy was violently criticized by the public works interests, but it stuck.

---

*To give psychological weight to the difficulties to be met by supplicants, I had the question "WHY?" (in three-inch letters) framed and hung on the wall behind my desk, so each one had to face it. The "why" became a ritual. Why do you have to have this money? Why will it cost so much? Why must we have it now? Why can't you do less? Why should it be done by the federal government? Why can't somebody else do it as well or better?

Eventually all of the government units fell into line, but there were some difficult contentions. Arthur Flemming fought vigorously and eloquently for many of his HEW programs and spent six full days alternating between the deputy director and me in his appeals. He believed so sincerely in his money requests that at one juncture I said, "Arthur, every time we disagree you put me in the position of appearing to be against health or education or welfare. I don't like that posture, but there must be limits even to those programs if we are to stay solvent." His reluctance to yield to compromise bore down so heavily on me during that period that Kathleen coined the term "Arthuritis" for my fatigue when I came home at night after long sessions with him. I never learned what he called me. Eventually we worked out an agreement after a long but candid struggle.

Meanwhile, we kept firing more questions and more doubts to Eisenhower about specific military projects. He met with Secretary of Defense Neil McElroy and other defense and military officials on November 28, in my presence, and again on December 3, with both Anderson and me present and arguing. He then settled the Defense amount at $40.9 billion which, although higher than my hopes, was within a range we could handle.

Finally, the figures came together. Anderson and Saulnier raised their estimates of revenues to $77,100,000,000, and my staff worked down the expenditures to $77,030,000,000, leaving a paper-thin surplus of $70 million. It was the best we could do. The budget was austere and severe, but not heartless. We had proved that even with so many uncontrollable commitments, there were ways to cut and save, or to generate revenues, to make ends meet. Eisenhower was so delighted that he announced the balancing of the budget the minute we had a final figure, on December 22, almost a month before it would normally have been made public. My proud staff held a bureau-wide ceremony and presented me a red football jersey with the black number 77 on front and back.

Getting this done was not without personal strain. Beyond the physical and nervous effort of the constant analyses, meetings, and tough decisions, there was an emotional stress on me that others never saw. There was not a night that I did not go home and brood over the human, social, and national security aspects of the decisions that were taking form. I was the last man who would want the safety of the country to be in jeopardy, whatever the cost. And yet, with every program, I had to press for the answers to the question "why?" The "why" followed me to bed, and I found myself wondering whether I was being too hidebound in my political philosophy. Were we overdoing the fiscal-conservative idea? There were moments of doubt, but in my thinking I always came back to one conclusion: in government fiscal matters there is no tolerable alternative to conservatism. It is a discipline that can be ignored only at the risk of continuing inflationary deficits and, if allowed to lapse for a long period, at the peril of the nation's economic and political survival.

The budget exercises could not be carried on in secrecy. As the news leaked out that we were trying for a balance, there was a strong initial wave of support in the country, exemplified by this excerpt in *Time* on December 1:

> But the real meaning of the Administration's effort to balance the budget lies not in whether or not it actually succeeds. A balanced budget, in and of itself, is no cure-all. It is instead the principles of government that lie behind the attempt, the refusal to accept inflation as inevitable and budgetary elephantiasis as incurable, that makes the effort of deep and lasting importance.

I took hope. Perhaps the country was ready, after all, for a demonstration of sound fiscal policy.

Nevertheless, negative political reaction was predictable as soon as we released the details. Senator Kefauver of Tennessee called the result "dishonest"; Senator Clark of Pennsylvania said it was a "cheapskate policy and a way to disaster." Senator Monroney of Oklahoma said it was "wishful thinking." Others used more or less cynical expressions. Some members of the press called it unrealistic, impossible, phony, and a mere bookkeeping exercise. One respected reporter, Raymond Brandt of the *St. Louis Post-Dispatch*, bet me ten dollars that it wouldn't work.

Sending a balanced budget to the Congress was only the first step. The second was to make it stick, and that was bound to be tougher. The Democrat-controlled Congress obviously wanted to spend more, quite apart from their unwillingness to let Eisenhower win the contest. The hard-pressed agencies of the executive branch were eager to accept larger appropriations if their friends in the Congress voted for them. Many of the special-interest groups were unhappy with what we had done and served notice that they were going to contend for more. Another truism evolved: every dollar saved was a dollar someone expected to get.

If we were to succeed, we had to make a real fight for it. I discussed this on several occasions with Eisenhower and Anderson as we got close to the opening of the congressional session in 1959. We all agreed that no president or budget director could halt the perennial increases in spending until the people at large woke up to the dangers in that trend. We had to arouse the public to dust off the old-fashioned criterion of ability to pay and put it back on the mantelpiece.

What followed was 1960's Battle of the Budget. There had been many budget battles before between the executive branch and the Congress, almost annually, but this one took on a scope and an intensity that caused the press to dignify it with capital B's, and to report its status with every change in the wind.

Our strategy was to bring the public on our side and through them to influence the Congress to hold the line. Our informal design was that Eisenhower would stress economy in government in his speeches and press conferences, and would veto any significant breaches by the Congress; Anderson would try to protect the dollar by reassuring the other nations that we were serious about fiscal responsibility; Saulnier would bolster the economic arguments at every opportunity; and I would go on the stump across the land, arguing for a balanced budget to protect national solvency.

From the moment I became director, I had made speeches to the public and held conferences and interviews with the press. This was a new practice. Traditionally, the budget director was supposed to have a passion for anonymity. *The Washington Post* noted that "in the past budget directors have spoken only occasionally," and *Business Week* commented that in seeing reporters I was doing "something no budget director has done since Frank Pace had the job in 1949." I was breaking the pattern by going public, and initially I saw three possible worthwhile results in doing so: cushioning the shock that the bad 1959 figures would cause when they came out; influencing the Congress to go easy on new spending that would make matters worse; and laying the groundwork for a grassroots drive for economy once the recession was over. I did not take this extra activity on without consulting with Eisenhower, who encouraged me to go ahead. I reported this to Sherman Adams, the president's top assistant, so he would know what I was up to. His advice was typical Adams, terse and solid. "If you believe in it, do it. If you don't believe in it, don't do it, because you won't be convincing."

I had no lack of conviction, so I went ahead. Deficits were not to my liking. I believed that a government could not be strong without being fiscally sound. Budgets should be balanced, not necessarily every year but at least over a cycle, with some reduction of the national debt. In 1958 I had spoken out against a tax cut on the grounds that it was not needed to combat the recession, and against emergency public works projects because their major impact would come too late, after the economy had turned upward. I had also argued broadly for fiscal sanity and order, pointing out that there was no free lunch in Washington, and that everything that was spent had to be paid for in someone's taxes, sooner or later. I had decried wasteful spending, annual deficits, and a growing national debt as a deplorable pattern of passing our extravagances on to our children and succeeding generations. I maintained the proposition expressed to me by Eisenhower that "we can wreck this country by fiscal irresponsibility just as much as by military carelessness."

I traveled somewhere almost every week, sometimes oftener, to address business, civic, and professional groups—in Los Angeles, Raleigh, Cincinnati, Detroit, Oklahoma City, Miami, Minneapolis, Chicago, and dozens of other places. I was interviewed on local television and radio shows wherever I went, and also appeared nationwide on *Face the Nation*, *Open Hearing*, *College News Conference*, and *The Voice of NAM* (National Association of Manufacturers). I wrote letters whenever possible to newspapers, and articles for magazines. I submitted to press interviews as time permitted, including two that were printed at length by *U.S. News and World Report*. I faced the military by addressing the annual Secretaries Conference of top officials of the Defense Department, and the military services at Quantico, Virginia. I met often with members of the House and Senate on pending legislation and testified before the Joint Congressional Economic Committee, the Senate Finance Committee, the House Appropriations Committee, and various legislative committees. At such times, I sometimes had to take positions that I knew were unpopular, such as urging a hold-down on increases in veterans' benefits or a postponement of pay advances to government employees. I made taped interviews with many members of Congress on the budget.

Less easy to convey was the failure of the economic policies that had caused these developments. Despite popular belief, the desperate efforts of the Roosevelt years to overcome the Great Depression of the 1930s had not succeeded. Only the advent of World War II had stimulated the economy to a recovery. Keynesian theories about spending more or cutting taxes to stimulate the economy, in the hope that resulting enlarged revenues would bring everything into balance, had not worked. We had to convert all of this into the simple question of whether a government can live on debts any more than can a family or a business, without risking its strength and its future. We had to convince people that in the long run more would be achieved in national welfare and security by frugality than by extravagance, through holding down the heavy burden of interest on borrowings, the heavy overhang of national debt, and the heavier tax of inflation.

I spent a long time working on ways to dramatize the nation's predicament. My brilliant executive assistant, Bill Carey, had a flair for writing and drafted most of my speeches; between us we evolved a series of expressions and phrasings as we went along that gave each talk a separate character and avoided the dullness of repetition. The attention they attracted was reflected in widespread publicity for speech after speech that essentially carried the same plea.

One difficulty in speaking to most audiences was in getting them to sense that whatever happened in Washington directly affected them. I wanted to break down their feeling of remoteness from its affairs and the resigned belief that they couldn't do anything about it anyway.

I continued to describe the trend: "The federal debt and the budget-making process are steadily getting out of hand. Uncle Sam has been living on credit cards, budgeting for one year at a time while we enact laws which mortgage our future income over many years and sometimes for decades. We are taxing current earnings to pay for many benefits and services legislated in past years, while we go on adopting new benefits and services without considering how we will pay for them when they become due."

I outlined it this way: We spend great sums on interest charges on our national debt, but we do not reduce the principal. We carry on massive federal programs that state and local governments could do better.

We perpetuate federal programs which have long met the objectives for which they were created. In many ways the federal budget today is saddled with yesterday's priorities instead of anticipating tomorrow's.

As time went on, there were occasional murmurs of disagreement from some public sources, and I addressed myself to them: "Today there are many who challenge the idea that we should strive for a balanced budget at all. There are those who say that it is not important whether revenues equal expenditures. They contend that our economy is expanding, that a balanced budget is just old-fashioned, and that a little inflation is a good thing . . ."

Also, I went back often to confront the delusion that a little inflation might not be unpleasant. Eisenhower chimed in to emphasize that point with this prediction: "If we just let prices go up, never pay our government bills, the day will come when the housewife will take a market basket full of money to the grocery store and bring back a pocketbook filled with groceries."

I invoked the specter of the Soviet challenge, taking my cue from a statement by Eisenhower on January 10, 1958: "We need to gird ourselves for economic war with the Soviets." By this time it was accepted that Khrushchev's threats to bury us were not threats of war but threats of economic conquest. Recognizing this, I said, "Khrushchev's attack and his promise to bury us is aimed straight at the American dollar. A strong economy, with balanced budgets, is the basic answer of the free enterprise system to Soviet Russia's economic challenge." In the national mood of the times, this was not an unworthy topic. *The New York Daily News* in an editorial of support became so extreme as to say, "The spend-and-spenders are giving aid and comfort to the enemy in time of war, which makes them traitors under the constitutional definition of treason." I would not go that far.

I tried to make it clear that we were not fighting solely for a one-year victory: "1959's battle of the budget is not really a fight over the budget for one particular year, but a serious search for the wisest route to economic strength."

As short punch lines I sometimes quoted Eisenhower: "Thrift is one of the characteristics that has made this nation great; why should we abandon it now?" Or I used my own version: "Let's remember one lesson from history. Economic soundness may not guarantee national greatness, but no nation can hope for greatness without it."

Obviously, these quotations are not from one speech but are selected excerpts from a series of them as the campaign progressed. The final plea, expressed in one way or another, was always for the listener to tell his representatives in the Congress that he wanted government spending held down and the budget respected.

Month by month, we won more and more support from organizations, individuals, and the media. Editorial endorsements came from the daily and weekly press, across the spectrum, from *The Wall Street Journal* to the *Local Daily News* of Westchester-Paoli, Pennsylvania.

Directly and indirectly, I continued to war against immediate proposals in the Congress that would destroy our chances of staying on target. Through Senator Bridges of New Hampshire, I listed legislation in Congress with a chance of passing that would throw us off $3 billion or more in 1960. In September, I announced that Congress had already boosted the year's spending by $597 million. Publicly, I pointed out, "Right now there are bills in Congress that would add $30 billion to the cost of government and reduce its income by $10 billion. To me this is a strange and destructive sort of arithmetic."

The result was more than gratifying. The audiences at my talks, the press reports, and the hundreds of endorsing editorials had an impact that fully confirmed the force of an aroused public opinion. An avalanche of letters, in many thousands, came to individual members of Congress; more thousands came directly to the White House and the Bureau of the Budget, encouraging us and asking what they could do to help. The results began to appear. Legislation was postponed or revised in Congress to save money. Appropriations for the year were even reduced slightly (although not enough to offset the failure to enact our proposed postage increases and to produce other necessary revenues). When the Congress did overstep, Eisenhower vetoed the bills and the vetoes were upheld; in all, his vetoes saved $100 million in 1960 and $5 billion in future years. Our crusade was having an effect.

It was a team effort. Eisenhower fought constantly, at Cabinet meetings, in press conferences, and in speeches, for conservatism and in particular for our 1960 budget, on the theme, "No doubt there are many ways to fight inflation, but there is only one way uniquely within our power to do, and that is for us to put our own fiscal house in order."

In June 1959, before the beginning of the new fiscal year, I saw enough favorable signs to raise the estimate of the 1960 surplus to $300 million. In September I reported that this had probably evaporated because of congressional enactments for new spending. It continued to be a cliff-hanger. In our Mid-Year Review, published after the end of the congressional session, the best I could see was a thinly balanced surplus of $95 million. In November I announced that the odds had shifted against a balance because of a prolonged steel strike. But in January 1960, when we issued the 1961 budget, we still found possible a $200 million surplus for fiscal 1960, which had five more months to go.

In May, I forecast a surplus of $200 million to the House Ways and Means Committee. In June that began to look like $600 million, and when the books were finally closed after June 30, the surplus came out at $1.1 billion (later reduced retroactively to $650 million). The economy had improved better than expected.

The "impossible" Battle of the Budget had been won. There had never before been a sharper or more significant improvement in the budget in the space of one year. It was one of the few times in history that expenditures had been reduced from the previous year, except after a war. The press generally hailed it as "a remarkable feat," "an astonishing result," and used other equally commendatory words. Columnists Roscoe Drummond and Inez Robb included me among their nominations for vice president. Newsman Brandt of the *St. Louis Post-Dispatch* paid me his ten-dollar bet.

There had been no time to relax during the past year, and there was none now. Long before we knew the results of 1960, we had to complete and send to the Congress a budget for 1961. As early as June 1959, Anderson and Saulnier had emphasized to the Cabinet that a balanced budget and a sizable surplus in 1961 were more essential than in 1960, and that the risks of failure to achieve those objectives were much greater. With an advancing economy, we could look for higher tax collections, and there was room to relax slightly on the austerity. The new budget we prepared showed a surplus of $4.2 billion, yet it provided for a strengthened defense, with emphasis on missiles and the most modern weapons; a doubling of the space program; selective improvements in civil aviation, scientific research, tax enforcement, and the development of national resources. In his budget message Eisenhower called it "a reasoned, powerful appeal to a mature people to act responsibly on the threshold of a fateful decade."

While we were still in office, we had to fight for the new budget, even though less than half of its life would be within our term. Almost at once, a restless Congress, prodded by special interests, began to show signs that many members believed that once was enough. Also, the fact that it showed a planned surplus as high as $4.2 billion seemed to be taken as an open invitation to spend most of it ahead of time.

The difficulties soon began to come to life. *The Washington Post* started to oppose our policies in a series of critical editorials and articles, and eventually attacked my "doctrinaire preference for deifying individual freedom of economic choice, whatever the consequences for collective national needs and programs."

In August, a month after the beginning of the 1961 fiscal year, I announced that the hoped-for surplus of $4.2 billion for 1961 had already been reduced to $2.6 billion as a result of new bills passed by the Congress. In September I said glumly that the surplus was almost gone. In October, in the Mid-Year Review, it was estimated at $1.1 billion, with the blame divided equally between increased expenditures voted by Congress and a slump in estimated corporate tax receipts. In January 1961, as the Eisenhower administration left office, we still predicted a surplus for the year, but it had been whittled down to a scant $79 million. Unfortunately, even that was soon gone after we departed. Incoming president John F. Kennedy had campaigned on a platform that promised increased spending for defense and welfare, so he proceeded to ask the Congress for supplemental appropriations.

Even more fatal for 1961 and future years was his deliberate public repudiation of the Eisenhower fiscal beliefs. In a speech in June of that year at Yale University, a few days after announcing that he would ask Congress to reduce taxes, he denounced as "myths" the premise that budget deficits were inherently bad and that inflation was a danger.

In January 1961, a few days before he left office, Eisenhower presented to the Congress the budget that we had prepared for the year to end June 30, 1962. As was the case in 1960 and 1961, it also proposed a balance, with a forecasted surplus of $1.5 billion. Kennedy, with his more liberal policies, rejected this budget and ended up with a final deficit of $7.1 billion for the year; all of this shift was due to higher spending and none to revenue losses.

The failure of Kennedy to hold the line was, of course, disappointing. I had taken great satisfaction in having prepared three consecutive budgets for the country that proposed a surplus of revenues over spending. I had no doubt they would have been achieved if Eisenhower had been able to continue in office or his successor had carried on his policies. That would have made possible either a small payment on the national debt or an earned and justified tax cut. More importantly, I felt we had set a new pace for the government that proved that it would have been possible to keep the budget under control for many years to come.

In contrast, the policies and circumstances in effect in the administrations after Eisenhower left office, through presidents Kennedy,

Johnson, Nixon, Ford, Carter, Reagan, and Bush, enlarged by new spending initiatives piled on by reckless Congresses, the Vietnam War, and a particularly large loss over several years from a virtually unregulated savings and loan industry, wiped out hopes of a balanced budget in any subsequent year up to now. The on-budget deficits in that long string of thirty-four years added up to $27 trillion—and are still growing. These circumstances set the stage for the incredible deficits of $60 billion a year in the term of President Gerald Ford and a continually growing string of multibillion-dollar deficits under the succeeding presidents.

Actually, our conservative fiscal policies of 1958–60 were validated by the course of subsequent events in the years immediately after. None of the disasters predicted by our adversaries came to happen, and 1960 ended with the nation in a strong position, and with inflation for the year at only 1.5 percent. A contributing element had been the coordination of fiscal policy and monetary policy during this period; under the Federal Reserve, the cast of monetary policy was toward a strongly disinflationary stringency. The inflationary psychology in the country was eliminated. The fiscal and monetary actions of these years provided a basis for inflation-free sustainable economic growth.

The recession of 1957–58 taught some lessons on the extent of responsiveness of the budget to economic events. When a downturn occurs in the economy, the unfavorable budget impact is much more serious than anyone honestly expects it to be. With an upturn, the results are much more favorable than experts believe possible.

We also confirmed our belief that the fiscal devices that gave the biggest boost to the economy in calendar 1958 and 1959 were the built-in stabilizers, principally unemployment insurance and lower tax revenues.

In 1960, which was an election year, there was heavy pressure from some directions for a tax cut. Nixon, who was then vice president and a candidate for president, favored one, but if he pressed the issue very hard it was outside my hearing. Eisenhower was reluctant to go along because he did not want to give up the balanced budgets that were in sight, and he was determined to end his term of office having honored his platform pledges of fiscal responsibility. Nixon was disappointed in the negative decision, and I think he subsequently may have blamed it for the loss of the election, although he never said so publicly. In retrospect, I think it probable that he was right politically and that he may have become president eight years before he did if a small popular tax cut had been proposed by Eisenhower and enacted by the Congress. Insofar as the national interest was concerned, Eisenhower's contrary decision was sound, because when his successor took office inflation had been curbed and the base had been built for what turned out to be one of the longest periods of continuing low-inflationary prosperity in the country's recent history.

We had provided the right medicine for the country. It was a calamity that our hard-won fiscal policy did not survive the change in administration. In the latter half of the 1960s and through the 1970s, the 1980s, and now, halfway through the 1990s, the evil results we had feared and fought to prevent came about after all as a result of continuing deliberate fiscal laxity, with spending and deficits growing to astronomical proportions.

Ironically, when Kennedy took office, a blueprint with a contrary result was available to him in the form of a report from me to Eisenhower, prepared by the staff of the Bureau of the Budget, analyzing the budgetary potential over the next ten years under various stated levels of growth in revenues and expenditures. It showed how annual surpluses could be achieved comfortably during that entire period.

# CHAPTER SIX

# Working with Eisenhower

No matter how able and thorough his staff may be, the budget director himself must have a working knowledge of every appropriation item each year in order to make requisite decisions and be able to defend them to the agencies, their constituencies, the president, and the Congress. One error of judgment can lay him open to unbearable criticism, and his best-founded decisions can be manhandled out of shape and sense by the political opposition and the pressure groups. The congressman who fails to get something his district wants needs someone to blame for thwarting him, and the man who guards the purse strings is the one easiest to attack.

Most of the criticism during my term as budget director was in good grace, but sometimes it was exaggerated or flamboyant. I'll never forget Congressman Dan Flood of Pennsylvania, irate at the bureau's action on the defense budget, accusing me of trying to run the Pentagon and proposing to the Congress that I be given a military uniform with seven stars lighted by neon.

On another occasion, when I was testifying before the House Appropriations Committee, Congressman Otto Passman of Texas, in his customary sarcastic way, tried to downgrade my budgetary skills by asking, "Mr. Director, you're a bookkeeper, aren't you?"

Modestly, I replied, "I prefer to call myself a certified public accountant."

His biting reply was, "What's the difference? Down in my country they are called bookkeepers until they get to the big cities; then they call themselves accountants."

Passman was overwhelmed by the backfire, after I talked to a few friends high in the American Institute of CPAs. Within a week he had heard sharply from almost every CPA in Texas, Louisiana, and adjoining states—by wire, phone, or letter—in protest of his belittling of their profession. By that time he'd had enough and pleaded with me to call them off. He was more polite to me in future hearings.

In the spring of 1960 *The Washington Post* in an editorial called me a "one-eyed bookkeeper" for "looking at only one side of the ledger" in fiscal matters. Senator McGee of Wyoming made that a battle cry in June on the floor of the Senate because of my suggestion that a proposed pay increase for government employees be deferred for a few months, and other members of the Congress followed suit. For our next New Year's Eve party at our house, which naturally was on June 30, the end of the government's year, all our guests were given eye patches to wear and we had a great joke about it.

There were many other times that I was the whipping boy of members of the House and Senate, but no one taught me as much about how the game of politics is played as Lyndon Johnson, majority leader of the Senate. He was a total political animal. He could be ruthless or compassionate, practical or idealistic, petty or noble, as he judged the political advantages of the moment. I met him for the first time a few months after becoming director, when I was getting more and more frustrated with the difficulties of convincing members of the Congress of the need for economy in government. Bob Anderson, who had just become secretary of the Treasury, was a close friend of Johnson and suggested that it would make my work easier if Johnson knew me and I knew him. Anderson took me to the senator's office and we spent an hour together, talking about current budget issues and ending with the usual picture-taking for the papers back home in Texas. Johnson was very amiable and assured me that he was sympathetic to my job.

"Lady Bird and I paid $600,000 in taxes last year," he told me, "so I'm as much interested in government economy as you are. Taxes are high enough and I'm against bigger spending." He said he would cooperate whenever he could with my efforts, and would call me if he had any ideas of his own for saving money.

About a month or so later Johnson fired off a vitriolic attack on the floor of the Senate at the "narrow-minded" director of the budget for blocking a favorite project. It was blistering in its criticism of me for ignorance, ineptitude, and every other crime of stinginess at the expense of the nation. I was amazed. It was so far off-key from the friendly attitude of our visit that I began to wonder whether he even remembered meeting me at all. Then another week went by and he sought me out at a cocktail party on the Hill. He was warm and cordial, and before I could protest he blandly said, "Mistah Director, I said a few things about you on the floor the other day, but don't pay them any mind. That was just some politics for the folks back home, and it's not personal at all." I accepted the explanation, but never ceased to wonder why it is necessary for the political game to be so bizarre and so inhuman.

Some of my earliest experiences as director taught me how earth-shaking small problems could sometimes be, even to people in high positions. I had been in office only two days when I got my first call directly from the president on the red phone.

"Stans, I've got a big problem over here," he started, "and if I don't get it straightened out quick, all hell will break loose."

I shuddered at the obviously monumental size of my first assignment from him, but spoke up bravely. "All right, Mr. President. What can I do to help?"

"Well, I've got this fine secretary here, Ann Whitman, and she's a grade fourteen. I just found that Seaton's secretary over at Interior is a fifteen. If I don't get that fixed right away, I'll lose the little hair I've got left."

With the help of Rocco Siciliano, special assistant to the president for personnel management, I saw to it that Ann Whitman got her pay advanced to grade 15 and thereby resolved that national emergency. After it was done I mused that no matter how important he may be, or how worldwide his responsibilities, even a president of the United States has to pause to deal with the human crises around him.

I never forgot the first telephone call I received from Lyndon Johnson following my visit to his office. It was about two months later.

"Mistah Director," he began, "when you came to see me I promised you that if I ever saw ways to save money I'd let you know, and I've got somethin' here that just came up."

I moved to the edge of my chair. This was just what I needed, something in the hundreds of millions of dollars, which it surely had to be to attract his attention. I was eager.

"Senator, I'm glad to hear from you, especially with ideas like that."

"Well, here it is. Mah position here as majority leader of the Senate entitles me to a Cadillac automobile," he continued, "and mine is due to be turned in for a new one. Now Ah just found out that this will cost six thousand dollars, but the White House rents its Cadillacs for the president for five hundred dollars a year. So Ah want you to call the president of General Motors and tell him to rent me a car the same way, and we'll save all that money for the gov'ment."

I did, of course. The president of General Motors was concerned about starting a precedent that would spread to the Senate minority leader and then to the equal officials of the House, but he also sensed some delicacy in refusing, and Johnson got his leased Cadillac. I wondered at the time whether he thought this would bring down his taxes, and later, when he became president and embarked on an economy campaign of turning out the lights in the White House for savings that could only be in pennies, I was the least surprised person in the country. He was being true to form.

The budget of the Department of Defense was our prime concern because it made up more than half of the total we had to deal with, and the ideas of the military researchers for new strategies and new weapons were always far beyond financial reach. Coping with the ambitious plans of the Defense Department was always difficult and the arguments were usually so persuasive that it was sometimes hard to retain confidence in a negative position. But again the problem was getting the best value for the money spent—or the "biggest bang for the buck," as my predecessor, Percy Brundage, was accustomed to saying in such cases.

The immediate post-sputnik era brought out an unbelievable number of marginal weapons proposals, some new and some taken off dusty shelves or out of long-closed files, some realistic and some pipe dreams. We in the bureau sometimes had a feeling that many were tossed out just to challenge us to see whether we could get them stopped. Our job in such cases was to marshal the questions and doubts and feed them to the president and his own military staff in the White House; hopefully, this would lead to his decision to not go ahead or to slow down. Sometimes our mere threat to take an issue to the president was enough to cause a military service to retreat as if it knew it was on unsound ground. For us in the bureau it was a real advantage to have a president with a military background who could see through the enthusiasms of these ideas to the realities of warfare. By the process of relying on Eisenhower's military judgment, we succeeded in gradually killing off a number of favored but doubtful projects in the Pentagon, and I am confident that their demise did not at all weaken our national strength. Only in this manner were the defense costs kept from skyrocketing immediately after sputnik.

Perhaps it shouldn't be said, but many times our budget experts learned about the doubts and inadequacies of Army projects from the Navy or Air Force, and vice versa. The rivalries were unbelievably persistent, and each service often fought for its own money by belittling the projects of the others, tipping us off as to the known or suspected deficiencies.

We also posed some very broad questions in 1959, such as the necessity of keeping five divisions of the Army, with their support forces and dependents, in the European theater so long after World War II; and the overkill capacity of present and proposed bombers and long-range missiles; and the future of a surface fleet, in which a single nuclear weapon of the enemy could wipe out a multibillion-dollar investment in one nuclear carrier and its planes. These were obviously subjects for the president and the National Security Council that could not be resolved in one budget exercise.

A confrontation with the Navy turned out to be somewhat easier, most likely because the military establishment didn't have the will to fight. In 1960, a congressman sponsored and promoted into legislation a bill to build a nuclear icebreaker, at a cost estimated at $60 million. It was in the early post-sputnik era of open fear that the Soviets were moving ahead of the United States in scientific achievements. The nuclear icebreaker rode through the Congress on that wave, with little visible opposition. The only apparent argument for it was that the Russians were building one, so we had to build one too. The Department of Defense conceded officially that there was no military necessity for the United States, so far from the Arctic, to have an icebreaker with nuclear power, and that other military needs had much higher priority.

When the bill came to the president's desk, the Bureau of the Budget had, as customary on all new legislation, a few days' time in which to make its recommendation to the president as to whether to sign or veto. We recommended a veto, on the grounds that there were many other national requirements of higher rank to call on the government's finances. The Navy, which would have had the responsibility to operate the ship, urged that the president sign the bill.

The president called both sides into his office, and a navy official argued eloquently for the importance of preventing the Soviets from getting a posture superior to us in any field of endeavor. To clinch his argument he said, with some haughtiness, "After all, Mr. President, it's only sixty million dollars!"

I abandoned most of the technical argument that my staff had prepared for me and merely pointed out that the secretary of defense had given me a letter saying that there was no military requirement for the ship, and that if we were to try to excel the Soviets on every meaningless front, we were certain to accentuate the cold war. On the money point, I ventured, "It's true, Mr. President, that this is only sixty million dollars, but if we can stop seventeen items like this we will have saved the taxpayers a billion."

Eisenhower looked up in interest, and then stared at the ceiling for a second, mentally checking my arithmetic. "By God, Stans, you're right!" he said and, taking up his pen, wrote a big NO on the briefing paper on his desk.

Probably the largest single item that yielded to the bureau's insistence on competitive justification was the B-70 strategic bomber. It was an extravagant concept for designing and building a supersonic high-altitude plane, capable of flying long distances at 2,000 miles per hour, to be powered by high-energy boron fuel at fantastic cost. Strongly pushed by the Air Force, it had generated considerable support in the Congress as a follow-on to the B-52.

By the fall of 1959 a total of $300 million had already been spent on research and development and another $360 million was being asked by the Air Force to initiate construction. The eventual cost would have been many billions of dollars. The bureau recommended to the president that the program be scrapped, and after studying the proposals, he at first agreed. The Air Force, in desperation, at the last minute induced him to keep it alive to the extent of $75 million more for research; this amount appeared in the 1960 budget, but the Congress later raised the figure substantially. Nonetheless, the project expired within a year or so. I drew quite a bit of personal criticism at the time for my part in this demise, but after a year the whole idea was considered discredited and it was forgotten.

The bureau's judgments were not all in one direction, and it gave its enthusiastic support to projects it considered most worthy. Among these was the Polaris submarine, able to fire bomb-carrying missiles from below the surface in waters anywhere in the world, which became a major element of our subsequent defense posture.

As a result of these decisions, and leaks as to how they occurred, a considerable debate grew in Congress as to the power of the Bureau of the Budget to control the military posture of the government. There were outspoken charges that we had put a money ceiling on the Department of Defense and that we were weakening the nation's defensive strength. The press reported various stories that Defense wanted more than $43 billion for 1960, and I was insisting on holding the amount to $40 billion and was causing the abandonment of a number of essential weapons programs. The Senate Preparedness Subcommittee held a hearing in July 1959, at which I was called on the carpet, and another hearing was conducted in July 1961 by the Subcommittee on National Policy Machinery. In both cases, I denied that I had ever put a ceiling on the department, but admitted that I had questioned the validity of many spending proposals. I said boldly, too, that I "did not accept a presumption that the defense budget must necessarily increase" year after year. The requirements had to be evaluated anew for each budget in the light of new conditions.

On the subjects of both the overall budget and its individual programs, I insisted that the president make the final decisions, but I acknowledged that the Bureau of the Budget was a constant gadfly, raising questions, challenging assumptions, and insisting that things be done in the right order of values.

Eisenhower did not like to have to deal with these tough budget questions. In fact, he had an obvious dislike for the pressures and timetables of the budget process, one part of which was that he usually had to give up most of New Year's Day each year to review the budget message, which had to go to press then in order to be ready for the Congress right after it convened on January 20. Brundage and I met with him in Gettysburg on January 1, 1958, on the fiscal 1959 message, and this schedule was followed by me on the three succeeding budgets that I prepared. Before then, of course, the details of the allowances to each agency had been approved by him and he had dealt with many appeals that ensued.

However, he was never casual in budget matters. He sought to be as fair as possible when the requests were reasonable, but he could be dogmatic and profane when he felt that proposals were unsound or contrary to his previously expressed policies.

Two of his faculties impressed me greatly, and made him easy to work with. He was always decisive, and he had a fantastic memory. Once he had listened to both sides of an issue, he did not temporize but came up with his answer right away, and it left no doubt as to what he had concluded. He did not slow up the works while we waited for his decisions.

I learned about his retentive memory early in the game, and it was awesome that a man who disliked figures as he did could remember them so well. On one occasion in his office we got to talking about an appropriation account for a particular kind of medical research. I mentioned that the new request was for $260 million, and he came right back and said, "We gave them $175 million last year and I thought that was high." I had to go to the records when I got back to my office to find out that he was exactly correct. He demonstrated this kind of recall over and over again.

While he had strong opinions and expressed them forcibly, he would always listen to reason—provided it was brief. In September 1958 at one of our meetings he vented his disgust at the size of the bureaucracy. "I want a ten percent cut in all civilian employment by next June, across the board," he said.

I knew from my experience in the Post Office what that kind of an order meant, and I knew it was unworkable. It was not possible to reduce by 10 percent the employment in government hospitals or prisons, or in the post offices, or in the FBI, or in the Coast Guard, or in many other units, without destroying the services. It made no economic sense to reduce the Internal Revenue Service or the U.S. Customs Bureau by 10 percent, since they produced revenues generally in proportion to the size of their staffs. But some cuts were possible almost everywhere.

So I said to him, confidently, "Mr. President, that's been tried a number of times and it has always failed," and I told him why. "It's demoralizing and it produces a deterioration in services until it forces a countermand. I don't think you want that kind of a fiasco. But if you will issue an order calling for a two percent reduction in jobs in every unit of government below what they have the money to pay for, without firing anybody, I believe it will work and it will produce more in savings than an abortive plan that would be embarrassing." He saw the point and agreed. Each month thereafter I presented to a Cabinet meeting a chart showing the changes in employment, and at the end of the year the total was down exactly 2.2 percent from the number covered by appropriations.

We did the same thing again the next fiscal year, 1960, and once more it succeeded. As a result, the total civilian employment was held at the same level of 2,355,000 at the end of three consecutive years, even though the money voted by the Congress would have paid for almost 100,000 more jobs. For fiscal 1961 we asked for a 3 percent decrease below funded employment, but the new administration that took office in midyear went in the other direction and government employment increased again.

Only once did I put money into the budget for something an agency hadn't requested. Being disturbed by what I considered overemphasis on the single monthly statistic of percentage of unemployment in the nation's workforce, I asked the Department of Labor to make an in-depth study of the characteristics of the unemployed. I thought the lawmakers ought to know much more about how many people were voluntarily out of work, how many were temporarily unemployed between jobs, how many were new entrants, how many were unemployed in families in which the head was employed, and so on. The picture of the unemployed as a static mass, merely increasing by new layoffs and decreasing by those getting jobs, was, of course, fallacious. It was an ever-changing group of individuals moving between working and waiting, usually soon able to find a new job to replace the one lost or given up; the proportion of long-term unemployeds was usually small, which is another way of saying that the average period of unemployment was relatively short. Evidence of the free movement of workers existed in the fact that most of the time only half of the unemployed were persons who had left their jobs involuntarily; the other half consisted of people who quit voluntarily or had just entered or reentered the workforce. This circumstance of free mobility, permitting people to take their own sabbaticals or shift around to increase their earnings, is one of the strengths of our system. I wanted to see this type of information pinned down and expanded, and then disseminated to the lawmakers, because I was confident that the periodic counts of unemployed, standing alone, were a gross exaggeration of the social need to be resolved. I also wanted to see some work done on a national computerized roster of unemployeds and jobs available, to assist in increasing mobility. The Department of Labor somewhat unsympathetically took the $300,000 I gave them for this purpose, and I never learned after I left what came of it. There have since been some gradual refinements in the definition of the unemployed, such as excluding the military from the workforce, but I don't know whether many of the questions I posed have been resolved and whether the extent of free choice in unemployment is well measured.

There were many frustrating experiences with the Congress on spending issues that regularly threatened to upset our objectives. It was, and is, a favorite tactic of the Congress to put a politically desirable but economically objectionable program within an authorization or appropriation bill that is otherwise satisfactory to the president, who then finds it very difficult to veto the bill as a whole.

On one occasion in his office he was feeling particularly disconcerted after a series of end runs on his budget by the Congress, and said so in his usual purple words. I shared his disgust at the erosion of our plans.

"You know, Mr. President," I said, "sometimes I think that what this country needs is a dictator for five years out of every twenty, to undo the excesses that the public forces out of the legislators. Then we could start again to please everyone." It was an absurd thought, and so intended, but Eisenhower was intrigued and his answer was almost wistful.

"Maury, you may have something there. Now, if you can come up with a sure way to get the dictator out of office when his five years are up, I'll go along with you."

I'm certain that many presidents and many directors of the budget have felt equally bothered by the difficulty of keeping democracy from undoing itself by excessive demands on the public purse.

I believe, however, that the recent presidents, with the exception of Eisenhower, have themselves unwittingly created many of the budget problems that beset them. It all starts with the promises they find it desirable to make in their campaigns for election, and their wish to keep some faith with those promises when they reach office. Once in, they seem to fall for the fallacy that they can keep the budget under control over a four-year term if they merely go along with major increases in the first year. The delusion is that at any given time there is a point of satiation, a level of spending that will satisfy the proponents of current causes. What they find is that, once having gone along with the demands, all they have accomplished is to raise the plateau from which the next demands will be made. There is no ultimate satisfaction. Programs feed on themselves.

This leads to another observation. As they are pressed day by day to approve new projects, the presidents I have observed seemed singularly unaware of the aggregate cost of what they had set in motion. Eisenhower acknowledged this. It is easy, in subjective discussion of one item after another, to agree to many of them, without a realization of how much they amount to in total. I have said on more than one occasion that what our presidents need most is an old-fashioned adding machine on their desks, so they can punch in the amount every time they buy a spending idea, and then glance at the total once in a while to see how much they have authorized.

Realistically, it is extremely difficult to reduce the budget for any one peacetime year below the amount for the preceding year. There is too much built-in momentum in existing growing programs already voted by the Congress to make that possible. But I did feel, and still do, that it would be possible to recover from cyclical deficits by keeping the total of the spending at the same level for a period of several years while income grows. Holding the overall amount even would minimize the severity of cuts needed in some programs to equalize built-in growth in others, while at the same time forcing careful selection of priorities among existing expenditures. This process would eventually assure a balance and some debt reduction without severe disruption to any worthy activities.

The space program was one that gave me, as budget director, a case of the jitters. The post-sputnik hysteria had removed all chance of orderly and rational consideration of costs and benefits, or of selective and efficient operation. The public seemed to be in full demand for its leaders to come up with efforts that would regain immediate preeminence in space for the United States. It was a rallying cry that enlisted many of the members of Congress into supporting an attitude of "the-hell-with-the-cost-let's-get-it-done," and budget limitations were something to be ignored in that kind of clamor. A civilian space agency was created to centralize the effort, and NASA's appropriations grew from $137 million in 1958 to $372 million in 1959, to $567 million in 1960, and to $975 million in 1961. In the meantime the Air Force still had its own space programs costing about a billion dollars a year. Waste and disorder were inevitable with such rapid growth, and I wanted to see a leveling that would permit orderly planning and discipline.

In preparing the 1961 budget, I suggested to Eisenhower that he propose in the budget message a uniform level of effort of $1 billion a year for the next five years as a reasonable amount to spend for a program of such uncertain national benefit. He did not want to make such a future commitment, and this amount was soon overrun anyway by those pressing the national urgency to outdo the Soviets. When Kennedy came into office in January 1961 and made his famous "man on the moon by the end of the decade" promise, the expenditures jumped to $6 billion a year. The total eventual cost of the moon walk was not far from the estimate of $40 billion given me in 1960 by Keith Glennan, the head of NASA. The huge expense of this incredible achievement may have been justified by what it accomplished in national morale, international prestige, and scientific byproducts, but through it all I did not change my early conviction that the speedup was not worth the costs it added. A more orderly and less expensive result would have been achieved at a slower and more even pace. There is no way to know whether spending the better part of the excess money on the earth's surface for domestic purposes like medical and health research might not have been far more beneficial in tangible terms for the American people.

There were a few matters that were of such a secret character that the bureau had little to say. These concerned the Central Intelligence Agency, of which Allen Dulles was then the head. At that time the CIA was a vastly more powerful entity than it became following the imposition of restrictions on it in the 1970s. The peak of its authority and influence was probably during the Eisenhower years, with Dulles in charge. Its decline began with its Bay of Pigs fiasco in 1961. It hit bottom after the moralistic purge that followed Watergate, even though its part in the Watergate series of events was actually minuscule and almost wholly irrelevant.

Dulles was a pleasant, gentle, likable person, quite in contrast to his stern, unhumorous brother, Foster, who as Eisenhower's successful secretary of state kept the nation on constant alert against the militant threat posed by the Soviet Union. Allen had a quiet, grandfatherly air, with white hair, a white mustache, a dark pipe, and rimless spectacles—not at all the way one would expect a master spy or intelligence chief to look.

Considered an able administrator despite almost continuous rivalries among his top subordinates, he was so nearsighted that when he had to refer to a paper at a White House meeting, he took off his glasses and held it within two inches of his eyes. Each year he presented in that manner a budget for the CIA's overt and covert activities, the details of which were disclosed in the budget bureau to me as its director and only one other staff aide. The money to cover these activities was included in several appropriations of the Defense Department, which in turn were reviewed under special confidential procedures of the House and Senate appropriations committees. In those days, secrets could still be kept from the public.

In the summer of 1960, Dulles came to me with a special request. He needed $15 million, he said, to supply and train a group of exiled Cubans in Central America in preparation for a guerrilla invasion that would attempt to overthrow Castro. I wanted documentation of some kind, but he adamantly refused, saying the only person outside his agency who then knew about the project was the president. It was money for which no conventional accounting would ever be made. I rebelled, because this seemed to go beyond even the deepest of the covert activities that I knew about. Dulles was irate. "If you question my authority," he said, "go to the president and ask him. If you question my judgment, that's none of your damn business. I know what I'm doing." His long and powerful tenure had made him somewhat contemptuous of budget directors.

I went to President Eisenhower in considerable dudgeon about Dulles's high-handed tactics, but he told me quietly to calm down. "I authorized him to spend the money, but I did not authorize any specific military action by the anti-Castro Cubans. That will have to come later, and I won't give it an okay unless I am convinced it is essential and that it won't fail."

The rest is painful history. When Eisenhower retired, the decision went over to his successor, John F. Kennedy, who quite promptly approved an invasion of Cuba by Cubans from offshore, with United States naval and air support, but at the last minute cut the air strikes and air cover so substantially that the whole escapade ended as a hopeless disaster. The invasion force was decimated and its survivors surrendered on April 19, 1961. The United States was disgraced; its complicity was known to the world.

An earlier set-to that I had with Dulles over top-secret spending plans ended more fortuitously for the country. He came to me one day early in 1960 with a request for $25 million to build a new super-spy plane that would fly at supersonic speed and at high altitudes over foreign countries, carrying specially designed high-resolution camera equipment to take photographs of defense installations, troop movements, and nuclear plant activities. Its principal target was, of course, the Soviet Union.

The new plane was to be a successor to one then flying, known as the U-2, which he said was highly successful in gathering valuable information on Soviet strengths and weaknesses. The CIA was concerned that Soviet antiaircraft defenses were reaching closer and closer to the plane's ceiling of about 80,000 feet, and wanted a new craft that would fly so much higher and faster that the risk of interception would be postponed for another ten years or so. It would take several years to design and build one.

Dulles made it sound easy, but I questioned the price of $25 million, considering the much higher costs of military aircraft. He countered: "We developed the U-2 for less than $20 million, and we need only to improve its performance to get what we want." I knew this was unrealistic, and that Dulles was either naive or trying to deceive me. Low-balling the cost of a project or program was and still is one of the common tactics in Washington to get it past the resistances in the budget process. Our experts in the Budget Bureau told me that a plane built to the CIA's intended performance standards might cost as much as half a billion dollars.

Over Dulles's objections, I passed this information on to President Eisenhower. After brief deliberation, and probably some independent checking, he decided to go ahead even though the $25 million would be only the down payment. His conclusion was, "This is something we may well need, and anyway it will be worth the investment to advance the state of the art for our air forces."

This time Dulles and the CIA were right in their planning. In May 1960 the U-2 plane piloted by Francis Gary Powers was knocked out of the air by a near miss from Soviet antiaircraft guns, and its further value in Soviet airspace was vastly diminished. A better plane was needed.

The first production model of the new plane was not delivered to the Air Force until 1965, long after I had completed my term as director. Early flights of the sleek SR-71 Blackbird high-altitude reconnaissance spy plane demonstrated a speed of 2,193 miles per hour—Mach 3—at a height of 85,126 feet. On one publicized occasion it flew from New York to London in one hour and fifty-five minutes. I was not around the Budget Bureau long enough to know the final cost tally, but it was many times Dulles's first estimate of $25 million.

As the 1960 election date approached, and realizing the uncertainties of politics, I considered it possible but not probable that Nixon might lose. This thought led me to the idea that the bureau staff ought to prepare position papers, with alternative options, on every conceivable pending public issue, to be available to a new president, or in any event to a new budget director. We set to work early in October on these papers to allow as much time as possible, since they had to be compiled concurrently with the 1962 budget that alone was a burdensome task.

When Nixon got wind of this, he hit the ceiling and demanded it be stopped. If the press and the public heard about it, he argued, they would consider it an admission that we expected him to be defeated, and he wanted none of that. We did continue some of the work thereafter, with Eisenhower's approval, but in very low key; after the election we stepped up the pace, finally producing several volumes that made it possible for the new administration to get a running start. The ninety or so thorough papers were as non-partisan as the nonpartisan staff of the bureau could make them. It was the first time this had ever been done on such a scale, and seasoned observers said it was the smoothest transition ever made up to then. As new president, however, Kennedy was extremely critical of the budget left to him and of the previous administration's policies.

Looking back across the years at my experience in the Bureau of the Budget, I feel four memorable impressions: the extraordinary competence of the career staff; the stern seriousness of the work, almost never broken by lightness or humor; the cynicism that grew in me as I appraised the tactics of the special-interest groups whom I came to consider collectively as "the spenders"; and, above all, the high respect I acquired for the qualities and character of Dwight Eisenhower.

The work was heavy, arduous, and demanding. Alone among the members of the Cabinet, the budget director shared little in the social life in Washington. His schedules of work, especially during the budget season (running roughly from September through January) were murderously long, averaging seventy to eighty hours a week. There was the tension of constantly saying no to sincere requests of able public servants who could not be satisfied with what was available, and the continuing abuse from the politicians and special interests for not meeting their expectations, with the press always eager to print the unwarranted attacks. These factors made a very difficult job almost overwhelming. Unlike most other employment, the satisfactions were infrequent; the only important one was in achieving the ultimate result of planning and executing an effective budget, and that could be accomplished only once a year. Nevertheless, the sense of importance of the work to the country and the privilege of working closely, almost on a daily basis, with the president of the United States made it exhilarating.

I paid a price for this, though, in neglect of family life. There was little difference to Kathleen and the children between a husband who had been away from home two thirds of the time building up an accounting firm and a husband who worked ten or eleven hours a day, seven days a week, and came home dog-tired from tusseling with the nation's financial problems. While they were always understanding, and their complaints were really solicitude about the wear and tear on me, I knew that we missed many of the husband and father relationships that should have been a part of our lives. I realize now that these conditions may well have caused some of the educational difficulties of the children and other turmoils of life adjustment they passed through. While they surmounted all those, and each grew up in time to be a well-adjusted, happily married parent, I have come to regret my own neglect, as a result of my perceptions of the demands of public service, of possibly doing more to smooth the way for them.

In the fall of 1959 I had thoughts of moving elsewhere before the close of Eisenhower's term. The position of secretary of commerce was vacant by reason of the ghastly political assassination done by the Senate on a really fine patriot, Lewis Strauss, in refusing to confirm him for that position. I was bold enough to suggest to Jerry Persons, the man who had succeeded Sherman Adams as principal assistant to the president, that I felt qualified for it and would like to be considered. He came back to me two days later.

"The president says there is no doubt you could handle the Commerce job, but he would like you to stay at Budget because he needs you there a lot more," he reported. With that compliment, I withdrew the application and stayed where I was through the term.

There were few light moments in the bureau, at least at my position. On the occasions I left Washington to make speeches, I often started out my talks by saying that I had no humorous stories to begin with "because nothing funny ever happens in the Bureau of the Budget." It was my best line.

Occasionally a serious event would occur that upon later reflection took on a much funnier tone. One I remember was on a day I planned to leave my desk late in the afternoon to go dove shooting with some friends. When my driver picked me up that morning I put my hunting clothes in the back of the car, together with my 12-gauge shotgun in its case. An hour or so after I arrived at work my executive assistant, Bill Carey, rushed in with word that my driver had been arrested and my presence was needed in the inner parking lot at once. What had happened was that he had become curious to see my gun, and had taken it out of the case, put it to his shoulder, and was trying it out for size by pointing it in various directions, all at the exact moment that Eisenhower was due to pass on his way to his weekly press conference in the Executive Office Building. The Secret Service pounced all over my driver, and he and I were thoroughly lectured before they gave up. To hear them tell it, only the fact that I had no ammunition in the car saved us from lifetime incarceration or hanging.

To my good fortune I missed one event that would have been troublesome to justify. General Thomas White, chief of staff of the Air Force, called me one day to invite me to go along on a three-day trip to Greenland. After a quick inspection of the base there, he offered, we would fly in a helicopter to Labrador and do some salmon fishing. I accepted at once but the next day, after some reflection, called him and said I didn't think it would be judicious for me as budget director to accept such an offer from one of the agencies that was a heavy claimant of funds. Besides, I said, one thing I didn't need was another cynical story in Drew Pearson's column. He laughed, but didn't press the invitation. Sure enough, about two weeks later I picked up the paper and read Pearson's caustic report that a fishing party headed by General White had just crash-landed in Labrador in an air force helicopter, at considerable cost to the government for rescue and repairs.

Pearson did write a critical account about me in October 1960, alleging that I was in a conflict-of-interest position with respect to some oil leases in Alaska. The story had been written for him by a freelance reporter to whom I had not paid much attention, and it was so wrong that it was libelous. Rather than blow off steam about it, I phoned Pearson and invited him to meet with me so I could show him the documents on the matter, and he accepted. I appealed to him to retract the story, urging that it would add credibility to his reporting if he admitted an error once in a while. To my astonishment, his column for the day before Christmas not only did contain a full withdrawal of the charge but also included glowing remarks in praise of the work I had done as budget director. It was one of the few times that Pearson ever did apologize.

Admiral Hyman Rickover, the crusty but dedicated senior advocate of nuclear power in the Navy, once tried to give me a hard time. Like many people who achieve prominence in a particular field, Rickover gradually assumed the arrogance to speak about topics for which his qualifications were dubious.

While I was budget director, I challenged him once when he professed knowledge that I suspected he didn't possess. There appeared a news report of a flamboyant speech he had given in which he charged that hundreds of millions, perhaps billions, of dollars were being wasted by the military services. This seemed like something a budget director ought to learn about, so I phoned him and asked him to come to my office.

When he was ushered in the door, he paced quickly to my desk, planted his feet, shook his white-haired head defiantly, and blurted out, "I'm not afraid of you!"

Momentarily taken aback at this ploy, I recovered quickly and said quietly, "Well, I'm not afraid of you, either. Now let's talk sense about some serious business."

That preliminary testing over, I got to the subject of the meeting and tried to pin him down. He insisted his statement was correct, but he finally admitted that he could not give me any particulars to back up the wild charge. The confrontation was a waste of time.

This was merely an example of the kind of exaggerated rhetoric he became noted for, which sadly detracted from the credit due him as an innovator in navy weaponry and father of the nuclear submarine. He would have been more impressive had he stuck to his knitting.

As we began late in 1960 to put the 1962 budget into shape, I wanted to show a substantial surplus. Eisenhower encouraged me in this, so I continued the fairly austere pattern of the preceding two budgets. However, by this time I had realized that the president could not carry the onus of a "no new starts" policy and gave that up. Some new programs and public works were included. In pressing for savings I asked Tom Gates, secretary of defense, to go back over his figures one more time to see if he couldn't bring them lower. After what must have been deep travail for him, he phoned to say that he would surrender another $200 million. When I failed to respond warmly, he burst out with, "Can't you even thank me?" Not until years later when Tom and I joked about the incident did I realize how the intensity of the budget job could distort one's sense of proportion and sense of humor.

In retrospect, it was a uniquely gratifying experience to work so closely with Dwight Eisenhower. He was a great human being, and a much better president than he is usually credited with being. Unfortunately, his two serious bouts with illness broke his stride, and unplanned events such as the U-2 incident with the Soviet Union prevented him from being the peacemaker that he wanted to be. But, all in all, he was the president who was right for that particular time in history, which seemed to call more for stability than for innovation. His years as president were good years, among the very best in our history. We had peace and order, with a sense of security at home and abroad. There was a high degree of unity in the nation.

Unfortunately, he was criticized by some for not being enough of a politician, particularly for not building the Republican party while he was president, and for not being more positive in his support for Nixon in 1960. I think I know the reasons for both: perhaps naively, he felt that good government, like virtue, brought its own reward. If he did a good honest job as president, he expected the credit to rub off on the party. He would not make decisions solely on political grounds. In 1958, he was forced by the Congress to either sign or veto an economic development bill within the week before a special election in Maine. There were communities in Maine that would have benefited from the bill, and the pleas for him to sign it and thus ensure a Republican victory were strong. But he felt that it was a bad law and the only course of honor was for him to veto it. He did so and bravely took on the criticism for losing a Senate seat for his party. That was his code and he adhered to it.

In 1960, he wanted Nixon elected to succeed him and I have no doubt that he would have done anything physically possible to help bring that about. But he didn't want to force himself on Nixon, especially believing that Nixon should run on his own and be free to agree or disagree with the Eisenhower record. So he waited until he was asked. Many people think that came too late, and that a bigger effort by "Ike" would have put Nixon across. There was obviously misunderstanding between the two as to his intentions, and Eisenhower's doctors wanted his activity limited, but I know that he was all out for Nixon and was terribly disappointed when Kennedy won.

Eisenhower could be profane at times under the conflicting currents of the presidency, as could almost every other president confronted with the daily mass of matters requiring hairline decisions and the knowledge that there was no one else to resolve them. He was often torn between his own essentially conservative views and the more liberal beliefs of some of his appointees. I never heard him engage in vulgarity or obscenity, although he could cuss a blue streak when irate. He did not often praise his subordinates directly for good performance, but he frequently spoke favorably to others about persons he felt had done well. He was, by all measures I apply to people, a splendid and beloved man, and I was proud to be a close part of his administration. I never found occasion to doubt his character or integrity. His sole aim was to do the right thing for the country. He was uniquely forthright and direct, never devious. His mind was sharp and his questions were precise, sometimes cutting.

His personal magnetism was legendary and I was privileged to observe it often, in the Cabinet, in our private meetings, and before the public. In 1960, at my request, he agreed to address the annual meeting of the American Institute of Certified Public Accountants in Philadelphia. He invited me to accompany him on his plane, so that we would have some time to review what he had planned to say, and then to ride with him in the backseat in his open car from the Philadelphia airport to the meeting hall. It was an incomparable occasion; people were lined all along the way, six deep in the downtown area, cheering and applauding. They were not there out of curiosity. I could feel the affection and respect of these thousands, there to express their devotion, and saw it glowing in their faces.

He insisted on a tight organization of the presidency and on an orderly way of resolving problems. If he had to listen to one side of an issue, he wanted the other side present. One of his innovations was to require that all policy papers considered by the National Security Council be accompanied by financial appendices. He would not make spending commitments without having consulted the Budget Bureau. Whereas budget officials of prior and succeeding administrations sometimes learned first about new programs in the newspapers, he wanted his budget director in on the discussions and decisions. His Cabinet meetings were on a regular schedule, agendas were prepared in advance, position papers were circulated beforehand, and those who attended were able to organize their responses ahead of time. The meetings were fast-moving and effective, with little random talk. The same procedure occurred in the National Security Council.

Although my relationship with Eisenhower while I was budget director was more than cordial, it was somewhat formal and could not be considered a close friendship. That came after he left office, when each spring I would pay him one or two visits in Palm Springs and we would sit for several hours at a time at his home or country club talking over our past experiences and relating them to current events. We knew each other much better and more warmly then. On the last of these occasions he promised me one of his oil paintings, which became a very prized possession when it was delivered to me after his death.

I never really found out until later how highly he rated my work. In his memoirs on the presidency he referred to me as his "able Director of the Budget," and that four-letter adjective was high commendation. In his book *Waging Peace*, written after leaving the presidency, he referred to the 1960 Battle of the Budget with this uncharacteristic but pleasing prose: "Under Maurice Stans, the Budget Bureau went to work with a determination and dedication that amazed as much as it delighted me. He deluged the Cabinet and when possible the public with statistics that made truly fearsome ogres of the gaudily garbed promises of the spenders."

But no greater encomium could have been given to me than his recommendation to Nixon on the day after the successful election in 1968. Nixon's associate Robert Finch was also present when Eisenhower, then in his terminal illness at Walter Reed Hospital, told Nixon that he had only two things to ask of him. One was to treat the retiring Lyndon Johnson as considerately as Johnson had treated him after his presidency. The other was to give an important place in the Cabinet "to that fellow Maury Stans, who is one of the ablest and finest men I have known in government."

There was one other word of praise that helped to make those three years in the Budget Bureau memorable. It came from the first Senator Harry Byrd of Virginia, for many years known across the country as the symbol of fiscal responsibility in the federal government. The autographed picture that he gave me in 1960 is inscribed "To the best Budget Director in my time." It was the ultimate acclaim.

# CHAPTER SEVEN

# Kennedygate

While the interregnum between Eisenhower and Nixon kept Kathleen and me out of Washington, it gave us some of the best years of our lives. It brought a few emotional and physical tremors, but by and large we lived days that were happy and adventurous.

In the first four years we dwelled in California. Our children reached maturity and one by one left the nest. We had a spacious one-story home in the foothills of Flintridge, just beyond Pasadena, and we kept in physical trim by daily swims in our pool and frequent climbs in the hills. My work, first in commercial banking and then in investment banking, gave me the challenges of two new careers in rapid succession. Social life was relaxed and unaffected, with occasional dances and parties and more frequent bridge foursomes. I took golf lessons and played some rounds at Annandale Golf Club, never with much success.

At the instigation of others soliciting my participation, I became active in local Republican circles, joined several clubs, took on some corporate directorships and a college trusteeship, raised money for charities, accepted special assignments on state and county commissions, rapidly became a working member of the community, and served as finance chairman for Nixon's 1962 campaign for governor against Pat Brown. For a year I spent my spare time as a syndicated newspaper columnist for the Times-Mirror Syndicate specializing in

Washington affairs. Through all these various pursuits we made many new and lasting friends.

By car on weekends, we explored the attractions of California. Best of all, we were able to take long vacations and especially to indulge our urge for adventure by frequent explorations in remote Africa. Our children were with us on two of them and these experiences brought us closer together than we'd ever been.

Not all the vibrations were positive, however, and there were some unexpected traumas. After two years with one employer I found it necessary, for reasons that might be euphemistically described as political incompatibility, to look around for another. Kathleen had to endure serious surgery several times, and a couple of our children had personal problems that gave us some temporary stress. But these negatives did not diminish the pleasant glow of a happy middle age for us both in surroundings and with people we enjoyed.

After these four good years in California, an opportune business merger induced us to move to New York into an apartment on Fifth Avenue and me, into an office on Wall Street. This brought another change of lifestyle. Childless now, we explored the world of restaurants, the theater, the suburbs, and the beaches. New friends came into our lives. We traveled still more within the United States and explored more deeply into Africa. Gradually, I worked my way back into national politics, with the growing hope of ultimately returning to Washington in another Republican administration.

In New York, too, there were unpleasant interruptions but we took them in stride. Wall Street went through ups and downs, and the firm I was with had to struggle its way through an early book-keeping crisis in 1965–66 when its computers lost track of millions of dollars in assets. Despite any temporary setbacks, the four years in New York were pleasant ones. They ended with our family all in fine health, three of our children happily married and one finishing college, my finances in good condition, and my appetite whetted for the next experience in Washington as a member of President Nixon's Cabinet. Kathleen said about this time, as she viewed our past and future, "Our cup runneth over."

A closer flashback at that period shows some interesting vignettes and brings out an untold story of unique personal crisis.

With the sponsorship of John McCone, who was then head of the Atomic Energy Commission, I accepted an offer from the Los Angeles–based Western Bancorporation (then briefly known as

Firstamerica Corporation and ultimately to change its name again to First Interstate Bank) to be its president and a director, effective in 1961 after we had taken a two-month vacation. It was an empire of banks scattered over eleven western states, originally put together by the famed Amadeo Giannini, who also had separately built the Bank of America (then the world's largest bank), and several other financial enterprises. Altogether, WBC had twenty-four banks and several hundred branches, and $5 billion in resources.

I also kept a close interest right along in developments in the federal budget, continuing through the Kennedy and Johnson administrations. It was particularly saddening to observe Kennedy throwing aside our careful work in ensuring that government finances were in balance when he took over and blithely entered a new era of willful overspending.

When Kennedy submitted his budget to the Congress in January 1963 for fiscal 1964, showing a deficit of $11.9 billion, I was asked by Congressman Frank Bow of Ohio, ranking Republican on the House Appropriations Committee, to review it and offer my suggestions. From that, there evolved a procedure whereby I spent several weeks in February of each year through 1966 working anonymously in Washington, without compensation, in analyzing the budget and making suggestions for savings. On some of those occasions I was assisted by Robert Merriam, my former deputy director of the Budget Bureau. Each year I had the exclusive use of room H-252 on the upper level of the east side of the Capitol building for this purpose. There I went over each appropriation line, considered it in light of my knowledge and conviction, and recommended an amount to be cut and the reasons for it. This was all worked into a series of tables for the Republican members of each subcommittee on appropriations in the House and Senate, with my suggestion for reductions listed, defended, and totaled.

This help was gratefully received by the Republicans, who found it very useful, since they had practically no staff to conduct such studies. The work had varying degrees of success, depending on the changing fiscal mood of the country and the Congress. It had its greatest impact on Kennedy's 1964 budget, which showed spending of $98.8 billion; this would have been the largest amount of peacetime spending in the nation's history, and it foretold still higher levels to come by asking for new authorizations totaling $108 billion. After three weeks, I produced data showing how the Congress could cut the authorizations between $10 and $15 billion. When this was announced as a goal by the Republican leadership, it got a lot of publicity and drew a considerable amount of favorable response from the shocked public.

My participation was, by this time, no longer a secret. According to the conservative *Human Events*, the "administration leaders reacted angrily, for they fear Stans, whose voice commands national respect." This was evidenced at Kennedy's press conference on April 3, at which he responded bitterly to a suggestion publicly made by Eisenhower that he consult with Stans to learn how to trim his budget. Kennedy laid on my fiscal beliefs the blame for the largest peacetime deficit in 1959, the largest outflow of gold, two recessions, and the highest peacetime unemployment. It was so ridiculous that I did not reply. The Republicans were outnumbered three to two, but the Congress did end up by cutting the 1964 authorization by about $8 billion, or 8 percent, probably the most severe peacetime reduction ever made up to that time.

In May 1965, as a result of stimulation by Eisenhower, a Republican Coordinating Committee was formed, with Ray Bliss as chairman, to express the party's position on current public issues. In addition to Eisenhower, its membership consisted of four previous presidential nominees, and about thirty congressmen, senators, governors, and officials of the Republican National Committee. I was named chairman of a Task Force on Fiscal and Monetary Policies. With valuable help from George Champion, a New York banker and my vice-chairman, and economist Raymond J. Saulnier, Jr., and with good staff assistance, we produced in the next three years four extensive booklets on fiscal and economic policies. These papers, to which I gave an immense amount of time, were adopted by the full membership of the Coordinating Committee almost without change. Each was written in a format that laid the responsibility for economic failings on the Democratic administrations and in parallel gave the Republican alternatives for each topic. These papers emphasized concern about rising costs of living and the dangers of a continuation of the fiscal and monetary trends.

After barely more than a year at Western Bancorporation I came a cropper because of my political expressions. Not for a long time did I learn the full background of my downfall, and it turned out to be a tale of unbelievable political arrogance and abuse of power at the highest level in Washington. While I have never publicly revealed the sequence of events and how they bore down on me, the experience was of such pronounced significance in my life that it is an overwhelming part of these memoirs. It was one of the very few setbacks I ever encountered in my business career. I am able to recount it in full detail because I made and retained daily records of each of the discussions with the persons directly involved.

Since banking was an entirely new experience, in a technical sense I lacked some of the qualifications to be a banker. My judgment on credit risks was short and probably poor. I knew little of the internal operations of a large bank and nothing about the mass handling of trusts and investments. None of this was expected to be fatal to my future, however, because my understanding with the chairman of the board, Frank King, was that for a considerable time at least I should become the public relations figure for the holding company and its member banks. I moved carefully in that direction, to be sure I was on the right track. Whenever I was invited into a public or political responsibility, I was careful to consult with him before accepting. He encouraged me to make speeches to many groups, to give interviews and write articles, to engage in political endeavors on behalf of candidates and the Republican party, and even to produce my weekly newspaper column, which soon reached forty major cities. All this was thoroughly publicized, with me always identified with one or more of the affiliated banks. It served its purpose well, since many officers and customers of the banks commented on my public activities with strong favor and I heard no remarks to the contrary.

During this period, I was of course also managing the internal affairs of Western Bancorporation, visiting its subsidiaries and serving on their various boards.

When this had gone on for a year, in mid-April of 1962, I reviewed my program for several hours with King on a quiet afternoon during a bankers' convention in White Sulphur Springs. He was commendatory of my results and expressed no instance of dissatisfaction. He then suggested that the time had arrived for me to take a more direct part in banking by moving from the upstairs office of the holding company to the officers' floor of United California Bank, its largest subsidiary. He confirmed specifically that he intended to work a few years more and then would expect that I would take his place as head of WBC, UCB, and its entire combination.

Only a few weeks later, an unexpected and violent storm broke in full fury, leaving me utterly bewildered at the turn of events, and soon out of a job.

Scarcely ten days after the White Sulphur Springs conversation, I joined King in a routine meeting in his office to review some pending matters. In the discussion, King casually made some comments about my political actions; in retrospect, as events unfolded they became much more meaningful than I perceived them to be at the time. He said quietly that while in New York on his way home from White Sulphur Springs, he had received a phone message from Asa Call, the head of Pacific Mutual Insurance Company and the dominant director of WBC, who reported that John McCone, a former director of WBC and currently the head of the Central Intelligence Agency, had expressed concern to him from Washington about my political goings-on. According to King, Call indicated that there was a danger that these activities would induce retaliation against the company in some way by the Kennedy administration. King intimated that this in fact may have accounted for questions just raised by the Department of Justice about WBC's recent exchange of stock with minority holders in the National Bank of Washington, a subsidiary. I couldn't believe that, but I promised to reconsider my schedule of forthcoming appearances. I mentioned that my next speech was to be in Seattle in June to the Republican National Committee and would be off the record; I would go ahead with it but would work out with him a new set of criteria for future appearances if he thought it desirable.

On May 7, King and I had lunch in Call's office with him. Call stated forcefully that he was concerned as a director and large stockholder that my political activities were harming the company, not by loss of disagreeing customers, but by creating the risk of government retaliation. He recounted his talk with McCone, stressing McCone's closeness to the president and the attorney general. In particular, he said that on the day he received McCone's phone call, Bobby Kennedy had invited McCone to his home for breakfast and there had raised the question of what Stans was doing, and that they then had a three-way talk by phone with the president; following this McCone had telephoned Call to raise with him the questions that Call then relayed to King. Call refused to say whether he thought McCone was expressing his own conclusions or was carrying a message from the White House.

In response to my questions, Call shook me by saying he believed I should either give up my weekly column and all political interests or withdraw from the company. I offered to air the subject before the Board of Directors but both Call and King dissented, saying it ought to be worked out among ourselves, one way or the other. Call stressed several times the possible harm to the company from Washington if I persisted. I agreed to think things over and come to a conclusion, after an opportunity to talk with McCone and a few of the directors.

Ten days after my meeting with King and Call I reached McCone by telephone. He said he believed that as president of a large corporation I was putting myself in a vulnerable position by writing articles critical of the administration. He insisted that this was entirely his own observation and represented natural conclusions that would be drawn. He continued that the administration had bitter feelings toward its opponents and that "these people know how to use power." His advice was to discontinue.

In a reply to a question, he said my participation in the Nixon governorship campaign had nothing to do with the situation. "Nobody in Washington gives a damn about Pat Brown," he opined.

He said his advice was personal and was based on how I could best do my job with the company and avoid criticism from within and from Washington. My alternative, he said, was for me to disagree and "stir up a fuss for First Western, a WBC subsidiary, on other items."

"Just stop being a columnist," he insisted.

Still not recognizing the seriousness of the threat, and aghast at the idea of knuckling under, I sparred for time. On May 29, while King and I were in Minneapolis calling on bank customers, I asked for another week or two to reply, and he agreed, saying I should take as long as I needed.

On June 20, after searching consideration, I met again with King. Speaking from an outline, I reviewed my actions and our various past conversations about them, and said that while I deplored the pressures, I was prepared to yield in large part to the demands. King acknowledged that I had not undertaken any political work without his approval, and that my columns had been valuable to the bank, since there had been many favorable and no unfavorable comments about my outspoken views. He did say, though, that Governor Brown and others had complained to bank officers about my working for Nixon against Brown.

Referring to my prepared notes, I said that I was not aiming at a political career, but wanted to stay with the bank; that I didn't like to be muzzled or threatened and didn't want to give up all political activity; that I felt the column would wear out by the end of the one-year contract, at which time I would not renew it; that the Nixon campaign would be over in November and I would continue until then, relying on the assurances of McCone and Call that it was merely a local affair; that thereafter I would operate under agreed criteria for speaking engagements designed to be of value to the banks; and that I would want to continue to work from time to time as a member of political committees or participate in off-record political engagements. I thought this met the conditions expected of me and should dispel all concerns. I was wrong.

At this point in the interchange, the climate of the conversation suddenly changed. King dropped his normally mild demeanor and became sharply critical, as if he had been steeling himself for an unpleasant task. He told me abruptly and for the first time that some of the directors were unhappy about my work for the bank, implying "serious mistakes" in judgment. He named three such items: my unfruitful negotiations for the sale of a subsidiary, the First Western Bank; my recommendation to increase the WBC dividend; and my proposal to form a Small Business Investment Company to serve small business customers of the WBC network of banks. I reminded him that he had agreed with all these propositions when I discussed them with him prior to presenting them to the board, and that the board itself had approved them. He insisted, nevertheless, that I had not displayed a "banking attitude" in moving ahead on these fronts.

Confounded by this obvious reaching for reasons to discredit me, I now began to understand my predicament. I told King I was certainly not interested in staying in the job if there was serious dissatisfaction. I could sense that despite his own abhorrence of the use of political force, despite his advance approval of my actions, and despite his April commendation of my work for the bank, he had found that he was under heavy pressure to jettison me. When I asked for other particulars he reverted to the political side, saying that my talk in Seattle to the Republican National Committee on June ll had ended all hope of a solution that would preserve my job. He had that word from Call.

In a way, I had no reason to be surprised at the reference. I had been assured that the Seattle meeting was closed to the press, so I pulled no punches before the party members in accusing the Kennedy forces of fiscal irresponsibility and mismanagement. I reiterated the charge that there was no way the federal budget could be balanced in their four-year term if they persisted in the direction they were headed. The words got out and made bold headlines across the country. King's suddenly aggressive confrontation was obviously an immediate and direct consequence.

In this conversation and one a week later, King made it definite that the die had been cast and I would no longer succeed him as head of the WBC system. He dismissed my proposed working relationship for the future and said he saw no way out other than my resignation. The extent of the desire for me to leave quickly was evident when we came to discussing a date for my departure. It was not agreeable for me to stay until the end of my contract in April 1963, but I would be paid up to then if I resigned promptly. I offered to resign in November, but this was not satisfactory. I suggested leaving in September, after I had taken my scheduled vacation; this too was rejected. My resignation was wanted forthwith, at once. King told me on one occasion that "top levels" in Washington were waiting for me to resign. I threw in the sponge and agreed to leave promptly but not until after I had one more conversation with Call, who clearly was the person holding the strings being pulled from Washington by John McCone at the direction of the Kennedy brothers.

It was not a satisfactory meeting. Call wanted to play "cat and mouse," and spent a long time reminiscing before even allowing me to open the subject. When I finally did, he said he would "go along" with King's conclusion that it was too late for any acceptable plan involving my continuance with WBC. He was evasive on the reasons for the sudden change in attitude toward me and toward my performance on the job, insisting that he couldn't say more than he already had. When I reminded him that the whole subject had originated with his conversation with John McCone, and repeated the report of that conversation I had received from King, including McCone's meeting with Bobby Kennedy and the three-way talk with the president, Call confirmed it precisely but waffled by stuttering that he did not mean to imply that he knew that there was any connection between that and the sequence of events or that McCone was carrying a message. However, he did comment that if I stayed with WBC there would be antitrust action by the Department of Justice against First Western Bank. Since First Western Bank was a subsidiary of WBC, I assumed he had misspoken: "You mean Western Bancorporation, don't you?"

"No," he replied positively. "I mean First Western."

He also reverted to the pending Justice inquiry about the WBC exchange offer for stock of National Bank of Washington, concluding that it had much more serious implications than I had attributed to it.

Like King, he assured me of his personal respect and friendship and said he would help me find suitable employment elsewhere. He insisted that I resign at once.

On June 30, searching for a friendly straw, I met McCone in his home in Washington to review the situation, expressing bewilderment as to what was going on. When I phoned him from Philadelphia, as arranged, he raised a new issue: that I had breached ethics by buying shares of stock of National Bank of Washington at a time when WBC was working on plans for a tender offer to its minority holders. This was an absurd allegation, because I had been required to buy the shares of this and another subsidiary in order to qualify under local laws for election to their boards of directors. Upon hearing that explanation, he withdrew the charge with some embarrassment. As for the main topic of my continued employment, he stated he had found a variety of things involved in the relationship that could not be ironed out and he hoped there could be a quiet termination. He concluded cryptically that I should consider that "this is a bad period for people—with the market upset and all—and maybe they were inclined to be more critical than normal." He would not elaborate, other than to concede that he was talking about the administration.

King, Call, and I had another meeting on July 2. It was fruitless except for King's confirmation that my purchase of stock in National Bank of Washington, referred to by McCone, had been proper and had been made with King's knowledge and agreement. King was apologetic. I asked for reconsideration of the decision that I should leave, but Call dismissed it cavalierly. "The platter has dropped," he said; "I hope you won't fight it." Both again offered to help me find another job. King volunteered to let me use an office, secretary, car, and driver until I found another connection.

I submitted the resignation on July 20, for acceptance by the board of directors at its next meeting on August 20, and left with Kathleen for a long adventure in Africa. Some of the directors later expressed to me their bewilderment at my departure from the company.

Upon my return, I began to pick up reports in the community about my surprise resignation. Author Ray Moley told Robert Finch, the lawyer whom I was consulting with daily, about a conversation with Call, in which Call said, "Stans was too active politically. His Republican National Committee speech and his column were not consistent with banking. First Western would have had an antitrust suit if the column had continued."

In the same month Leonard Ettelson, a Chicago lawyer, reported to me a conversation with Homer Livingston, head of the First National Bank of Chicago. Livingston told him he was greatly surprised to hear of my resignation as "[o]nly recently King had said Stans was the man to succeed him."

On September 18, at a luncheon I arranged with King at the California Club, so we could make an open show of friendliness to curb possible rumors, he made some very revealing statements. He volunteered that McCone had been "very anxious" to know when my resignation was effective so he could tell Bobby Kennedy about it at once. He then said that the first thing McCone did after I resigned was to phone Bobby Kennedy and the president and tell them Stans was out. I told King I considered this significant and that I deplored such misuse of power by government officials against a person because he spoke out on public issues. I said I was sure there were more forces involved than I knew about. King agreed and said that while he had told me all he knew, there had undoubtedly been close communication between McCone and the White House all along, since the Kennedys were both intensely interested in getting the word immediately as to what happened to me and when.

New shocks came along as I searched for employment. Some promising opportunities evaporated following favorable interviews, presumably after my background had been checked, but for a while I could not pin down what had occurred to change the atmosphere. Then the story unfolded. One of my interviews was with John Schiff of Kuhn, Loeb & Co., investment bankers in New York, to consider me for a partnership, upon the recommendation of our mutual friend, Lewis Strauss, a former partner of that firm and a former nominee for secretary of commerce. My meeting with Schiff and his associates went well and I felt very optimistic about being invited to join his firm, until a few days later I received a phone call from Strauss.

"Maury, the Kuhn, Loeb thing isn't going to work. The word is out that you have opposition in the administration in Washington. You have some highly placed antagonists."

I reeled. Was this to control my destiny? Was this to be a nonending vendetta? Strauss went further. He wanted to expose the whole affair, but I disagreed, because doing that would surely upset my hopes for any new connection. "All right," he said, "I won't make a public issue of this now, but I am writing a memo on the sources of my information and the details and putting it in my files, so you or I can have it available in case it becomes important someday to make a disclosure."

I did not see value in a public confrontation, either then or later when Robert Kennedy became a candidate for president. The incident had distorted my life for an unsettling period until I found a new course, but I saw no possibility of gaining in a counterattack. There was no way I could fight back. I could have been ruined, politically, economically, and socially. It would have been futile heroism to take up arms. I had to live for another day. Anyway, I presumed that the principals would readily deny any charges I might make, although fourteen years later King did confirm to me at lunch his various earlier statements about McCone's function as intermediary and the persistence of Jack and Bobby Kennedy in demanding that I be discharged at once, under threat of antitrust action if that were not done. Years later also, Lewis Strauss's son read to me the memo his father had written about the incident, still preserved in the files after Lewis's death.

Another company I was in touch with regarding new employment was Transamerica Corporation. At the instigation of Henry Salvatori, a respected Los Angeles businessman, I met with Horace Brower, a leading factor in Transamerica. When Salvatori followed up with Brower a few weeks later, Brower told him, "The people in Washington are down on Stans and out to get him," and since TA had regulatory problems from time to time, "[Stans] would not work out in the company." Salvatori reported this to Bob Finch who passed it on to me. Brower repeated this directly to me when I approached him, and he expressed his regrets.

In any event, the cloud followed me, hanging low. A similar result occurred when it was arranged for me to be interviewed for the post of financial vice president of International Telephone and Telegraph Co. in New York. The "headhunter" who had scheduled the appointment, a partner of Boyden Associates, contacted me in embarrassment and dismay at the last minute to cancel it, after I had traveled all the way from California to New York, saying that Harold Geneen, the chairman of the board, did not want to go ahead because of "political implications"; he feared his company's government contracting might be jeopardized if I were employed.

A longtime Chicago friend, William J. Froelich, a Democrat and well-respected lawyer, undertook around this time to check with Henry Crown to see whether I would fit into General Dynamics, which Crown controlled. A few days later Froelich called to say that he was told "Stans is not the man because he is too political."

On December 11, I visited Strauss in Washington. He confided that the original source of his information had been Earl Mazo, columnist and author, but he did not know who had told Kuhn, Loeb about the administration's curse on me. Strauss was irate about the whole affair, and said it was a typical Kennedy maneuver, and that he would like to expose it. I said again that I did not want that done because it would merely prejudice my job-hunting. He offered to have his friend J. Edgar Hoover check it all out, but I objected for the same reason. At the close, he said he had kept his word about putting a memo in his files and would add to it anything he heard later.

In January 1963, Robert Merriam, my former deputy in the Bureau of the Budget, reported that McCone told him "Stans has learned that banking and politics don't mix." In February, writer Ray Moley told Robert Humphreys of the Republican National Committee that Stans was fired because of fear of antitrust action against First Western by the administration. Moley's source was Call, with whom he was friendly and on whose recommendation he had bought stock in WBC. Moley also said that Call had told him as early as the previous May that "Stans is on the way out and doesn't know it." Surprisingly, there was no media publicity about the circumstances of my departure from banking, although several press people besides Moley had the story. Charles C. J. Murphy of Time-Life told Strauss at lunch one day that a *Time* reporter on the West Coast had come up with the story on the Stans firing, the gist of which was that McCone told King that the administration regarded Stans's criticisms as "dangerous to the national credit." According to Murphy, McCone also said that the removal of Stans would head off an antitrust case for Western Bancorporation. This conversation with Murphy was recorded by Strauss in a memo on December 20, 1962.

In March 1964, columnist Roscoe Drummond, seated next to me at a dinner in Washington, said it was no secret that I was still seriously out of favor with the attorney general.

That's the unembellished story. A president and an attorney general of the United States, with the director of the CIA as middleman, demand of a dominant director of a major banking system that its president be fired, without consideration by its board of directors, under threat of antitrust actions against the company or a subsidiary by the Department of Justice.

To say this unraveling of discoveries was a traumatic experience would be a gross understatement. The distress was not so much at having to seek another job; I had full confidence that I would find something equally to my liking, although that self-assurance began to wane after the disappointments started to mount as I found myself tarred as a target of political hatchery. What shook me the most was that such a thing could happen in my country, the modern-day United States. It seemed more like a throwback to the autocracy of the Middle Ages, or at least to the fearsome risks of political life in the South American nations, or Stalin's Soviet Union where bald power was regularly employed to destroy opposition.

One day I was the highly respected president of one of the world's largest financial corporations, with a six-figure income, fulfilling a lifetime goal in a position of prestige and influence. The next day I was out of a job under circumstances never publicly known, leaving me under a handicap of negative inferences in finding another, ambitions thwarted and illusions shattered, not because of incompetence or misdeed, but because of political terrorism emanating from the highest level in Washington. I was a marked man because I had dared to oppose, to speak out on issues, to contradict those in power.

My opinions and quoted facts had carried weight in circles opposed to the White House. I was a factor to be reckoned with, a thorn in the side. So I was wiped out.

The suggestion by Eisenhower to President Kennedy that he go to Stans for advice on how to keep his budget under control; my weekly column in newspapers around the country raising challenging questions about current handling of government expenditure issues; the annual work I did for several years in providing recommendations for cuts in the Kennedy budget to the Republican appropriations committees in the House and Senate; and finally, my biting speech before the Republican National Committee's annual meeting in Seattle in which I predicted that Kennedy would never be able to balance the budget, piled one on another, were just too much to bear.

It is commonly quoted that the motto of the Kennedys in government was, "Don't get mad—get even." I often wondered how many others had received the same quiet axing. I have every reason to believe they practiced it with impunity. They certainly could not like anyone who was constantly nipping at their heels, and I fitted that description. They knew how to silence me and they did it.

# CHAPTER EIGHT

# New Jobs and New Explorations

Several months after my resignation from Western Bancorporation, I settled on a new business connection. It was waiting for me only one hundred feet away, in the long-established regional investment banking firm of William R. Staats & Company in Los Angeles. Staats operated through about twenty branches in California and Arizona, had a fine reputation, and its head, Donald Royce, was a longtime friend. At his invitation I became its president early in 1963. This was another change of life for me, at fifty-five, but I entered into it with full enthusiasm, visiting the branches, organizing committees to increase employee participation in policies, and trying generally to introduce new management and sales techniques. I also spent a large amount of time working on corporate financings and mergers for clients. The company had a long prosperous history and it regularly made good money.

Late in 1964, after I had been there less than two years, the company was invited into a merger with the prestigious New York underwriting firm of Glore Forgan & Co., and after brief negotiations the deal was concluded. It made a good relationship because Glore Forgan had major underwriting positions in Wall Street offerings and Staats had good distribution for such marketings and needed more of them. One of the understandings of the merger was that I would move to New York as president of the combined firm, which took on the clumsy name of Glore Forgan, Wm. R. Staats, Inc. to retain customer recognition of both sides. I did so on March 1, 1965, after resigning from and receiving farewell encomiums from all of the business, civic, and governmental relationships I had undertaken in my four years in Los Angeles. Altogether I resigned from fifteen different business and eleemosynary affiliations, but I continued to hold two corporate directorships and stayed on for several years as a trustee of Pomona College.

In many ways, Kathleen and I hated to leave Los Angeles. We had acquired a wide coterie of good friends, and I had achieved broad recognition in the business community and a solid place in civic affairs in a short span of time. Our living had been healthful and comfortable, and one measure of our pleasure with the mild Southern California climate was that our children all decided to stay there when we departed. But I had never shied away from a new opportunity, and Wall Street was enticing. I knew I was going into the big league of the financial world, and I welcomed the adventure that it offered. Nixon, who had preceded me to New York, warned me that it was "a fast track." I learned how true that was when I saw competing firms dropping by the wayside in Wall Street's bookkeeping crises of 1966–68; they collapsed because their primitive computers failed to keep up with the growing volume of business, and they lost control of their securities and money. Glore Forgan came through better than many at that time, mainly because the combining of the two firms and their computer systems in 1965 provided plenty of opportunity for trial and error before the explosion of volume occurred a few years later.

Business was generally good for the merged company and for me in the three years I spent with it in New York. In place of the personal attachments we had acquired in California, Kathleen and I settled down to enjoying New York's attractions. We calculated that within a mile of our apartment at Fifth Avenue and Sixtieth Street there were almost a thousand places to eat, and we set out to check them off, but we never got past the first 106. We saw every new play and musical comedy that opened, and took in many of the new movies. We spent weekends in the country or at the beach with friends, and made short driving jaunts into Long Island, New England, and New Jersey. In retrospect, it was a time of quiet, even-keeled living, with nothing more exciting than my two hospitalizations for surgery and the citywide blackout one day in 1965 when the power supply failed and we had the discomfort of being in an eleventh-floor apartment in the dark for twelve hours without working appliances.

Early in 1968 I took a leave of absence from the company to become finance chairman for Nixon's comeback try at the presidency. In that year, even though I gave very little attention to the Wall Street business, the fees to the firm from the closing of transactions that I had originated in preceding years amounted to more than $1 million, so I felt I had well earned my way. At the end of 1968, when I was designated to become secretary of commerce in Nixon's Cabinet, I formally withdrew from the company and received a payout of all my capital and earnings. Considering the subsequent sad fate of Glore Forgan Staats (being forced into a disastrous liquidation after a bad merger, six months after I departed) and the general distress then in Wall Street, I couldn't have gotten out at a more opportune time. I probably would have lost my entire life's savings in that affair had I stayed.

My lifetime belief in the law of averages had been vindicated. Good fortune had wiped out the wounds of ill fortune. I could renew my confidence in the future.

Interspersed with these several careers in banking and investments were a series of carefully planned vacation trips. From the time of our first vacation to northern Minnesota, which led us to vow to take our future vacations outside the United States, Kathleen and I learned increasingly about the excitement and pleasures of adventure travel. All of that exploded into a new world of exploration in 1948, when we made our first trip to Africa. From then on, with the exception of periods away from home strictly for relaxation, our attention was riveted on that continent, and this became a fixation that excluded all other places when we read a book by my friend Lewis Cotlow, a member of the Explorers Club in New York, entitled *In Search of the Primitive*, which ranged broadly through most of Africa but included some other remote parts of the world as well. He showed that there were still many lands occupied in great part by races and peoples surviving far away from the customs and amenities of our twentieth-century civilization. We followed his footprints in some countries and in others ventured way beyond them, returning each time to visit a different country or area for a month or more. Whenever possible, Kathleen and I traveled together and sometimes took our four children as they were growing up, but there were three or four times in which Kathleen's circumstances prevented her from going and I found other companions.

For this volume, I have chosen to give brief accounts of five of our nineteen expeditions, including two directly connected to Washington that tied me to political events in Africa involving the saving of American lives.

Our 1948 African safari was a brief one of two weeks in Kenya. It opened our eyes to a timeless world, centuries different from our lifestyle. Once we got beyond Kenya's capital city of Nairobi and its airport and central business district, we were wide-eyed with wonder at the herds of magnificent animals in their natural settings and the primitive people living as they had for thousands of years.

The Masai tribe was among the most colorful of all in Kenya, nomads who counted their wealth in cattle and would not sell them for the white man's currency, who lived in low huts made of wattle and cow dung, and whose main food was milk mixed with cow's blood (taken without injuring the animal). Their sex customs included a period of free love for teens, and they put their infirm aged out for the hyenas to finish. Their young boys became men by killing a lion with a spear. We saw all of that and much more. One tradition of the Masai was that if a man married, the other males of his formal age group had the right, upon visiting, to share his bride in bed. We had this practice brought home when one of the trackers on that first safari left us and stopped off at his home village because he learned that one of his buddies had just been married.

Our biggest thrill on that safari was on the first day. We were accompanied by an older friend, Harry Falk of Chicago, and had set out in an open safari car to scout the plains some distance west of Narok and near the Mara River. Our tent camp had been set up on the bank of a tributary and we had moved out at daybreak, before breakfast, to see the animals as they began to stir with the dawn. I cautioned our professional guide that none of us had ever shot an animal larger than a deer, so we didn't want to tangle with anything big on our first day.

That caution was quickly thrown to the winds. Our head guide, a reckless lad named Jerry Button, suggested that we shoot a zebra for lion bait, drag it over the plains some miles to create a spoor, and then leave it in a tree for the predators to find. We would then be on hand to photograph them feeding the next morning.

The zebra he selected fell heavily with my one shot to the head. It then was pulled behind the car with a stout one-inch rope, and we had gone with it only a short while when one of the African scouts yelled, "*Mmbogo mkubwa*," and Button called a hasty conference. It was a big black buffalo just entering a patch of forest, a distinctive trophy for the area, and he wanted me to "take it." I hesitated but, relying on his confidence, set out with a heavy .600 rifle that I had not yet had time to try. In the darkness of the woods, my aim was not accurate, and the two-thousand-pound animal crashed out in the opposite direction with a severe wound behind the lungs, not enough to bring him down. With his immense strength he took us on a long chase of several hours and then created some tense excitement by doubling back on our trail. I had to shoot quickly as he charged from the rear, but I was fortunate this time and dropped him within five feet, still breathing on us menacingly.

Meanwhile, Kathleen and diminutive Harry, who was all of five feet two, had awakened to the fact that they were alone in an open car on an African plain, with no guns, and with lion bait at the end of a twenty-foot rope. Sure enough, after a short while a lioness with five cubs got the scent of the zebra and came out to investigate. Kathleen and Harry were frightened half to death at the thought of the lioness entering the open car and finding them more tasty than the zebra, and in a panic they tried to escape by moving the vehicle. But with the heavy drag it couldn't move faster than a walk, and the lioness and her family kept coming at the same leisurely pace. In desperation Harry finally stopped the car, edged out with his tiny penknife in hand, and sawed away at the rope until it parted, hoping all the while that the lioness wouldn't come closer. She didn't, and Harry then drove the car as quickly as possible to a hill, just a few minutes before Button came back on foot to collect them. Eventually, we all got together again, but my heroics with the buffalo were of no interest to Kathleen and Harry. They'd had their own exploit for the day. It had been more than enough for Harry, and he left the expedition for good the next morning, taking one of our cars back to Nairobi and the safety of civilization. We learned later that the danger from the lioness was imaginary. She would never have fed on human flesh with a zebra dinner so close at hand.

The rest of our trip was a revelation in the multitude of displays of wildlife and the interesting insights we picked up from numerous tribes of natives as to their ways of life. We collected very few animals, just enough to provide the necessary meals for us, our professional hunter, and his native staff. In all, this adventure brought us to a level of excitement that could have only one possible outcome: the booking, before we left Kenya, of a second trip, to last three months in early 1950.

Our 1950 safari began in Nairobi with two professional guides, six keepers of the household, and four truck drivers and porters. We set out on a course that ultimately took us on the first known automobile trip to make a wide sweep around Lake Victoria; after scouting the central and western sections of Tanganyika, we swung northward to parts of Uganda, then west into Ruanda-Urundi, and north to the eastern part of the Belgian Congo. Among other things, we visited the seven-foot-tall Watusi warriors and, less than a hundred miles further on, the Pygmies, in both instances enjoying pleasant visits with the tribes in their own villages. We then turned eastward, passing the famed Mountains of the Moon and the north side of Lake Victoria, and finally continued back to Nairobi.

An unexpectedly valuable tool on this trip was a Polaroid camera, the first in East Africa wherever we went. It was absolute magic to the natives, many of whom had never seen themselves in a mirror; often it took the insistence of his friends to prove to an individual we photographed that the print was really his likeness and not actually his own skin. Even in the larger communities close to Nairobi where tourists had appeared in the past and pointed black boxes at them, the natives had never before known what came out. Wherever we stopped to take an attractive shot of a scene, or a person, we were besieged by people calling out in Swahili, "Nataka pitcha," wanting a picture of themselves.

Our experiences with the camera were incredible. In the Albert National Park in the Congo, an askari wanted a picture of his wives, and when I agreed he ran to his village and brought back eight of them. I gave him two group photos but balked when he let me know what he really wanted was a separate one of himself with each wife. At the border between Uganda and Ruanda-Urundi a hyper-conscientious Belgian customs officer found flaws with our identification papers and auto permit and refused to let us cross. I resolved the impasse by producing an instant picture of him at his desk, after which he invited us to his home for dinner so I could take photos of his wife and children; the next morning he stamped all our papers. A few days later he sought me out at our hotel in Usumburu, eighty miles ahead, just as we were turning north, and entrusted me with enough francs to buy him a Polaroid camera and some film and mail it to him after I returned home.

The most bizarre of all these Polaroid experiences occurred out-side a native village in western Uganda. We had set up our tent and made camp for the night, when the nearby chief came over and pre-sented us with a local type of food. In return, I found a few trinkets to give him and topped it off by presenting him with a picture of himself. There was the usual process of slow identification, followed by his feeling his skin to see whether any had been removed in the transfer to the piece of paper. Finally reassured, the chief left proud-ly for his village holding the photo at arm's length ahead of him.

The next morning I was awakened right after daybreak by noisy argument and turmoil outside my tent. When I stepped out I was confronted with a wildly decorated character in animal skins and feathers shouting loudly and threatening me with his spear. I with-drew quickly under the protection of our professional hunter until he could fathom the commotion.

It all became clear. I had not only practiced witchcraft in competi-tion with the village witch doctor, but was accused of doing harm to his chief. It took a long while before emotions cooled and voices dropped to where I could safely demonstrate the camera to him by taking pictures of our own party. Then, as an inspiration, I put the camera in the witch doctor's hands, pointed it at the chief, and showed him the button to press. When he found he could duplicate my magic in front of his boss, his hurt pride was assuaged and he wanted to take pictures of everyone in sight. After he had used up several rolls of film I had to plead "nkwisha," which meant that the supply was exhausted and the spell of the magic had been broken.

As time went on, there was a gradual enlargement of the scope of interest of each exploration after we made an alliance, in 1952, with the Museum of York County in Rock Hill, South Carolina, to bring back a trophy male of every species we encountered. Their persua-sion was based on the argument that every such specimen had a unique educational value. If it were correct that there was no full exhibition of all of the African animals in any one place, this was the opportunity to create the only such collection in the world. I accept-ed the challenge to carry it on until we attained that goal in 1995.

During the years when I was working under Eisenhower, we did not have a major trip to Africa until 1960, a time that was historic there principally because it was the year in which the Belgian Congo became an independent nation under the name of Zaire. This trip crossed the country from east to west and was a nightmare of unbe-lievably bad happenings, but it ended well. Among other things, we drove across a large part of the country, visited its gold-mining area, and had an unplanned but very thrilling stop with the primitive Bakuba tribe and its territory. I became a citizen of the country, had to escape our impossible guide from Rhodesia, then organize and equip with men and provisions a new safari in the eastern part of the country where we eventually collected Africa's most elusive game animal, a bongo, a beautiful striped antelope that hides out and sleeps in the daytime and feeds only at night.

This offbeat adventure began when our white hunter, an Irishman named Paddy from Salisbury, Rhodesia, was a day late meeting us at the airport in Luluaburg, in the western part of the Congo, leaving us stranded and unable to converse in the local French. When he did arrive, he was without one of the guns we needed, but with a mass of chairs, tables, Spode china, a three-hundred-pound refrigerator, a cast-iron bathtub, and four cases of corn flakes, all of which we didn't need on a fast-moving safari. Since a gun could be bought only by a bona fide resident of the country, I was unable to obtain the shotgun we needed until the mayor took pity on me as a distinguished visitor and certified me as a citizen of the town so I could get a license to make the purchase. He rationalized that our intended safari of thirty days into the depths of the nation was long enough to qualify me as a resident, and ordered that I be entered in the city's "Book of Populations" while I waited.

We progressed through a frustrating comedy of errors that included daily flat tires, the wrong maps, frequent sojourns for hours stuck in muddy roads, erroneous directions, engine trouble, separations of our safari car from the lorry, and sundry misadventures brought about because neither Paddy nor I spoke French or any of the Congo dialects. All this went on without our getting even a hint of where to find a bongo. With halting communications we once spent several days in hopeful pursuit of an animal the natives seemed to call a pongo, only to find it was about one tenth the size of the fellow we sought. After two weeks of this farce, as I was about to give up the quest, Kathleen and I noticed an abrupt and frightening change in Paddy's personality and his actions. He became brutal toward the natives and irrational in conversation with us. We were so concerned about our safety that I bribed his young assistant to load our luggage after dark and take us to the nearest American mission, an estimated hundred miles behind us, leaving some traveler's checks on the bed to pay for the trip in full so Paddy wouldn't want to chase us.

There was a surprising sequel to all this. Several years later when we were in Salisbury, I asked about Paddy and learned that he had never returned alive from the Congo. He had died along the road from a brain tumor, which of course explained his erratic behavior.

We didn't find an American mission but we were rescued by an American anthropologist, Alan Merriam of Indiana University, and his wife who were living in the Basongye village of Lupupa, across the Bubububu River, researching the native residents. The Merriams generously took us in for a few days and then drove us one hundred miles south to an airport where we could get a plane back to our starting place.

One conversation in Lupupa was memorable. Merriam introduced me to the village chief who offered to take us hunting at night. The hunt was tiring and useless, without a quarry in sight, but it paved the way for a visit with the chief the next day. An elderly-looking man of an age hard to guess, he had told Merriam about many of his life's experiences, one of which was cannibalism. I pursued the subject with the chief, asking how it was that he sometimes ate human flesh. Was it to celebrate a victory in war? No. Was it a ceremony to the gods? No. Well, why did he eat the meat of other people? The answer was unequivocal, "Because it tastes so good."

We still had two weeks of our safari left, so I decided to make another attempt to find the animal we wanted. A kindly fate intervened in the form of a friendly Sabena Airlines local manager who suggested that we visit the picturesque Bakuba tribe about a hundred or so miles to the north. The Bakubas are artisans. Their woven Kasai velvets made from wood fibers, and their wood carvings are strong on angular geometric designs and are among the most beautiful of traditional African artwork. When he offered to take off from work to drive us, we happily accepted.

Along the way, we met Dr. Mark Poole and his wife, Sara. He was an American physician associated with the Presbyterian missionaries in the central Congo and his wife was a nurse. His mission post included, in addition to classrooms, five hospitals in which he cared for about four hundred patients, with the help of locals he had trained. In addition, he had a small Cessna plane that he flew to four outposts, each about fifty miles away. There he had established additional nursing centers where again, with the help of trained locals, he paid weekly visits to treat hundreds more. All these activities were in the territory of the Bakubas, a very primitive tribe headed by a heavyweight king called Mabintshi Makena.

King Mabintshi, following tribal custom, was entitled to one wife from each of the 537 villages in his domain. These wives he kept in a maze of thatched grass huts in a large royal compound in Mushenga, a few miles north of Poole's compound at Bulape. They embraced a wide range of ages, from very young beauties of probably twelve or thirteen to older women who looked to be in the seventies but were probably much less.

His palace was a simple thatched hut of considerable size, perhaps thirty by fifty feet, with several rooms. We were not invited to enter the building but were led to a wide-open window frame, three feet in height and six feet in width, above a foot-high threshold, inside which he held court while his visitors remained just outside. There were no handshakes, merely a series of nods as we were introduced through several interpreters, from English to French to the Bakuba tongue and back. At a gesture from His Majesty, low stools were brought and we poised on them only slightly above his level as he sat with his four-hundred-pound bulk about three feet inside the hut on a woven grass carpet covering the sandy soil.

His reception of us on short notice demonstrated a special affinity for distant visitors from the land of America, which we attributed to the excellent accomplishments of the American medical and teaching missionaries. Undoubtably another American contribution was a large framed color picture of himself that was produced for him by his aides upon a clapping of his hands and a single word. He displayed it fondly and proudly. It had been taken by *Life* magazine for a feature story a year or so before.

The conversation was minimal, because he volunteered little and we could not think of much to say. Searching among our possessions for something to present to him as a gift, I came up with a small two-inch silver penknife and a bright blue bandanna handkerchief. He was immensely pleased with both, made evident when he immediately brought forth from deep within his massive flabby body a long rolling belch, a traditional sign of pleasure. He then presented us with a well-used but worthy piece of the unique Kasai velvet, and invited us to witness a formal dance of his wives. There were about fifty of them, bare-breasted and heavily skirted, who performed rather well considering that they were the ones who were fat and aged. The younger wives, I learned later, were doing their customary work in the fields.

The bottom line of this memorable experience developed when the new government in Kinshasa sent word to the wives that they were no longer bound to traditional tribal customs and were free to leave the king and return to their own villages. A majority did so, leaving the poor monarch to live out his days with only two hundred wives, and these unfortunately the older and less attractive ones. I wonder whether he considered this one of the benefits of modern civilization. Mabintshi Makena died about ten years after our visit.

To my good fortune, one of the two times I ever caught dysentery in Africa was on the return trip from the Bukuba country to Luluaburg; our route took us directly to Dr. Poole's central mission and hospital. His knowing diagnosis and treatment abolished its agonizing discomforts in a few hours. In a very surprising and unexpected way, I repaid the favor a year later when I became a link in a chain of shortwave communications between him at Bulape, his brother in Texas, and the State Department in Washington, during the time of the tribal terrorism in 1961 that followed closely after independence.

Rioting and civil disobedience were everywhere; whites were being ravaged and killed by rampaging tribesmen, tribes were fighting each other, and anarchy reigned. The military forces were uncontrolled and in mutiny. Foreigners were in flight. Poole and all the persons in the ten missionary stations of the American Presbyterian Congo missions, including sixty-five children, were in the path of destruction, as some of the murderous waves headed north from Luluaburg into the Bukuba country. The situation became critical on July 9, when the missionaries lost all outside contact with the capital of Leopoldville, other communications were cut, and mutinous troops held the airport at Luluaburg and the roads between there and the missions.

It was at this juncture that Poole in desperation sent an SOS by shortwave to his brother in Texas asking him to get in touch with me at my office in Washington to plead for help. As soon as I received the message I communicated with officials in the State Department, urging government intercession, and a rescue chain was set in motion. Belgian paratroops cleared the Luluaburg airport; Poole made repeated dangerous trips for several days from daylight to dusk with his tiny Cessna to bring the missionary Americans to safety, a few at a time; a U.S. Navy DC-3 flew from Rhodesia to Luluaburg and back several times to carry on an airlift until all were safely out of the country. Poole came immediately thereafter to

Washington to thank the government and me for the prompt and effective rescue work, which may well have saved many lives.

The uncertainty, tension, and sheer excitement of these African explorations cannot be portrayed in words. Each one took a toll or brought a boon in emotion, and each one qualified as high adventure. The trips were a marvelous counterbalance to the dread discipline and heavy pressure of government office at an executive level, and despite misadventures and odd events I always returned to my desk from an expedition refreshed. As Kathleen put it, we went to Africa to unthink, and it worked.

As the years elapsed, our African travels took us to places that were more and more distant and primitive. Having embarked in this direction, we headed for countries barely known to the outside world, certainly not to its mobs of rowdy tourists. Our trips almost invariably involved rugged traveling over plains and through forests, staying in tented camps, hunting early and late hours, and testing our physical stamina in tracking animals both remote and rare.*

Despite the busy times and unsettling events in Los Angeles, Kathleen and I managed to take two safaris of a month each during the five years we lived there, one in 1962 in southeastern Angola and one in 1964 in northern Bechuanaland. On both of these we took our four children. These were wonderful family affairs, and the intimate experiences of tent life in a land of thousands of animals and hundreds of peaceful indigenous peoples—the Hereros, Ovambos, Damaras, and Bushmen—cemented the family closely together. As Terri put it later, "I finally came to know my parents."

Getting to the lower inside corner of Angola wasn't simple. We went via Salisbury over immense Lake Kariba to Livingstone by scheduled airline, and then took two small charter planes to a newly built airstrip just across the Luiana River in Angola. Our little puddle-jumpers were the first aircraft to land at the "airport," which had been cleared in the sandy savannah country, wetted down with water carried for miles, and tamped into a secure-looking surface that our pilots were not sure would survive the first landings. However, we settled down in a cloud of dust, without incident, and taxied to the end of the strip, where we were greeted by hundreds of applauding residents of nearby villages, who had come to see the

---

*At no time did we ever collect one that was protected by local law or international covenants.

massive noisy sky-bird that disgorged walking and talking people from its side.

On this safari, we spent most of our days in a permanent camp, and this did not have the rustic thrill of tent life. Our hunting was successful, and we had gathered a splendid collection of local fauna for our Stans African Hall collection when disaster struck. On the second to last morning, as we breakfasted in the dark at four o'clock so we could get an early start for a distant area, we were suddenly alarmed by one of the men yelling "fire." We rushed from the dining table into the open to see a sky-high blaze that lighted our dismayed faces as we saw the drying shed irretrievably lost in flames. Built with grasses and parched tree branches, about forty feet long and twelve feet high, it had been used to air dry the trophy skins and horns. There was no chance of saving anything in the intense heat, and we stood helplessly watching the building evaporate in five minutes before our eyes, taking with it all of our hard-earned treasures. The next two days were gloomy and we ended the safari in sadness. The fire had evidently been started by a flying ember from a random brush fire miles away.

The following family trip, to Bechuanaland in 1964, more than made up for the disaster and disappointment in Angola. It was the safari of safaris, and our white hunter, Harry Selby, was every bit the wonder that author Robert Ruark had said he was in his famed books on Africa. We camped for a time on the shore of the vast Okavongo swamp, one hundred miles long and thirty miles wide, a body of crystal-clear lakes and streams amid sandy islands and peninsulas. The waters, which came from the mountains of Angola, contained fighting tiger fish who battled at the surface with mighty vigor until their hearts literally collapsed. The surrounding land areas had thousands of lechwe, tsessebe, buffalo, wildebeest, and warthog, and hundreds of kudu, sitatunga, giraffe, ostrich, zebra, sable antelope, roan, reedbuck, elephant, and other game animals, plus occasional lion and leopard (in Africa, animals are not spoken of in plurals). I used up thousands of feet of cinefilm in a short time, filming the better-known animals and the rarer aardvark, honey badger, and porcupine, and the majestic greater kudu with their spiraling sixty-inch horns. This was untouched country that had been opened up to outsiders for only a year, and we goaded Selby into allowing us to explore places neither he nor any white man had seen before. Each new piece of woods, each new clearing, and each new view of the swamp had fantastic numbers of unmolested wildlife. We stood speechless many times to watch immense herds of three thousand buffalo thundering in clouds of dust through the bush, or a dozen graceful reedbuck sprinting through the shallow water in their rocking-horse gait.

Wonderment was on all sides, and we inhaled it fully in this last awesome frontier. We did very little shooting, and it was really with an inner reluctance that we killed a few of the common animals for food for our family of six and working retinue of twenty-two, and one of each new species for our museum. We caught fighting tiger fish until our rods broke, returning the sharp-toothed bony fish to the sand-filtered perfectly clear water of the streams, in which we could see the bottom twenty feet down. We took time to admire and film the bird population, from fish eagles to various hornbills and sacred ibis and many other varieties, including green pigeons and fruit pigeons. It was a natural paradise, unspoiled, and we took care not to spoil it.

After twenty days along the Okavongo, we picked up our belongings and drove south into the fringes of the Kalahari Desert. Here we met some of the surviving Bushmen, and saw more unique and spectacular animals like the gemsbok and red hartebeest, as well as thousands of graceful springbok.

While we were later living in New York, I found time for another trip in 1965, this one without Kathleen. My companion was the former ambassador to Luxembourg, A. Burke Summers of Washington, who had been in Africa several times before. A polished gentleman and world-traveled sportsman, he helped to keep our safari dignified under all contingencies, except for the night when I was driven out of my bed and indiscriminately bitten by thousands of tenacious black safari ants. I was wholly irate when he broke down in hilarious laughter at my physical gyrations instead of helping me to pick off the bloodthirsty insects. Dancing with pain and slapping at my furious tormentors with both hands, I saw nothing funny in it.

This safari was in Chad, and we carried the official Safari Club flag No. 82, filming our exploits as carefully as the conditions permitted. This film, entitled "Wonders of the Sahara," is in the Explorers Club library in New York. Chad is part of the old French Equatorial Africa; it is dotted in the northern regions by former outposts of the old French Foreign Legion, once occupied by "Beau Geste" characters, but now taken over by the Chadian army. Our white hunter was Claude Vasselet, a slight, wiry, middle-aged Frenchman who had left Paris seriously ill and come here to die ten years before. Thin, lithe, and tough now, he guided us from Abéché in the eastern part of the country northward past the outposts of Biltine and Oum Chalouba to the end of the trail at Fada, well within the Sahara. On the way we collected the beautiful fawn-colored desert animals like the addax, scimitar oryx, dama gazelle, and dorcas gazelle, getting record-book specimens of each one, again for our museum. We survived thirst, auto breakdowns, desert mirages, sandstorms, and the fatigue of 120-degree days without serious misadventure. In the desert, we sometimes passed caravan after caravan of camels carrying one-hundred-pound loads of natron from dead lake beds, or dried dates from oases, in either case a three-hundred-mile, thirty-day trip to carry about ten dollars' worth of goods on each animal.

When we came to Fada we still had ten days left on our calendar for a planned camel caravan of our own, north into the Ennedi Mountains and beyond in the Sahara. It took a full day of heated bargaining with the camel owners to arrive at terms and another half day to load our supplies and ourselves.

A camel ride must be one of the worst anatomical punishments known to man, and it was relieved only partially by the red rubber doughnut, the kind that hospitals use after surgery, which Kathleen had foresightedly sent along from Washington. We traveled about six to eight hours a day, with twenty-five camels, and nine cameleers in attendance, breaking at times for lunch or just to dismount and walk to relieve sore muscles. At nightfall, we made a light camp in the open, making sure to station our folding beds at least a mile away from the noisy, smelly camels and their loud, argumentative owners.

On one such night we camped late in the day on a white sand wadi, a flat dry riverbed about three hundred feet wide. We were so dead tired and sore that we merely washed a bit, had a quick sandwich, tumbled onto our cots in the bright moonlight, and immediately fell into heavy sleep. I was awakened at what seemed about midnight by the strange sound of an animal lapping water, which struck me as being entirely out of place in this setting. Rising in my bed, I discovered I was a mere ten feet away from a big hyena boldly drinking from the washpan we had left on a low stool when we retired. He heard my movement and departed instantly for the thorny brush bordering the wadi.

Relieved, I went back to sleep, only to be awakened once more after a few hours by the same sound of an animal lapping up a liquid, but this time less noisily. I mentally credited the hyena with real astuteness, but when I peered over in the moonlight, quietly this time, I found myself looking right into the eyes of a magnificent male leopard, drinking from the same pan. Slowly and carefully I reached for a weapon but the leopard's alert ears heard my movement and he departed in a few bounds into the thorns. I slept fitfully the rest of the night, awakening now and then from gory dreams of bare-handed struggles with desperately thirsty and desperately hungry beasts.

At dawn, I was up first so I could track the two animals to learn how they had come to find that small pan of water. The hyena had crossed directly from the bushes forty feet away on the bank of the wadi, but the leopard's tracks showed that he had entered the wadi about four hundred feet upstream, walked down the center of the sand, and then trotted over to the head of our two bunks before turning to the water pan. The tracks even showed that he had stopped and swung his rear legs around to put his nose directly over the top end of my bed. I'll never know how long he stood there contemplating the situation, but I give thanks for my good fortune that he was more thirsty at the time than hungry.

There was a tragic sequel to this hunt in Chad that was almost fatal for our white hunter, Vasselet. Through an astounding coincidence I played a part in saving his life.

Five years after our safari with him, Vasselet was guiding a party of Mexican hunters in southern Chad. While he and his assistant each took several hunters in safari cars in different directions in search of the Lord Derby eland, their camp was raided by a force of fifty bandits on horseback, who killed one of the skinners, and brutalized and wounded several other workers. The raiders then waited in ambush for the return of the hunters, and when the first car arrived they terrorized and wounded several of the occupants and took their guns, ammunition, and valuables. Vasselet, tipped off by one of the camp boys who escaped, drove to the nearest police post for help. The raiders, after a long wait, took everything of value in the tents, then departed.

The police identified the group as a band of revolutionaries and called out the army, who caught up with them and reportedly killed every one. Vasselet's trouble began when the authorities discovered that some rifles and ammunition stolen from him were unregistered, a violation of the strict Chadian laws. He was tried, found guilty, and sentenced to serve an indefinite term in a grimy, cold, infested prison. Fearful that he would not survive, his wife wrote to me and others among his past clients, asking that they request the American ambassador in Fort-Lamy to intercede with the president of Chad. The ambassador acknowledged my personal letter to him and replied that his previous efforts on Vasselet's behalf had been fruitless but he would take up the case again in view of my interest, but without much hope.

The ambassador's gloomy reply arrived about a week before a White House dinner at which President Nixon entertained all the heads of state who were in New York to observe the twenty-fifth anniversary of the United Nations. As secretary of commerce, I was present with Kathleen. Mingling with the guests, we renewed our acquaintances with Emperor Haile Selassie of Ethiopia, President Anastasio Somoza of Nicaragua, and quite a few others. This brought us by design to the French-speaking president of Chad, with whom I talked through an interpreter. I told him I had enjoyed my safari in his country and hoped to return, and we exchanged pleasantries. It would not have been appropriate, I thought to myself, to bring up the Vasselet matter in this setting, so I started to move on, but the president interrupted me by taking my arm. "I received your letter on behalf of that hunter, and I will do something about it when I return," was all he said, and I thanked him. Immediately upon his arrival in Fort-Lamy the president released Vasselet on condition that he and his wife leave the country at once without taking anything with them. Perhaps no other set of circumstances could have brought about so fortunate and prompt a result. Vasselet was extremely grateful for my intervention, which in this fortuitous way, saved his life. He and his wife moved at once to Australia, leaving all their goods behind.

Africa meant peace and surcease for us from workaday efforts, and a month there every year or so brought rejuvenation to us, as others find theirs on the Riviera, or in Switzerland or Miami Beach. Africa meant turning the calendar back a thousand years, it meant following the trails of Stanley or the great explorers, it meant memories of Livingstone at Ujiji, and of Tippu Tib and the ivory trade and Zanzibar and Timbuktu and the outposts of the French Foreign Legion. It meant races and peoples in their last generation before the advancing reach of civilization—the Masai, the Somalis, the Turkana, the Basongye, the Wagenia, the Bakuba and scores more that we visited and pitied for their poverty, even as we deplored the shock waves that modernization would soon bring them. It meant the hordes of animals of the plains, the jungle, the desert, and the waterholes, which we knew would gradually yield to the same march of human progress.

Africa meant the vulturine guinea fowl and yellow-necked francolin, the sand grouse and greater bustard, the flamingo and ibis, and the myriad other strange birds of the air, the woods, the marshes, and the lakes. It meant the mysteries of the Zimbabwe ruins, the grandeur of Victoria Falls, and the modern miracle of man-built Kariba Dam and Lake Kariba. It meant the tales of "China" Gordon fighting at Omdurman, the Coptic churches carved by monks a thousand years ago out of the living rock at Lalibela in Ethiopia, and the slave traders moving out of Mombasa. For me, the two years spent in Africa on nineteen expeditions, most of them with Kathleen, were life's most exotic and memorable adventures.

Africa was for us a hundred or more tense or thrilling experiences like those I have told here. It was a thousand vignettes that come back to mind of the moments of beauty and peace and tragedy and discovery. Our daughter Terri sitting under a baobab tree with a washrag and bowl, cleaning the faces of the black babies outside a tiny native village in Angola, while their mothers approved smilingly through the barrier of language. The village on an island in the Luiana River where half of the residents had been born with diseased or blinded eyes caused by the blackfly. The Masai nicking the neck of a cow to draw blood painlessly to mix into a milk cocktail. The women everywhere with corn rows or other elaborate hairdos, the styles sometimes held in place by cow dung. The last of the wooden-lipped Ubangi women. The Wagenia tribesmen fishing dangerously on flimsy platforms over the fast-rushing Congo. The bloated four-hundred-pound Bakuba king seated on a grass mat in his oversize hut to receive visitors. A Pygmy mother soothing a crying infant. The massive crocodiles of Murchison Falls. The grace of a cheetah on the open plain at Manyara.

The pathos of a seven-ton elephant at Samburu trying to raise and bring back to life the empty carcass of another, long dead and picked over by vultures and hyenas. The distress we felt at having natives beg us for the white man's pills, any pills, that would relieve their headache or toothache or other pain. The massive walking rhythm of Ahmed, the elephant so distinguished in size and ivory that Kenya made him a national monument. Kathleen with me sleeping in the open, lions roaring in the distance, under the uncontaminated African sky whose stars are just above the treetops. Being stranded in the jungle in the Congo with two native guides who spoke no English, separated by a mapping error from our main party, hungry and thirsty beyond desperation, yet afraid to eat the pieces of manioc they offered because I knew that if it had not been fully cooked it would be poisonous to me. At the end of the day, the magnificent red sunset over the vast desert sands. All these scenes and a thousand memories more will live with me vividly as long as I am here to remember.

After I became a public figure I was criticized on some occasions because I engaged in big game hunting. It was not true. From the beginning I set a policy that I adhered to on all my expeditions. I would kill a necessary number of the plentiful species, like gazelle or impala, to feed the persons on the safari. Beyond that, I would shoot only one each of trophy animals, aged males with large horns or unusual characteristics, often those too old to run with the herd. These we brought back and had mounted by skilled taxidermists in realistic settings for the Stans African Hall, whose unique collection is attended by thousands of people a week, many of them excited schoolchildren in nature classes.

My answer to the critics is that in their natural state in the wild, these animals can be seen only by the privileged few who can afford to go to Africa. My effort through the years was one way of preserving the primeval beauty of scores of species and subspecies so they can be seen, studied, and admired by hundreds of thousands of young and old every year. If I am wrong in this, all the natural history museums of the world are wrong. Collecting for a museum is not in contradiction with my conservationist commitment. In my early days in Washington, I was one of the organizers and a trustee of the African Wildlife Leadership Foundation, of which Russell Train was its first president and a dynamic manager. Through the years it has financed and conducted a large number of programs in wildlife conservation in Africa, including schools for wildlife management, educational activities on the value of wildlife, antipoaching and law enforcement work, and other measures to preserve these valuable treasures for future generations.

The passing of centuries had not yet brought about much fundamental change in Africa when we paid our first visit in 1948. The European colonial powers of Britain, France, Portugal, Spain, and Italy still held sway over most of the continent; Germany had been forced to give up its colonies after losing World War I—Tanganyika to the British and South West Africa to a League of Nations mandate. The colonial boundaries, which had been drawn without regard to tribal ranges, were generally ignored by the nomadic peoples in their annual migrations for food and water for themselves and their herds. Some of the young men of Kenya and other British colonies, and perhaps a few from elsewhere, had seen fighting service in World War II and through that a few scenes of life in the white man's world; some had received rudimentary educations from missionaries, and some had attained low-level civil service status. But a massive proportion of the population was uneducated, eking out a meager subsistence under the harshness of nature, living in grass huts in primitive villages, adhering to ancient customs and taboos, migrating with the seasons, and in contact with few whites. Most of the trading in the bush was by Indians and Goans, Middle Eastern Arabs and European expatriates, who sold in shabby dukas the beads, spices, printed cloths, enameled pots, and similar objects that were the earliest intrusions of the outside world.

Beginning about the time of our first safari, history began to speed up. Independence came to colony after colony; education, communications, and transportation began to advance; and more trade goods became available. The greatest change was in the cities, originally settled and built by whites, which began to receive waves of natives escaping from traditional tribal homelands to the excitement and hope of a better way of living. Nairobi was typical of many cities throughout the continent. A sprawling community of Europeans and Asians, who owned the housing and shops, employing Swahili-speaking blacks in domestic and clerical jobs at petty wages, it had a countable population of under 120,000 on our first visit. By 1980 that had grown to 850,000, with a substantial base of tourist revenues augmented by a growing commerce in manufactured goods under the free-enterprise government of onetime Mau Mau leader Jomo Kenyatta and his successors in the presidency. In the countryside, natives had acquired most of the prolific crop-producing lands of the white colonials, but millions in the bush and jungle still lived in a noncash economy of bare subsistence.

Kenya's per capita income in 1980 was still under $1,000, and its government was hard pressed to temper the local expectations of an abundant life under independence. In the process, most of the Asian merchants were driven out, and many whites gave up their homesteads at depressed prices and left for Europe. Crime and violence flourished under the unsettling conditions of housing shortages, heavy unemployment, and fluctuating prices of goods produced for

export. Other countries, most of them less developed than Kenya—
such as Somalia, Chad, the Central African Republic, Zambia, and
Tanzania—were much worse off.

In two years of in-depth travels in nineteen countries in east, central, and southern Africa, I invariably appraised the state of development, the conditions of the economy, and the prospects ahead. I
could see little hope that these grossly underdeveloped nations would
achieve peace and quiet in several generations, after a standing start
from thousands of years of tribal antagonisms; or that, with high
birthrates, they would obtain more than a small measure of improvement in living standards in that time, with so few ways to generate
the capital needed to produce economic and social progress.

Most of the native governments were headed by inexperienced
and lightly educated leaders. Many were heavy with corruption. The
concept of building a nation, infrastructure and all, was beyond their
comprehension. At best, dictatorships or military governments were
the only means of providing whatever social and economic discipline was possible. Democracy, Western style, in the absence of centuries of trial and error, was a hopeless dream for the few who even
understood it. As the years pass and the Idi Amins are driven out
and the Nyereres withdraw, some gains occur, but the militant tradi-
tions and hatreds of tribalism still provide an unstable base for
improvement, bound to come slowly and insecurely for generations.

In a Cabinet meeting in Washington in 1970, after one of my
expeditions, President Nixon called for my observations. What I said
was generally along the following lines:

As our minds agonized over the future of the unfortunate millions
on the African continent, we always came back to one firm conclusion. Independence at the time and in the manner in which it was
granted to these poor, illiterate people was a catastrophic injustice.
Life would have been much more just and history more compassionate if after World War II the colonial nations had accepted mandates
of fifty years or so to guide and bring the Africans to a planned and
seriously targeted level of education, production, modernization,
and comfort before turning them loose.

# CHAPTER NINE

# Moving into the Nixon Cabinet

The setting was dramatic, but somehow the proceedings didn't start auspiciously for me. It was December 11, 1968, and a victorious Richard Nixon was about to unveil the Cabinet to take office with him on the following January 20. One of the large meeting rooms of the Shoreham Hotel in Washington had been converted into a television studio, with a central stage on which Nixon was almost circled by a wide arc of easy chairs. Here he would introduce, one by one, the thirteen seated persons to take over the twelve Cabinet departments and the Bureau of the Budget for a period of time described on the official appointment scrolls as "for the pleasure of the President."

This was to be a momentous day in my life. After confirmation by the Senate as secretary of commerce, I would be, I had told my children, just ten heartbeats from the presidency in the line of succession.

First of all, I had difficulty getting to the meeting from New York. As the time approached, Kathleen and I were both fighting the Asian flu. It showed no signs of letting up and I doubted that I could make the trip even though I desperately wanted to be present. My staff, however, insisted that I absolutely had to go; and on the previous

135

day they had chartered a small jet that would avoid most of the airport inconveniences and allow me to recline while on the way. With these arrangements made, I undertook to be on hand, even if it meant I could just hang on during the ceremony and then go right to bed in Washington. Kathleen, however, was even sicker than I was, and it would have unduly risked her health to travel. Since each of the appointees was expected to bring a spouse, I did the next best thing and phoned our daughter Maureen in Los Angeles, who was delighted with the idea of being my companion for the event and flew overnight to Washington.

On the day of the ceremony, after I had summoned my reserve strength to go to the airport and board the jet, the pilot discovered that for some mechanical reason he couldn't take off. An associate scouted around the airport for several hours before locating a replacement plane, and chilled and fatigued, I finally arrived in Washington with only an hour to spare. Without time to eat or rest, I took more aspirin and joined the other Cabinet designees in a side room. My temperature was around 103.

Most of my Cabinet colleagues were new to me, but some I had met before. Bob Finch, who was to head Health, Education, and Welfare, was an old friend from California days. Bill Rogers, the designate for secretary of state, was the only one besides me who had been a member of the Eisenhower Cabinet, in which he was attorney general. Mel Laird, to be secretary of defense, was a good friend whom I had known as a key member of the House Appropriations Committee. I had met John Volpe, new secretary of transportation, on several occasions and we were more than casual acquaintances; in fact, I had unsuccessfully backed him to Nixon for vice president at the Republican convention in Miami Beach. John Mitchell, to be attorney general, was the one, next to Finch, with whom I had the most contact, working for almost a year in the 1968 election campaign, he as campaign chairman and I as finance chairman.

So I knew five of the Cabinet members quite well. The others were almost total strangers, although I had been introduced once or twice each to George Romney (HUD), David Kennedy (Treasury), and "Red" Blount (Post Office) before this occasion. My principal meeting with Blount had occurred several weeks earlier in my New York apartment, after Mitchell had asked me on behalf of Nixon to meet with Blount and encourage him to accept the Post Office position. My two years in that department under Eisenhower as deputy postmaster general apparently made me best qualified to sell Blount on taking what was known to be a very troublesome and politically tough spot. I did not tell Blount that it had earlier been offered to me and I had turned it down. I did not know George Shultz (Labor), Cliff Hardin (Agriculture), Wally Hickel (Interior), or Bob Mayo (Budget) at all. But on this occasion we became at once a congenial, warm group, full of the spirit and enthusiasm of the day. I tried not to show how lousy I felt, but my sneezing and coughing were noisily evident.

When the signal came, we all moved onto the television stage and took our seats, the wives seated behind each nominee. Maureen was with me, eager and fascinated. I was doing my best to relax and appear alert, but there was a strong draft in the room that found me right on its path and this made me increasingly feverish and uncomfortable. At long last the program began.

Nixon spoke for a few minutes on the importance of the Cabinet and the effort he had made to find the best available man for each position, and then began his introductions. Starting first with Rogers, an old friend of his, the president-elect extolled his background and diverse abilities for about two minutes, speaking entirely without notes, and then introduced him. As he moved from one to the other, Nixon continued from memory to describe the job, the man and his unique qualifications, and finally presented him by name. I was eighth in protocol order, and when he came to me he praised my work for Eisenhower and in the business world and then ended astonishingly without mentioning my name! I was so befogged with my discomfort by that time that I didn't even notice the lapse. The press did, however, and I became noted as "the man Nixon forgot." To compound the seeming slight, he overlooked mentioning my name again a month later when I was sworn in at the White House. I'm sure that on the first occasion he wasn't aware of the oversight; certainly he knew me well enough not to have forgotten my name. On the second occasion, he was presumably joking in making the omission, in a calculated response to the mass of publicity that resulted from the first incident.

Before Nixon's announcements of his Cabinet selections there had been considerable speculation to the effect that I would be named secretary of the Treasury; reports persisted later that I was unhappy that I did not get the post. These stories were grossly incorrect.

What actually happened was that about ten days after the election, John Mitchell invited me to lunch, and we met at the Metropolitan Club in New York. We talked about the election and many other things until coffee was served, but not about what I was waiting to hear. Finally, he opened up.

"The president would like you to be in his Cabinet. He would like you to be the new postmaster general," he offered. I didn't hesitate a second in replying.

"John, I was deputy PMG almost fifteen years ago and I don't feel that the Post Office should be my ball game again. It's a no-win situation. The PMG spends most of his time jockeying between labor negotiations for higher pay and Congressional hearings for higher postage. That badminton game is not my idea of a pleasant future. It would be more of a punishment than a reward."

It was bold of me to turn down the invitation, and I feared that Nixon might not be too pleased. "Please explain this to the president and tell him I'd be happy to serve anywhere else that he feels is within my qualifications."

Mitchell was astonished at my turndown but he pursued the new lead. "What would you like?" he asked.

"I've looked over all the Cabinet posts," I replied "and there are a number that I could handle, but only two I'd want. I'd be happy with either Commerce or Treasury. But please tell the president that if neither of these works out I won't be bitter about it." That last wasn't wholly true, but I was anticipating the possibility that he already had commitments for those positions.

Mitchell called me about a week later while I was visiting the Peter Flanigans at their Westchester County home in New York, and his message was short. "That Commerce job is available if you want it," was all he said. I told him I was delighted, and I was. I had long felt that the Department of Commerce had been so downgraded for many years that its prestige and responsibilities needed rebuilding. To my mind the opportunities for constructive work in Commerce were at least as great as those in Treasury, and I never regretted the president's choice. I could have handled Treasury, but it wasn't my only heart's desire.

My interest in Commerce had been sharpened during the campaign. I had suggested to candidate Nixon that one of the promises he might consider making would be to upgrade the functioning of that department and bring it out of the backwaters of the government. He had turned the suggestion over to his advisors on a Key Issues Committee of which Senator John Tower was chairman; with the help of a paper developed by Senator Charles Percy, a former successful businessman, the committee had prepared a document containing recommendations on methods by which the role of the secretary of commerce as a policymaker and innovator could be strengthened. While Nixon had not thought the idea useful for campaign purposes, I felt it was nevertheless a sound blueprint for his administration, and he later agreed.

It called for the secretary of commerce to be "an effective, responsible and responsive leader of the private business sector in this nation"; it specified that he should be a policymaking spokesman for the dynamic qualities of the private enterprise system. The secretary would be a catalyst for inducing greater contributions from the private business sector toward the solutions of general public problems, a stimulator of economic development through domestic business, and a prime promoter of American business abroad. This comprised an excellent charter and offered a real challenge that I wanted very much to take on. I believed that the secretary should not be simply a voice of business in Washington but a strong advocate and defender of the American free market.

Following the public introduction of his Cabinet, Nixon, a few days later, met individually with each of us for a few hours in New York to review what he foresaw as major problems and indicate what he expected of us. He echoed my desire to rebuild the stature of the Department of Commerce, which had sunk to its lowest level in the recent administrations, partly as a result of the shifting of some of its major units to the Department of Transportation and other government agencies, and partly because no president since Hoover had been business oriented. The discussion was general, but he encouraged me as secretary to speak out for the business viewpoint on public issues, and to do all I could to move Commerce from a defensive to a progressive posture.

Between my meeting with Nixon and January 20, I spent several days in Washington in the Department of Commerce, meeting my predecessor, C. R. Smith, and other officials of the department, and being briefed on the various operating functions and entities. Every one of the incumbents assured me of total cooperation in connection with the transition, and as the days went by they were all fully helpful in making the turnover. With my earlier experience in Washington, I knew the shock waves that went through a government organization upon a change in administrations, and I wanted to minimize them in Commerce as much as possible. To avoid a complete exodus from the top positions on January 20, I urged each appointed official to stay for an additional period until his successor was named and had time to be "broken in." Many of them did so and the transition went smoothly as a result.

Before being sworn in I had selected Rocco Siciliano, a former assistant secretary of labor and special assistant to the president in the Eisenhower era, to be my under secretary. He and I set to work at once to pick the rest of our top team, and it wasn't long before we found out how difficult that is.

Emulating Nixon's remarks at the introduction of his Cabinet, I intended to have the best possible person in each of the top positions in Commerce. There were about fifteen key appointments to be filled, and I wanted to make every one of those selections personally. These officials could then make the choices of top persons to serve below them. Altogether, there were only 114 positions that would be filled on a political basis by the president or the secretary, of which 50 were presidential appointments. The rest of the many thousands of employees in the vast department were career individuals within the civil service, protected by law against replacement by patronage.

I learned quickly what a difference there was between moving into the directorship of the Bureau of the Budget in midterm, as I had in 1958, and taking over a department upon a change in administrations. In Budget, I inherited a smoothly functioning organization. In Commerce, I had to build the top structure from scratch, but I could not give that undivided attention because from the day I took office there was a constant stream of demands on my time: congressional inquiries, budget hearings, masses of daily incoming and outgoing mail, innumerable telephone calls, people within the department wanting to discuss problems, White House meetings, press meetings, and public issues calling for attention. I didn't want to slight the selection process, so Siciliano and I worked out a division of effort between us to keep everything moving while we interviewed a number of candidates for each appointment. Gradually we filled the slots, but it was almost six months before the last of the top fifteen was found to my satisfaction and sworn into office.

I'm sure the general public believes there are a hundred good people ready and able to fill each such post. There may be, but there is no effective time-saving procedure by which such people can be known to those making the selections in this delicate but crucial undertaking.

I finally filled three assistant secretary spots with people I had known previously and for whom I had great respect, and every one of them—Larry Jobe, Robert Podesta, and C. Langhorne Washburn —did a sterling job in his term in Commerce. Larry Jobe was a bright certified public accountant, twenty-nine, and as assistant secretary of administration was the youngest person to hold that rank in the Nixon administration; among other things he modernized completely the archaic accounting system of the department. Bob Podesta was an established Chicago investment banker who had once run unsuccessfully for Congress. I selected him to head the Economic Development Administration, a post requiring frequent contacts and a good rapport with members of the Congress as well as a knowledge of business, and he fulfilled both requirements with distinction. Lang Washburn had been a Republican fund-raiser for some years, with an earlier background in public relations; his dynamic and innovative personality made him a natural for the United States Travel Service, which he headed with energy and imagination.

As for the others, the long time we spent in making our selections paid off. The first of these, James Lynn of Cleveland, an eloquent young lawyer, became general counsel and soon established a close relationship with the White House that made him a persuasive advocate for Commerce's point of view in legislative and organizational matters. The dean of the Thayer School of Engineering at Dartmouth, Myron Tribus, was our choice for assistant secretary for science and technology; he emerged as a strong advocate of technological enhancement programs as a means of holding our country's favorable position in international trade.

Harold Passer, an able economist with Eastman Kodak, became assistant secretary for economic affairs; he turned out to be unusually perceptive in projecting the trend of the economy and I quoted his views with confidence. Andrew Gibson was chosen to be head of the Maritime Administration; experienced and knowledgeable in shipping and shipbuilding, he successfully shepherded legislation that reoriented the government's policies toward those industries, to the satisfaction of the companies and their unions. George Brown, the director of marketing research for Ford Motor Company, was chosen to be director of the Bureau of the Census, and he competently steered the 1970 enumeration through some rough shoals. William Schuyler, a Washington patent attorney, headed the Patent Office and did an excellent job in speeding up its snail's-paced operations, and in understanding and handling international patent negotiations. Successors to my initial appointees were equally fortunate selections. Robert McLellan and Harold Scott, assistant secretaries for international and domestic trade, successively performed capably and acquired high respect in the business community, as did Bill Letson as general counsel, Bob Gottschalk in patents, and Jim Wakelin in science.

When I left Commerce three years later, there were only two or three of the top 114 appointees who had not performed as I expected. Every one of them was there at a substantial personal sacrifice; almost all could have earned double the pay in the private sector. Incidentally, all were younger than I.

Rocco Siciliano was an especially fortuitous choice as under secretary, because his years of background in the federal government, particularly in personnel matters, made him unusually valuable in the original selections of key people and in maintaining the continuing morale and loyalty of the entire staff. With both of us having had prior executive experience in the federal government, we had a considerable advantage over the other departments in hitting the ground running on January 21. When he left after two years I had no hesitation in promoting Jim Lynn to be his successor; Lynn not only performed well as my under secretary but later went on to earn two successive Cabinet posts as secretary of housing and urban development and as director of the office of management and budget.

While the name of the game was to put individuals who were both qualified and Republican in the major posts, I made a few exceptions. The principal one was Robert White, a highly competent career Democrat, who headed the Environmental Science Services Administration. I kept him on and, two years later, when Commerce was given responsibility for the National Oceanic and Atmospheric Administration and acquired major units from other departments to put into it, I again chose White as top man. He performed with distinction. Another was Dr. Alan Astin, head of the National Bureau of Standards, who had survived a bitter try by Secretary Sinclair Weeks to remove him about ten years earlier. Astin's subsequent record was good and he was within about eight months of retirement at sixty-five. An intermediary asked if I wouldn't allow him to stay in the job until then, and I agreed. When he left, I replaced him with Dr. Lewis Branscomb, a Democrat with strong scientific qualifications. Also, because they held jobs that required highly specialized technical knowledge, I did not attempt to replace the carryover members of the Board of Patent Appeals.

All in all, and with admitted bias, I believe we had in Commerce one of the most able and efficient executive groups of any government agency during the Nixon administration. By having a strong top team, we were able to give firm leadership to the entire bureaucracy, and bring from it the latent abilities and dedication that was merely waiting for the way to be shown. We had little of the public dissension or turmoil that unfortunately marked the departments of some of my colleagues, and our internal progress was not only smooth but gave the president little trouble or concern. And we succeeded in enlarging considerably the scope of responsibilities and functions of the department, and in breaking new ground on a number of fronts.

At the outset, I had much to learn about the wide-ranging activities of the organization. Fortunately, and to my immense gratitude, my predecessor had caused every major working unit in the department to assist in the transition by preparing a brochure containing full data as to its purpose, its authority, its programs and projects, its policies and its problems. Not only that, a group of top officials of the outgoing administration of the department had spent several months in a self-survey and evaluation of its functioning. Their report of December 1968, given to me when I first arrived on the scene, was an inch-thick analysis of strengths and shortcomings, its tone set by this opening paragraph:

> The Department of Commerce as presently constituted is neither a very useful Cabinet-level arm of the President nor a particularly vital force in economic affairs. The Department lacks a unified purpose.

I found Commerce to be a massive conglomerate of 25,400 people working in sixteen diversified agencies, their relationships to Commerce not all well known because many of them, like the Weather Bureau, the Patent Office, or the Bureau of the Census, dealt anonymously with the public. Beyond responsibility in the field of domestic business, Commerce also operated in the stimulation and regulation of international trade; but these two customary concepts of "commerce" comprised less than 4 percent of its budget. The department, in 1969, also included the Maritime Administration, responsible for developing and subsidizing our merchant fleet and shipyards; the Bureau of the Census, which not only compiled a nationwide head count every ten years but in between made many studies of agriculture, business, and demography; the Patent Office, which administered the system by which patents and copyrights are granted; the Environmental Science Services Administration (ESSA), the largest unit of which was the Weather Bureau, which monitored and forecasted climatic conditions and also conducted research into the modification of weather; an Office of Business Economics, to compile statistics and forecasts on the economy; an Office of Foreign Direct Investments, to regulate the outflow of funds from American investors into foreign countries; an Office of State Technical Services, to disseminate business know-how through state organisms; the United States Travel Service, with the one-way responsibility of inducing foreigners to travel in this country; the Economic Development Administration, with a program in hundreds of millions of dollars a year to stimulate economic progress and employment in depressed areas; five regional commissions with a similar task in geographically limited interstate regions but with a much smaller budget; the National Bureau of Standards, with many chores related to domestic and international standards measurement, scientific testing, and public safety; and a Clearing House for Federal Scientific and Technical Information, which had the mission of collecting and publishing the reports on scientific and technical research and studies across the government.

During the three years that I was secretary, there were some additions and changes in these organizations and duties. An Office of Minority Business Enterprise was created, by executive order of the president, to help build business ownership among the nation's black, Latino, Asian, and Native American minorities. The Office of Business Economics and some parts of the Census Bureau were merged into a single data-gathering and reporting unit of Commerce known as the Bureau of Economic Analysis. The Clearing House was recast into a National Technical Information Service, with an expanded range of publications and services. Because I could not see meaningful results from the Office of State Technical Services, I agreed with John Rooney, chairman of the House Appropriations Committee, to its termination at a budget saving of $5 million a year. An Office of Telecommunications was created, to assist in administration of the uses of the electronic spectrum by broadcast users of all types. By a major presidential reorganization, the Weather Bureau and other units of ESSA were combined with seven other entities from four other government departments into the National Oceanic and Atmospheric Administration, based in Commerce, with responsibilities in the fields of weather, ocean fisheries, marine minerals technology, mapping and charting, oceanography, and marine research.

These revisions and acquisitions increased the size and scope of the department for the first time in many years. In several prior administrations it had gradually been reduced by the transfers of functions and people to other agencies, especially Transportation. To the contrary, by the time of my departure in February 1972, Commerce had grown from 25,400 to about 35,000 employees. In between there had been 200,000 other persons working for a while on the 1970 census.

An idea of the size of the department was conveyed to me on one of the first days I was at work. Thinking it would be good to view Commerce from the side of its printed output, I asked an aide, "Would you pull together one of each of the publications that we produce in the department? I'd like to take them home some evening and look them over." He came back in an hour and gave me an unexpected answer: "We can have the first truckload over in the morning." I learned then that Commerce regularly published more than four thousand periodicals and reports, some weekly, some less often, some annually.

In order to form the department into a cohesive unit, I scheduled a plan of meetings so policy communications could be at their workable best. Each morning at eight-thirty, I met with my personal staff to review the day's schedule of events and any current crises. The head of any operating unit could also attend and present his immediate troubles and ask for guidance. This gave us quick management of new developments, and time to exert as much influence on them as we could hope to bring to bear, and it avoided a lot of unhappy surprises.

Commerce people had no difficulty in sensing when our basic thrust moved from the get-acquainted phase of the job to action. When I arrived I brought with me the WHY? sign that had been my slogan at the Bureau of the Budget and put it on the wall of my office. Less than sixty days later, I took it down and replaced it with a new one that said NOW! It meant simply that we had arrived at the time to get going with our new initiatives.

Every Monday noon I met at lunch with a regular group of about forty key people of the department. Frequently we had a speaker from the White House or another agency to brief us on a topic of mutual currency. In all meetings, we took time to go around the table and get each one's report as to pending difficulties, congressional hearings, White House actions, public relations, or other matters of general interest to the group. These were always fully attended.

Once a month I had a session of what I called my board of directors, the top dozen in Commerce. It was a day-long affair, usually on a Saturday and often away from the office, devoted almost wholly to long-range planning. Beyond all this, any one with a policy question or important matter to be resolved could always arrange a prompt meeting with me or the under secretary. At these occasions, decisions were made where called for and the responsibility fixed for carrying them out. With the caliber of men and women I had in Commerce, it was a wonderful experience to see how well this all worked and how much we accomplished in harmony.

I had some extramural responsibilities too. In our talk in December Nixon said that he would like me to keep a weather eye on the Office of Special Trade Representative, which was structured within the Executive Office of the president but physically separated, and also the Export-Import Bank and the Small Business Administration. He commented that these were all units that probably ought to be put officially under Commerce, but he didn't think this was politically possible at the time. After Henry Kearns was appointed to head the Export-Import Bank, he performed superbly and didn't need any watching by me, although I helped out occasionally in his battles with the Budget Bureau over how fast the bank should be allowed to grow.

I did make a gentle pass at moving the Special Trade Representative (STR) into Commerce in the middle of March of 1969, but word of the idea leaked out and there were instant battle signs from the State Department and some of the "free-trade" organizations. State objected on the strained grounds that "delegation of the function of the STR to a business-oriented department might well be interpreted abroad as a move toward protectionism."

I could see a time-consuming controversy developing along free-trade versus protectionist lines that would eventually distract the president, when both he and I had too many important undertakings to want to have our time diverted, so I withdrew the idea. With my concurrence, Carl Gilbert was appointed STR soon after, and we stayed in close communication, relatively without friction. I offered to give him and his staff office space within the Commerce building so we could work more closely together, but by that time the forces of suspicion had become so strong that he concluded it would be better if the physical move weren't made either. It was too bad, because the STR would have been a logical component of Commerce.

The Small Business Administration was a different matter and the appointment of Hilary Sandoval, over my protests, caused some grief for me and ultimately for the White House. I considered his business experience too limited to qualify him for the post and urged him to accept a different position, but he was adamant in his refusal. After he was sworn in, we met and talked many times, and I invited him to my weekly staff meetings. As a result, we developed a suitable degree of surface harmony while at the same time meshing our respective programs where they overlapped, especially in areas of minority entrepreneurship.

After he had been in office a couple of years, the White House turned against him because of some alleged erratic behavior, and I was enlisted to ask for his resignation. It was a distasteful chore since he was not well, and I felt sorry for him for that and other reasons. But he did resign, and not long after that he died of a brain tumor, which could very well have accounted for some of his inconsistent actions.

Nixon, on January 24, 1969, named a quadriad, to consist of the secretary of the Treasury, the chairman of the Council of Economic Advisors, the chairman of the Federal Reserve Board, and the director of the budget. The next day he named a Cabinet Committee on Economic Policy, including the vice president, the secretaries of commerce, labor, agriculture, and the Treasury, the director of the budget, the chairman of the Council of Economic Advisors, and Counsellor Arthur Burns, and gave it the task of blending considerations of domestic and foreign economic affairs. I attended all of the regular meetings of the Cabinet Committee on Economic Policy, but by accident I did miss the dramatic week preceding August 15, 1971, when the president announced his moves to halt inflation, including setting up wage and price controls, imposing an import surcharge, and devaluing the dollar. I had taken advantage of a quiet break in Commerce to get away for our only private vacation in three years. Phone calls from the White House to invite me to meetings on these topics did not reach me because my son Steve and I were out of communication at a fishing lodge on Great Bear Lake, near the Arctic Circle in Canada. When we returned to Edmonton on schedule on the afternoon of August 16, I found urgent messages saying I was due to be in Washington for a Cabinet meeting the following morning. An air force jet was sent to Edmonton to pick me up, and we traveled in luxury back to Washington on an overnight nonstop flight that arrived just in time.

An important legislative coup was in getting a new maritime law approved by the White House in 1969 and passed by the Congress in 1970. There had been no major maritime legislation since the Merchant Marine Act of 1936, and the intervening years had seen significant declines in the number of ships in our privately owned merchant fleet and in maritime employment. In view of this trend, there had been eleven serious attempts in the previous eight years to write a new law, but every one had floundered in disagreement. Subsidies for building and operating such ships were a heavy charge on the budget, and we wanted a new mandate from the Congress as to the extent to which they should continue. There was need for an overhaul of the technology of shipbuilding, to make our shipyards more closely competitive with those in Norway, Japan, and other shipbuilding nations. The formulas for paying operating and construction subsidies were so complex that claims were normally pending for ten or twelve years before final settlement, and a large backlog existed.

Our principal proposals were ably engineered by Maritime Administrator Andrew Gibson, and we succeeded in taking the government out of the shipbuilding industry, freeing shipping and shipbuilding as much as possible from bureaucratic shackles; and upgrading the size and condition of the U.S. merchant marine. We were fortunate. The White House and Budget Bureau under Nixon had not yet developed their later techniques for slowing down and nitpicking proposed new legislation, and taking advantage of the know-how that Siciliano and I had as to the legislative ropes, we got their prompt approval and the president sent our bill to the Congress in October 1969. It had the strong support of the maritime unions and the appreciative endorsement of the House Merchant Marine and Fisheries Committee, which had long been looking for a workable program. Very few amendments were made to what we presented and, amazingly, there was only one dissenting vote in each house of Congress.

An immediate and pressing irrationality that was thrust at me after I was sworn in was a furor over the national population census to be taken in 1970. The trouble had started in 1967 when Congressman Jackson E. Betts of Ohio, whom *The New York Times* called "one of the more obscure figures in the House," began a campaign "casually, almost absent-mindedly," by intimating in a speech that the census questions were an invasion of privacy. He knew better, but when that got applause he decided he had an issue on which to build, so he enlarged his criticisms from one speech to the next until he won the support of some organizations, some perennial cynics, and a confused portion of the public. He was a member of the House subcommittee on the census, but neither he nor any other critic bothered to mention that his subcommittee had already approved the census procedures and questions two years in advance of the enumeration date. No one mentioned that every question had been carefully weighed to produce valuable economic and social data, necessary for congressional legislation and valuable to state governments, educators, and businessmen. No one mentioned that the number of questions for 1970 was no more than in 1960 and much less than in earlier censuses. No one mentioned that in the history of eighteen previous decennial censuses from 1790 through 1960, not one person had ever found his confidential answers revealed to anyone else.

Nevertheless, Betts introduced a bill on the opening day of Congress in 1969 to limit the census to six questions to which answers would be required (name, address, age, sex, marital status, and relationship to head of household), and to allow the answering of other questions to be voluntary. This kind of arrangement would provide only a head count, and would invalidate the bulk of the economic and demographic data sought to be collected. About 110 other congressmen, caught in the wave of an enticing issue, sponsored bills similar to the Betts bill. Because they were labeled as "anti–big government" and "against government invasion of privacy," such bills had appeal to certain types of constituents. As I reported to the president early in March, passage of the Betts bill or a similar bill would have ruined the census, damaged our ability to make public policy, made social research almost impossible, and resulted in our knowing less about ourselves than any other major nation in the world.

In addition to the head count items, the census forms contained twenty-five questions to be answered by 75 percent of families and one hundred questions to be answered by only 5 percent of families, all to be selected on a scientific sampling basis. The United States had employed mandatory answering of census questions since the first one in 1790, and every country in the world that took a census required its citizens to respond. A voluntary census, according to experts we consulted, would produce answers that would be worthless or even deceptive.

Nevertheless, the hue and cry was picked up by columnists, editors, and politicians, and "the census is an invasion of privacy" became a slogan. A handful of publicity seekers and errant crusaders announced that they would refuse to fill in the forms. One question, designed to measure elements of living standards, asked about bathroom facilities and whether they were shared with another household. This was immediately distorted by columnists and cartoonists to read, "Whom do you share your shower with?" It was a sex-implied catch line that ballooned the public interest in the controversy and gave the objectors their best weapon, albeit a false one.

For a time I felt that it had the earmarks of a losing battle. I went over the forms and procedures in detail with our census people and found practically nothing to challenge or modify. We reduced slightly the number of families who would be asked to fill out the long form, and we changed the bathroom wording "shared with another household" to "used by another household." With this approach exhausted, I appointed a Decennial Census Review Committee of seventeen statisticians and other experts; Betts denounced it as a stacked group. I held a press conference defending the census, met with a number of House and Senate members, made speeches, and testified before the census subcommittee in both bodies of Congress. Nevertheless, the chairman of the Senate Judiciary subcommittee on constitutional rights, Sam Ervin of North Carolina, got into the act by asserting that he considered the census questionnaire to be an unconstitutional privacy invasion. The Senate-House subcommittee on statistics held a hearing on proposals to eliminate all penalties for noncompliance with the census, and I testified in opposition to it.

Others in the department worked diligently with me to slow down the growing criticism and keep it from becoming a public rebellion. The House actually passed a bill, somewhat modified from the Betts proposals but seriously detrimental to the scope of the census. Fortunately, the sophisticated heads in the Senate wisely sat on the measure until it was too late to stop the work from going ahead as it had been planned. April 1, 1970, came and the census was taken and tabulated, with little commotion or fuss, despite all the negative publicity. No one's privacy was violated. New techniques of enumeration were successful; the costs were kept down by using a mail count in urban areas as the first step, followed by personal checks at each place of habitation.

As usual after a decennial census, there were some publicized contentions by unhappy mayors and embarrassed local chambers of commerce that the count was incomplete and their city's population was much greater. Every complaint was carefully checked into, and evidence of undercounting was solicited and traced; very few errors were found, aggregating in each case less than 1 percent, although as in earlier censuses there was no doubt that the minority populations in large inner cities had not been fully enrolled, largely through lack of cooperation. Regretfully, we had to conclude that as many as several million individuals (later established by the Census Bureau statisticians at about 4.5 million) avoided identification and counting, probably because of marital and family support problems, fear of being approached by the law, or, in the case of many Spanish speakers, their illegal presence in the country. The Decennial Census Review Committee in August 1971, after having observed the census procedures at work, endorsed fully the planning and execution of the enumeration and the privacy that it had achieved. To secure total accuracy, or anything near it, would have been frightfully expensive.

To my mind, the opposition to the census was a mindless crusade and could have been harmful to the country had it succeeded in depriving the public of valuable data and the national, state, and local lawmakers of essential information to deal with the many facets of education, welfare, health, and business. It was a dreadful example of the willingness of some politicians and journalists to take a false issue, popularize a slogan to fit, and seduce the public into believing it might be valid. The census was completed without any breach of privacy and without incident except for a handful of dissidents who took their refusal to court and lost. The congressman who started it retired in the next election, and the question has not been seriously raised since, although it still arises in some form every ten years.

# CHAPTER TEN

# Fighting the Wars of Trade

An engrossing subject that soon came along to demand a considerable proportion of my hours for several years was the one of textile imports. It serves as a good illustration of how international relationships and domestic interests can clash, and how difficult it can be for an administration to negotiate and enforce a solution that ought to be apparent to both sides at first glance.

In the 1968 campaign, candidate Nixon had promised that if elected, he would take steps to extend existing international agreements on cotton textiles and apparel to similar items made of wool and man-made fibers, with the objective of imposing reasonable limits on the explosive growth of imports taking place in the latter categories, and to strictly enforce the present and future agreements dealing with them.

Nixon was not the only one to propose such an undertaking. His opponent, Hubert Humphrey, echoed him with a commitment that went even further, explicitly promising to go for legislated quotas if international negotiations failed.

The background of these promises rested largely on an unanticipated shift from cotton to synthetic fibers in the making of men's and women's clothing in the preceding five or six years, which in turn had precipitated an unexpected flood of imports of these man-made fiber textiles and finished garments into the United States. Imports of goods made of cotton were regulated and limited under multilateral and bilateral agreements dating back to 1962 between the United States and major producing countries.* These agreements had been worked out at a time when synthetic fiber fabrics had negligible acceptance, so there were no similar provisions controlling their shipments in international trade. In consequence, imports of these fabrics had grown from a mere 170 million square yards in measure in 1962 to almost two billion yards in 1968 and were accelerating rapidly.

The unfortunate result had been an acute decline in the fortunes of the American textile and garment industries and their employees; the probabilities of continuing enlargement of the import wave threatened them with dire consequences. These industries employed 2,400,000 persons, or about one out of eight of all those engaged in manufacturing in the country. Computations showed that they could lose close to 100,000 jobs a year if the trend continued. In certain lines of fabrics and garments, imports already filled more than 50 percent of the domestic market. Adding to the frustration of the American industry was the circumstance that the provisions of existing agreements limiting incoming goods of cotton were not being seriously enforced because of the State Department's reluctance to antagonize other nations.

Most of the imports came from four low-wage and low-cost countries—Japan, Korea, Hong Kong, and Taiwan—but with growing sources sure to develop in Singapore, Indonesia, Israel, Brazil, and other nations if the field were kept wholly open. Textile mills were being built in Ethiopia, where the going wage was four cents an hour, to produce goods for the world market. Current textile wages were 10 cents in Korea, 15 cents in Hong Kong and Taiwan, and 45 cents in Japan. American mills then paying $2.50 to $3.00 an hour could not survive such competition, since the United States was the only nation without meaningful limitations on textile imports. American labor generally was aligned in favor of protectionism insofar as textiles were concerned.

There were two potential routes to a solution. The first was Nixon's promise to cause existing international arrangements under GATT to be voluntarily amended by the various countries to put synthetics under the same type of limitations as cotton goods. This

---

*In 1960, candidate John F. Kennedy had campaigned on a platform calling for textile import restrictions, which he accomplished in 1962, but only as to cottons. Such limitations were negotiated persuant to a General Agreement on Tariffs and Trade (GATT) among the major nations of the world.

seemed attainable because Japan, the major producer, already had executed agreements controlling such exports to eleven other countries. The other course, implied as an alternative in the Humphrey statement, was to ask Congress to impose unilateral quotas on incoming goods. Nixon felt that the legislative route carried the danger that quota protection would be extended in the law by Congress to other import-sensitive industries, which would have been contrary to his basic belief in free trade between nations except in very unusual circumstances.

It became my lot to carry out Nixon's campaign pledges by seeking negotiated agreements.

In February 1969 Nixon went to Europe for his first trip as president and visited several of the major countries to cement relationships. When efforts were made by his hosts to get him involved in matters of international trade, he told them he did not want to get into that area but would send his secretary of commerce over shortly for that purpose. When I greeted him in the receiving line at Andrews Air Force Base upon his return, he said merely, "Maury, they're waiting for you."

Thus I entered into the discussions with other countries with sincere conviction. The selling countries had to be reasonable and accept limited growth of their products in our markets, or the costs here in business failures and lost jobs would bring certain retaliation against them by our Congress. If the percentage growth in imports was held a bit above the percentage growth in the domestic market, our industry would be caused to progress normally through domestic competition without excess from overseas. While there would still be business casualties, their number would be minimized and so would the shock to the economy. Having examined the figures in depth, I was convinced of the merits of such a pragmatic approach and developed the case along those lines for presentation in Europe to the major consuming countries and in the Far East to the producing countries.

I prepared well for the trip in a crash indoctrination extending over several weeks. I had to be conversant not only with the textile matter but with the full gamut of international trade issues, which included non-tariff barriers, border taxes, international investment limitations, and the initials that popped up everywhere, such as EEC, GATT, ASP, CAP, and VAT.

In Europe, Belgium and the Netherlands were encouraging but officially neutral, giving me the impression that their support was available but would mean nothing unless Germany, France, Italy, and Britain went along with us. In Germany, I got encouragement from some elements of industry but a flat turndown from the government. In Italy, France, and Britain, the reception ranged from cool to openly negative. *Time* magazine called my trip "Mission: Impossible," and this turned out to be the case. Nevertheless, it was a mission that had to be made, to set the stage for later developments. The experience was generally pleasant, despite a cold that I suffered all the way from Brussels through the next six stops to London. I had the privilege of conferring with the chief of state in every one of the countries I visited, except de Gaulle of France; at the time he was preoccupied with a referendum to come three days later that led to his resignation and retirement when he lost. In a detour in Belgium, the land of three of my grandparents, I was greeted as a hero on my visits to their hometowns, with bands, parades, speeches, and dinners in my honor. I responded to their exciting reception by proclaiming proudly in my opening response that "Ik ben een Maaslander." My pride of ancestry matched their pride in the fact that I held the highest post in the American government ever held by anyone of Belgian descent. To my great delight, I was presented by my hosts with a genealogical study of the Stans family going back to 1650.

The trip that followed a month later to the Far East was hardly more successful. Here I was to meet separately with the governments of the four major textile-exporting countries to try to get them to agree, bilaterally or multilaterally, to hold down their rate of growth of shipments to the United States. The purpose of my mission had been well advertised. In Europe, there had been three or four Japanese reporters with tape recorders at every one of my speeches and press conferences, so there was no secret as to the American objective.

On May 9, while I was in transit by air to the Far East, Congressman Wilbur Mills introduced a bill in Congress to limit textile imports. On the same day, following a flurry of lobbying by Japanese textile and labor organizations, their national legislature, the Diet, passed a unanimous resolution taking note of my visit and directing all its officials not to discuss textiles with me. It became evident there, as in Korea, Taiwan, and Hong Kong later, that there was no chance of reaching any agreements at the time but that the visits were a necessary preliminary to later talks that might succeed.

From the outset of my visit to Japan, tactics to thwart my mission were incredible. My first meeting was with Foreign Minister Kiichi

Aichi, a diminutive friendly man who spoke good English. I was accompanied by Stanley Nehmer, my knowledgeable deputy assistant secretary of commerce, and several staff people, and Aichi had an equal number across the table. After the usual exchange of greetings, he immediately referred to the Diet resolution and said that he would be pleased to discuss with me any subject but textiles. I replied calmly saying that I had come halfway around the world specifically to talk about textiles, and that while I was aware of the Diet resolution, I did not believe his government would refuse to listen to me while I presented a mutual problem, even though it would not want to reply at this time. Aichi acquiesced, with some obvious distress, and I went ahead with the full story for about an hour, and left with him a series of charts and statistics.

In several meetings with Minister Masayoshi Ohira of the Ministry of International Trade and Industry, I also received courteous treatment, even though his reactions were strongly negative. He made it clear that Japan could not, as an internal political matter, work out any limiting agreements on textiles unless the other three nation producers in the Far East were equally limited. He was confident that the United States would never be able to negotiate such agreements with them.

However, at a second meeting I requested to probe for some concessions, he did give me a proposal that Japan send a delegation of junior officials to the United States to confirm that our problem of meeting their price competition in the market was not due, as they contended, to obsolete manufacturing plants. This step was not a large one, but at least it was a clear-cut move that gave us an opportunity within a few months to eliminate one looming issue.

While tough as a negotiator, Ohira was personally very friendly and paid us the high compliment of inviting Kathleen and me and several members of our party to his home for a dinner. It was a traditional Japanese banquet, with course after course of excellent meats and fish, served at a low table while we sat on cushions on the floor. Since it was an unusually warm evening, Ohira had gone to the trouble of providing special air-conditioning for us in the form of an electric fan blowing over a huge cake of ice.

In Korea, the talks on textiles were more friendly but no more productive than in Japan. The government could not understand how the United States could do so much for it in military and economic aid and then propose to go in the other direction by forcing the "dismantling" of its fastest-growing industry. Korea said it wouldn't enter into any restrictive agreements unless the other three major exporters were more severely limited, since it felt that, as a protégé of the United States, it was entitled to preferred treatment. A concurrent set of separate agreements between us and the four countries was now evolving as the likely solution, and that would be a very drawn-out one, unless the United States was ready to take the alternative step of imposing limits on textile imports by legislation, or the president could take a more severe course and invoke his powers under a pertinent section of the Agricultural Adjustment Act to force a result, but that had little favor at this stage. The State Department, understandably, was violently opposed to any unilateral actions.

While in Korea, Kathleen and I had an uplifting emotional experience when we met for the first time our foster daughter, Youn Jum Ae. Fourteen years earlier, when she was five, we had undertaken to contribute to her support through the Foster Parents Plan. The amount of money we sent monthly was not large, but through the years Kathleen and our children had kept up a close and warm correspondence as Jum Ae grew up. When the Foster Parents Plan terminated her at the age of eighteen, we continued to send her letters and some money to provide courses in dressmaking and English. In all this time we had never seen her, and since we were on a tight schedule, we asked the American embassy to arrange in advance for her to travel from her home in Kunsan to meet us in Seoul. She was a sweet girl and, although timid in the overwhelming circumstances of our meeting at the Embassy, displayed a genuine, appealing personality. The local press took note of the relationship and ran front-page stories and pictures, and when I met President Park in his office the next day he complimented and thanked me, commenting with a smile that since the relationship had been going on for fourteen years it could not have been arranged just to adorn my official visit! Jum Ae spent almost two days with us, mostly with Kathleen, and left a deeply affectionate feeling in our hearts. We have remained in touch ever since. In August 1992, she and her husband and two sons came to the United States as our guests for an emotional two-week visit.

Taiwan was anticlimactic after Korea, and the textile discussions were parallel. No agreement was possible, and the government echoed the Korean question of how we could extend so much aid with one hand and try to take it back with another. In Hong Kong I met a repeat of the Japanese cold shoulder, in the form of a pompous British colonial officer whose reception was close to insulting. Only when I reminded him that I was an official representative of the government of the United States did he assume a civil attitude, and even then I made no progress toward securing a fair understanding of the problem. He kept insisting that final disposition would have to come from London insofar as Hong Kong was concerned, which we knew to be a red herring, since the British government's approval to any agreement reached in Hong Kong would have been pro forma.

After I returned to Washington from the two trips, I surveyed the textile situation with the president. It was obviously a more difficult matter than either of us had thought, and would take much longer to resolve, but I felt that the necessary beginnings of these complex international negotiations had been made. He agreed, and asked me to work out future strategy with Henry Kissinger, his foreign policy advisor. From then on, I was in constant conflict with the State Department, which held a twofold resentment: first at having the textile subject injected into foreign relations, and second at having anyone outside of its own walls handling the negotiations.

In the months that followed, State tried often to force a partial solution in the form of a "selective" agreement that would restrict some categories of textile imports that were especially heavy, but allow others to come in without limits. On three occasions State took this difference of opinion to the president and each time he ruled that the outcome had to be comprehensive. He did not want a halfway measure that would force him to deal more than once with uncontrolled imports while he was in office, and he did want to keep his word to the distressed industry that he would work out a proper and adequate solution.

On October 20, 1969, I wrote a memo to the president suggesting that the only way I could see to accelerate action was to use the textile issue in other negotiations with Japan. There were a number of monetary and territorial concessions relating to World War II that Japan was seeking from us at the time, and I didn't think the "give" should be all on one side.

With Prime Minister Eisaku Sato due to arrive in Washington in November to meet with the president, Henry Kissinger moved personally and openly into the textile front. The main purpose of the Sato visit was to document a United States agreement for the turnover of Okinawa to Japan. While the textile matter could never be allowed to seem to be an offsetting consideration, this was an opportune atmosphere for the subject to be settled.

Kissinger communicated with Sato in advance of the meeting, through an intermediary designated by the Japanese government (whose name I never learned), conveying various alternatives that I had outlined, a formula that I felt acceptable to our side and which Kissinger was assured would be acceptable to the prime minister. In substance, it called for a specific controlled annual growth of shipments of textiles to the United States above the level in effect for the year ending June 30, 1969. On the basis of this understanding, I prepared a detailed scenario as to how, independent of the Okinawa discussion, Nixon and Sato would meet on textiles and initial a memorandum outlining the formula. It would then be put into effect at the end of the year after implementing arrangements had been worked out by further negotiations of details at a working level.

But again a snafu developed. When Sato met the president from November 19 to November 21, he insisted that his understanding did not extend to as broad a formula as we had outlined. Nixon felt that Sato had found in the meantime that opposition in Japan to any limitations was so great that he could not deliver what he intended. Nixon told him that an agreement had to be found that was comprehensive in its result, even if not in form. There was some confusion as to where the subject was left, but Japanese officials confirmed some months later that Sato had promised no less than "to do his utmost" to provide an acceptable arrangement promptly.* The joint communiqué issued at the end of the Nixon-Sato conversations did not mention the subject of textiles. In any event, the carefully coordinated Kissinger plan did not become operative on its expected due date. The year 1969 closed with progress having to be measured at a glacial rate.

Late in March 1970, under pressure from all sides, Kissinger pushed the Japanese ambassador, Takeso Shimoda, for some action to carry out Sato's commitment. On March 28 Shimoda then presented the first proposal from the Japanese. It called merely for a one-year overall moratorium on their exports above an unstated level, but with no limits on specific products; during that year nego-

---

*In a note to me from Japan several years later a friend quoted a local version to the effect that the problem rested on Sato's use of the phrase *zensho shimasu* in his meeting with Nixon. The interpreter translated this as "The Prime minister will accomodate your wishes," whereas what Sato actually had in mind was "I'll do my best."

tiations were to continue "under normal procedures of GATT," with little assurance that they would reach a satisfactory result.

Nixon was outraged by the minimal proposal and sent word to tell the textile people to seek their relief in Congress. It wasn't clear whether he intended such action merely as a threat to force the Japanese to come to terms or whether he was hoping thereby to wash his hands of the whole affair. In any event, I continued to carry out talks with the industry and Congress, still seeking a way to a negotiated result; I was encouraged in this by the State Department, which did not want the matter to be resolved by an imposed law.

At about this time, Ohira was replaced as minister of MITI by Kiichi Miyazawa, apparently chosen by Sato as a realist who foresaw risk to Japanese-American relations in the failure of Japan to address the problem more constructively at home. I learned that a friend of mine, former assistant director of the budget Ralph Reid, was also a longtime friend of Miyazawa, and through Reid I made arrangements for him to come to Washington to meet privately with me in a sincere effort to bring the controversy to an end.

To make the occasion as informal as possible, we met in my Washington apartment with only the two of us present. Since Miyazawa spoke fluent English we covered the ground very quickly and thoroughly. He proposed fixed restrictions on the most troublesome categories, with the others put into a "basket" on which export limits would be imposed whenever the growth rate exceeded certain trigger points. It was the basis for a breakthrough and we probed it fully for five or six hours, considering terms and definitions.

At the end of the day, I felt confident that we had found a satisfactory conclusion. The main unresolved question was the period of the agreement, on which I wanted five years and he said he could not go beyond a year or eighteen months, with no renewals. I was sure that this could be compromised at three years, and that night I reported optimistically to the White House and the State Department on the day's events. We were to meet again the next day to finalize an understanding.

That evening it all began to come apart. Reid received a call from Miyazawa with a "clarification" that was actually a withdrawal on a major point. Miyazawa said he had misspoken. The next day he postponed our meeting, and when we finally got together some hours later there were further withdrawals by him that could only mean a breaking-off of the talks.

I asked the question directly: "Does this mean that we have no agreements left on any points that we discussed?"

"That is right," he said.

"And do you see any hope of a solution at this time?"

"None," he replied, unusual directness for a Japanese.

Reid's probes confirmed that fact. What had happened was that about twenty representatives of the Japanese textile industry had come as a "surveillance team" to Washington to follow the discussions, and they apparently exploded when Miyazawa reported to them at the embassy on the tentative agreements we had reached in the first day's meeting. Foreign Minister Aichi also had arranged to be in Washington at the time, to present a united front for any conclusions that were reached. I never learned whether he or Tokyo had the major hand in ending the talks, but I suspected that the heat became so intense for all concerned that Miyazawa was told to return without any agreement. It was clearly evident that in the Japanese culture of the time, organized business groups had the power to override the judgments of their public officials. The Japanese cabinet held an emergency meeting on June 25 presumably to review the new situation.

On June 19, in anticipation of Miyazawa's trip to the United States, Sato had written Nixon acknowledging the necessity of a settlement, provided it were understood that textiles were an exceptional case that would not set a precedent for any other exports, and provided there would be no expectation that any agreement reached would be extended at its termination. Without doubt he was trying to bring the Japanese industry around to accepting reasonable limits on their shipments, but he did not succeed.

Meanwhile a trade bill, providing among other things for quotas on textile imports, had begun to move in the House Ways and Means Committee. The State Department was strongly opposed to this legislated solution. On May 12, 1970, I testified on various provisions of the bill but, on instructions of the White House, asked the committee to hold off any action on textiles pending further attempts at negotiations for a voluntary result.

When I returned to the committee on June 25, right after the failure to come to terms with Miyazawa, I had authority to say that the president did not believe in mandatory quotas in principle but as an exception did favor having authority at this time to impose them on textiles only. Legislation moved ahead, although the Japanese, for a time, believed that it was merely being used as a threat and that its chances of passage by the Congress need not be taken seriously.

The Ways and Means Committee reported out a trade bill on August 21 that I told the president was clearly acceptable, even though it contained some features on matters other than textiles that he did not want. It resolved the textile problem by imposing quotas in a manner that fully met his expressed objectives. It also provided quotas on imports of shoes, which by then had become an even more serious case of import injury to our manufacturers. This brought forth a tremendous amount of flak, on the one hand from those who did not believe in any limitations on imports, and on the other from industries that felt they had an equally good case for being sheltered. The Congress, especially the members of the Ways and Means Committee, was deluged with protests.

The State Department continued to argue that all such provisions were intolerable in our foreign affairs, and the bill stalled. Nevertheless, a new minister of international trade and industry, Kakuei Tanaka, during a return meeting in Washington of the Cabinet-level Japan-U.S. Committee on Trade and Economic Affairs in September, acknowledged frankly that if a Japanese plan of self-imposed limitations was not worked out somehow at home, he expected the only outcome to be that the United States would impose unilateral restraints. Negotiations were at an impasse in the last few months of 1970, when a new round began between the Japanese ambassador in Washington, Nabuhiko Ushiba, and Peter Flanigan of the White House, with my continuing involvement behind the scenes.

Flanigan is a brilliant person and operated on this problem with high skill and diligence, working with Commerce experts to insure a technically sound result.

After several near misses, these negotiations came unglued in the spring of 1971, despite valiant efforts by Flanigan. On March 9, the Japanese rejected our proposals in an uncompromising aide-mémoire that sent everything back to the point of beginning.

The problem continued to enlarge. Imports of man-made fibers from the Far East grew to 2.8 billion yards in 1970. Employment in the textile and apparel industries in the United States fell 65,000 in 1970 alone. The situation was becoming more and more acute.

Yet opposition plagued us at every step. Free-trade organizations and their officials made frequent speeches attacking our endeavor as one that would mean higher prices for consumers. The Japanese lobby in the United States accused us of advancing the cause of a narrow segment of our economy while destroying the peaceful relationships with an essential ally in the Far East. Members of the Congress and individual businessmen engaged in private negotiations with the Japanese, conceding portions of our position without our knowledge or consent.

Confronted with a Hobson's choice among distasteful solutions, the president brought Peter Peterson, then chairman of the Council on International Economic Policy, into the battle. After exploring the history of the negotiations, and trying his hand himself without success, Peterson induced the president to include in his economic pronouncements on August 15, 1971, a private statement to the producing countries that the United States would impose unilateral restraints on textile imports unless "voluntary" agreements were worked out with them by October 15.

David Kennedy, the retired secretary of the Treasury, who had meanwhile become the United States negotiator and had struck out in his first attempts, was finally able, with the solid weight of the president's edict behind him, to reach detailed agreements in the next few months. Japan gave in first, followed by Korea, Taiwan, and then Hong Kong. These agreements met the president's original commitment to the American textile industry.

American industry and American jobs were greatly benefitted by the result. The serious decline in the fortunes of our textile industry was halted. Foreign goods continued to be imported in slowly increasing amounts, thereby giving the consumer the continuing benefit of lower prices without disruption of our markets and our economy. We had never asked for a cutback in imports. All we sought was a managed orderly marketing arrangement that did not destroy a basic American industry.

That being the case, why was the matter so difficult to resolve?

Many opinions have been advanced, but the one that seems the most logical is that we were up against a coincidence of historical timing that stonewalled any chances of concession on their part. By 1969 Japan had, after years of feelings of guilt and resignation following the war, developed a new sense of confidence and self-respect as a result of its remarkable economic recovery. This new nationalism found expression in a growing popular demand for greater independence from American influence. The reversion of Okinawa was one accommodation to that feeling. That being the new spirit, the American demand for textile controls provided a convenient cause for the Japanese to assert themselves in unison in opposition to the United States. The Japanese press was the champion of the mood of self-assertion, and the textile industry took advantage of that attitude to bolster and maintain its resistance. Only the threat of unprecedented unilateral measures by the United States brought it to an end. Once Japan yielded, the other producing countries fell in line.

The best wrap-up commentary about the long course of the textile controversy, and the international frictions it generated, came from the *Japan Times* in 1971: "The textile talks . . . were the most complex and most difficult of diplomatic negotiations the two nations have undertaken in recent history. The basic reason . . . is that negotiators on both sides were dealing with an issue that is primarily economic in nature as a political problem."

I wish I could report in this book that the agreements reached by the Nixon administration, made with such taxing difficulty and effort, provided a long-range solution to the problem. Not so. The lapse of time and continuing competition, in the face of changing economic forces, have repeatedly threatened the American textile industry with destruction by imports. Even in 1994, along with many other aspects of trade disputes with Japan, our enormous trade deficit in textiles was still causing serious harm to American producers and workers.

This long account of the textile battle of the era describes only one facet of international trade, which was a demanding topic during my three years at Commerce. Trade was important because of the gradual loss of our favorable balance of exports over imports, with 1968's surplus of $726 million being the lowest in more than thirty years. There was every reason to believe that unless ways could be found of reversing the antagonistic trend, it would continue to get progressively worse.

A vital essential to reversal of the trend was identification of its causes and agreement as to their relative significance.

Sorting out measures of cause and effect among these elements was not easy when we took office in 1969, but there was much valuable information available. In a back room of the department, I found a statistician-economist named Michael Boretsky, whose extensive analyses of our technological position in trade had theretofore been given scant attention. His work interested me greatly and I became convinced of its validity. Boretsky found that all imports and exports fell into four categories, and he computed an annual trade balance for each one. Comparison of these amounts showed that our trade balance on high-technology exports like airplanes, computers, chemicals, and the like, which in 1951 to 1955 had been in the annual range of $5.7 billion, had grown by 1970 to $9.6 billion. However, our trade balance in low-technology exports, which in the same base period had started at an annual surplus of $1.8 billion, had given way to a huge deficit of $6.1 billion. Meanwhile, our trade balance in raw materials, such as coal, minerals, and timber, had run persistently at a deficit of more than $2 billion, and this showed signs of increasing. The fourth category, agricultural products, had shown a small but fluctuating surplus of around a billion dollars a year, generally equivalent to the amount of our giveaways and soft currency sales of these items. In other words, our loss of net exports in low-technology goods and in raw materials was not being recovered fully in increased exports of high technology, and our position was worsening year by year.

Technology, then, was one possible key to our situation. To maintain and build a lead would take more research expenditures, especially since figures showed that Japan, Germany, and some other countries were spending a much larger proportion of their gross national product on research than we were. While I proposed various ideas for technology enhancement, and tried fliers on tax credits and similar incentives, only one of these really got off the ground for some years, the Domestic International Sales Corporation (DISC) export incentive.

Meaningful improvement in our export position did not come along until the president devalued the dollar, imposed an import surcharge, and set up wage and price controls in 1971. The really great push to our exports, however, came fortuitously for us with the subsequent agricultural shortages in the Soviet Union and elsewhere, which brought farm product sales to record highs.

Discriminations against imports (technically called nontariff barriers or NTB's) were almost universal around the world. The United States had some of them, but not nearly as many, and those it had were not as extensive or effective as those of the Common Market countries or Japan. We were more often the victim than the culprit.

It became increasingly evident as time went on that there were many differences of opinion in the administration over policy on trade and foreign investment, and it was very difficult to try to resolve them by dealing with one agency at a time. Recalling the very effective arrangement under President Eisenhower, whereby

Clarence Randall headed a Cabinet committee on international economic matters, I wrote to President Nixon on June 26, 1970, urging him to create a similar body. I believed that such a forum would provide the only sound way to coordinate efforts of the various departments and save the waste of time otherwise involved in settling policy debates. I proposed that it include the secretaries of the Treasury, commerce, labor, and agriculture, the deputy under secretary of state for economic affairs, and the chairman of the Council of Economic Advisors. Presumably as a result, early in 1971 Nixon did sign an order creating the Council on International Economic Policy and brought in Peter Peterson of Bell & Howell to head it. Peterson was successful in resolving many issues through CIEP, until he was named to succeed me as secretary of commerce when I resigned in February 1972.

It is impossible to quantify and total how much we were able to accomplish in trade policy in my three years. One reason we could not be as effective as we wished was that both the Nixon administration and I had to bear the suspicion that was attached to the label of "protectionist" that came with the textile negotiations. No matter how many times I insisted that I was a free trader at heart, as I did in dozens of speeches, I could not cast off the label. I honestly felt and said that the principles of free trade could not be an invariable rule but had to be applied with some flexibility.

Free trade was and is in fact a fiction. It doesn't exist anywhere in the world except possibly in Hong Kong, which is largely a free market. In other words, I favor "fair" trade, which is a pragmatic and more sensible concept.

Nixon was also reluctant to retreat very far from free and open trade and especially hesitant to impose import restraints. Despite almost overwhelming pressure on him to adopt restrictions on imported shoes, he refused to do so. The trade bill he submitted to the Congress in 1969 did, however, propose that he be given authority in extreme cases to retaliate against unfair trade practices of other countries. He called its provisions in that respect our "first full-scale attack against covert forms of protectionism which discriminate against American exports."

The Congress took intermittent and slow action on his trade proposals and did not get around to enacting them into law until 1974, and then with a considerable number of modifications. Most notable of its changes was a recognition of the pragmatic position that I had taken all along in textiles, that a dogmatic and inelastic free-trade policy could at times do unreasonable harm to employers and employees in this country. It set up an International Trade Commission to be a mechanism for establishing the facts and proposing to the president restrictions in the form of higher tariffs, quotas, or other relief whenever it was found that imports of a commodity had grown to the point that they constituted a significant threat to American jobs and business investment. It was a sensible resolution of this highly emotional problem.

In the real world of national prides, mercantile jingoism, and heartless competition, however, neither the forced restraint of textile imports nor the enactment of a statute spelling out trade policy could mean an end to conflict. Free trade is a worthy ideal, but it is a long way off in a global society of selfish peoples with selfish goals. Anyone who believes that the national interest will be served by unrelenting free trade is a foolish idealist. Constant compromise with protectionism is essential to balance costs versus benefits, until time achieves an ideal world of unselfish nations and peoples.

# CHAPTER ELEVEN

# An Equal Place
# at the Starting Line

A subject of nonroutine interest that claimed a considerable part of my time as secretary of commerce was the development of a program to stimulate business ownership by America's minorities. In the 1968 campaign, Nixon had promised to help "black capitalism," and right after he took office he named me chairman of a Cabinet committee to create a plan. Within a month, the committee had approved my proposals to establish an Office of Minority Business Enterprise in Commerce (OMBE).

From the outset, I became imbued with the strong vein of justice in the idea, and I gave more than a proportionate amount of my attention toward making it work. The statistics were compelling. In this land of presumed equality, 20 percent of the people making up the minorities owned only 4 percent of the business units; these were so small on the average that they held considerably less than 1 percent of the nation's business assets and sales. The imbalance was clear, and the stark fact was that the federal government had done nothing specifically to redress it.

We had to start from scratch and to some extent feel our way, identifying and building on our successes and jettisoning what didn't work. The American minorities at that time had been officially defined by Congress as including blacks (African Americans), Hispanics (Latin Americans), and Indians (Native Americans). A few years later it added Asian Americans. Considering their depressed and underparticipating status in the economy and social system, it was no exaggeration to state that they constituted the equivalent of a Third World nation of fifty million people within the boundaries of the United States.

Our basic premise was that there are four essential ingredients to successful business ownership: a qualified or qualifiable entrepreneur, a sound business idea or opportunity, adequate financing through a reasonable mix of equity and debt capital, and managerial and technical know-how. Contrary to the beliefs of most aspiring small businessmen who discount the other ingredients, capital is in most cases the least important, or in reverse terms more businesses fail because of inadequacies in the other three. It would not do, then, for the government merely to hand out money. We had to have a balanced plan that helped to bring the four ingredients together in each individual enterprise, and to screen out those in which a workable combination of them did not seem likely.

There was urgency in the president's command to me, and at the same time a sense of reality. "Both morally and economically," he said publicly, "we will not realize the full potential of our nation until neither race nor nationality is any longer an obstacle to full participation in the American marketplace." Privately, he said to me, "Maury, this is something long overdue and I want you to give it a high priority. Politically, I don't think there are any votes in it for us, but we'll do it because it is right."

In order to get going in a hurry, without wading through the long processes of congressional hearings and appropriations, I decided to begin with the tools at hand and not wait for new laws. This meant, in effect, that OMBE would start out as a vehicle for drawing upon existing resources of government and the private sector to provide opportunities, funds, know-how, and business orders for qualified minority owners to begin and to grow. Several ways were quickly at hand. Our research found that there were 116 different programs in 21 government agencies that in one way or another could be tapped to help minority enterprise by loans, grants, and technical assistance. We could see to it that these agencies cooperated fully with our efforts, but we could move much more speedily if we had behind us the power of an executive order by the president, calling on all departments and agencies to cooperate with OMBE in finding ways to allocate some of their resources, including both money and personnel to assist it for a few years. After that it would secure appropriated funds to plan its own program, secure personnel, and carry on rapidly without a break in momentum. We could push the Small Business Administration to provide constructive guidance along with more minority loans. It could use more extensively an existing law providing for set-aside orders from government agencies for small businesses. We could also ask business corporations engaged in franchising to do much more for minorities, even to seeking out and training applicants. There were many other plans, too, as we went along, all based on the premise that we in Washington would not create a new nationwide structure to deal directly with individual ventures, but by stimulating local resources to do so would in effect work at a "wholesale" level, providing resources, ideas, and exchanges of information.

Franchising had special appeal, because it was already in the position to provide several of the basic ingredients in our sketch of successful business: a business concept, some of the capital, and much of the guidance. If a franchising company made it a matter of policy, it could choose and establish minority franchises. This could create opportunities within a wide range, from General Motors dealerships to Kentucky Fried Chicken stores and gasoline service stations. This avenue was an especially intriguing one for building minority ownerships, because the companies provided standards of product and service as well as supervision, and these elements were clearly most in need. While some money was necessary, the soundness of the business idea and the infusion of know-how were even more important in the scale. The franchise concept thereby helped admirably to fill these gaps.

Next, a very small part of the government's purchasing power, directed to minority businesses, would be a very large factor in getting many of them off the ground and past the tough first few years. The statistics indicated that minority entities were receiving only a measly $8 million a year in competitive contracts from government departments and less than another $8 million through the existing set-aside program designed to benefit small businesses in general. These amounts could be increased manyfold.

Getting capital was the third problem we tackled. The Small Business Association (SBA) could make a more deliberate effort to provide funds to minorities. Programs like Model Cities in HUD could help. The Office of Economic Opportunity could do much more to provide concepts to help business ownership. But the bulk of the answer was in the private sector. Banks and insurance companies understandably shied away from the heavy risks in minority business loans, and had to be given encouragement and possibly incentives to do so. A considerable number of welfare-minded business corporations had set out on their own to help minority ventures as partners or associates, as sponsors, or as lenders without an ownership interest; but there was no organized body of knowledge as to experiences, as to successes or failures, or as to ways to improve results in general. Therefore, many of these projects were short-lived. A national center for interchange of information was needed. Also, a program whereby federal, state, and local governments shared the loan risks could cause a vast growth in bank and business support for minority owners. Out of this we evolved the MESBIC, an acronym that stood for a minority enterprise small business investment company; it was devised as a legally permissible variation of the regular SBIC, under the SBIC law, and this made it possible to move ahead at once without going through the slow processes of getting new legislation.

These were our initial approaches, and from them we developed a number of ways to help identify the right candidates for ownership, to validate their ideas, to provide them with capital and counsel, and keep an eye on their hurdles and accomplishments.

An increase generally in the educational and motivational levels of minority citizens would be an ultimate step in achieving real equality of opportunity, but we couldn't wait for that. We had to do the best we could with the available skill levels, by planning ways of enlisting competent guidance, and finding sources of funds and management assistance.

To improve my measure of the whole problem and the concepts for dealing with it, I made trips to about twenty large cities and met in give-and-take sessions with groups of blacks and other minorities. These were very difficult at first, and many times I was insulted and even threatened by persons who doubted the sincerity of Nixon toward minorities and believed I had no weight to cause anything to happen. Although this was discouraging, I took it all patiently and listened to the sober voices, especially those of black and Latino businessmen whose experiences made them worthwhile commentators. In some of these visits I was accompanied by other government officers such as Robert Kunzig and Hilary Sandoval, the respective heads of the General Services Administration and the Small Business

Administration; their presence was of real help in giving authenticity to what I was saying. On one trip to Atlanta, I raised eyebrows among blacks and whites by staying overnight at a black-owned hotel, an experience that was wholly comfortable except for the half hour I spent in a balky elevator.

From the beginning, a heavy skepticism about our programs arose from the simple fact that OMBE had no money of its own to hand out, and that its main value was the influence it could bring to bear to cause others in and out of government to act. That changed, however, as our studies worked down to the local level. There we found that our most likely success would come from working through the self-help economic development organizations that minorities had already established with local support in the larger cities.

As the months went on we crystallized our plans in many ways and got the means to carry them out. Late in 1971, after much cadging of funds and personnel within the executive branch and the business community, we sought a substantial appropriation of money from the Congress to allow OMBE to take a more direct hand in crafting the "delivery systems" in the local communities. We requested an appropriation of $100 million, which was apportioned by the Budget Bureau to $40 million in the first year and $60 million the second and was appropriated by Congress in that manner. Also, on October 13, 1971, the president signed a new executive order giving OMBE and the secretary of commerce more authority and direction to carry out its efforts. In October 1972, the Congress finally passed another law embodying our suggestions for broadening the MESBIC provisions to make that program even more helpful.

We saw two organizational needs in the cities. One was a larger number of well-managed and adequately financed business development organizations run by capable minority leaders, with assistance from majority businessmen. The other was local centers for the accumulation of resources of money, technical assistance, and opportunities, largely to come from the majority community, and the delivery of these resources to qualified recipients.

From the beginning, we had to absorb a lot of criticism from minorities that what we were doing was too meager, as well as some from commentators that we hadn't solved the whole problem in the first six months. We also had flak from a few eager-to-find-fault columnists who tried to make something of the fact that I had turned down some financing proposals advanced by my own staff members. There was no denying that I had, and if those columnists had spent ten minutes finding out how harebrained and unworkable some of those early ideas were, they would have been embarrassed at what they had written in their support. The Treasury quite properly looked askance, for example, at allowing OMBE to issue $12 billion in 12 percent notes to finance minority businesses, as well I knew it would, but I found we had to run some of these fantasies past Treasury just to have backing for my turndowns.

After six months with a Caucasian as head of OMBE I appointed a black, husky, and amiable Abe Venable, and found that his good liaison with the minority community made it possible to increase OMBE's credibility and mine. He resigned after two years to join General Motors and I again chose a black, John Jenkins, an attractive, eloquent young man whose solid dedication advanced immeasurably the acceptance of our efforts by the minority community and the successes emanating from those efforts.

As Venable and Jenkins have attested many times, I gave a lot of thought and hours, in and out of Washington, to making minority opportunity a reality. As the months went by the figures began to show what we were achieving, and in some respects they were astounding. The total of government grants, loans, and guarantees by program agencies rose from $200 million in 1969 to $472 million in 1972. The dollar value of government set-aside contracts skyrocketed from a beginning $8 million in 1969 to $243 million in 1972. More than 50 MESBICs were formed in 1972, with a private capitalization of $28 million which by borrowed leverage (through SBA and banks) made possible minority financial capital of $254 million. The number of black-owned businesses of all types grew from 163,000 in fiscal 1968 to 195,000 in 1972, and their receipts rose from $4.5 billion to $7.2 billion. The total receipts of all minority businesses jumped from $10.6 billion to $16.6 billion between 1969 and 1972. Franchising created thousands more new business owners.

Through all this, we concentrated on the basic formula of combining the man, the opportunity, the money, and the technical assistance. Our successes proved that we had the right combination, and the momentum of three years was strong enough to ensure that it would carry on. It would be absurd, of course, for me to claim that our program was responsible for the entire 19 percent increase in new minority businesses from 1969 to 1972, but a fair conclusion would be that our publicized national efforts created a climate in which business ownership became a new hope for the minorities;

and our tools and impetus, with the support of federal, state, and local government agencies and from the private sector, made more and more of these aspirations come true.

Minority-owned business is still in an early stage but the number is growing, as is the average size, and this is a validation of the cause we embarked upon in 1969. In this setting, it is not mere coincidence that the magazine *Black Enterprise* was able to report that out of the hundred largest black-owned businesses in 1975, more than two thirds had been formed since 1968, and out of the top forty-eight black-owned banks, twenty-five were founded in the same time frame. Similarly, *Nuestro Business Review* counted that every one of the top nineteen Latino banks, and twenty-two of the top twenty-eight Latino savings and loan institutions, were created between 1969 and 1976.

Carried on more by momentum for some years than by White House interest, progress continued on all fronts after I left Commerce early in 1972. Later censuses showed regular growth in the number and average size of minority-owned businesses. By mid-1976 there were eighty-two MESBICs with private capital of $45,266,000, making possible leveraged minority investments of close to a billion dollars. Franchises shot from 450 generating $67.5 million of sales at the beginning to 3,413 with $750 million of sales. The 8(a) program of government purchases eventually reached $1.6 billion under President Carter. At the end of 1976, minority banks had $1.4 billion of assets and minority savings and loan associations had $900 million. The combined gross receipts of minority-owned businesses, which had been $10.6 billion in 1969, reached $23 billion in 1977. The deposit base of minority-owned banks burgeoned until it exceeded $2.3 billion by the end of 1980.

At the instigation of Walter Sorg, a former printing company executive who joined OMBE early, we had midwifed in 1971 a National Minority Purchasing Council (NMPC), which under his direction became one of the most remarkably successful corporate efforts ever undertaken to advance a public policy objective. From its founding and with nominal funding, the NMPC succeeded in rocketing annual corporate purchases from minority firms from under $50 million in the first year to $20.5 billion in 1993.

One more gratifying result was that the expansion of the minority business units gradually led, as I had expected, to a natural evolution wherein more large and diverse firms came into being in areas previously unpenetrated—communications, transportation, construction, food processing, and mass-market entertainment. Not only blacks but Latinos and Native Americans and Asians began moving into the mainstream.

Objective members of the various minorities readily identify the OMBE program originating in 1969 as the first and only really successful start ever taken by the federal government to be helpful in a meaningful way in the cause of business opportunity for them. That work must go on for decades, and basic educational equality is an ultimate key ingredient, and with elementary business education and motivation comprising major components. Nonetheless, I am proud of what was accomplished in my three years toward reversing the long course of historical inequity.

The finest hour of my career in Commerce was the evening of February 24, 1972, a week after I had officially departed, when two thousand members of minorities from all over the country financed a testimonial dinner at the Sheraton Park Hotel in Washington, and showered me with words of praise and thanks and many mementos in token of their appreciation. In the course of a five-hour program, Senator Edward Brooke saluted the work I had done, as did many other blacks, Native Americans, and Latinos. Reverend Leon Sullivan, head of the Opportunities Industrialization Corporation and a black director of General Motors, said "Stans has opened doors that have been closed for one hundred years."

It was no less a tribute when in November 1972, as Kathleen lay critically ill in Walter Reed Hospital with a serious blood disease and receiving frequent transfusions, John Jenkins, the director, and eleven other members of the OMBE staff, most of them black, appeared at the hospital and offered to donate blood to help her! These were the kinds of rewards that erased all the frustrations and insults and cynicism in early days of OMBE and left me feeling warm all over.

Late in 1984, a group of almost a thousand black businessmen from all over the country, accompanied by their spouses, on their own initiative and at their own expense, gave a testimonial dinner in New York City for President Nixon and me, extolling our feat of establishing a flow of opportunities for minority communities; their films, booklets, speeches, and general attitude of praise and appreciation gave me a long-lasting feeling of exhilaration, and were gratifying also to President Nixon, who was much more accustomed to public encomiums.

The official tribute at the testimonial dinner was touching:

> Secretary Stans's commitment to his presidentially assigned responsibility to further minority business enter-prise was immediate and complete. He moved within government to develop programs and he moved into the minority community—into city after city, meeting after meeting, business after business. He welded bonds with his sincerity, his compassion, his eloquence, his devotion to the needs of minority business. He leaves a rather wondrous legacy of achievement for a too-long-neglected national priority.

Of all the verbal bouquets I have ever received, that expresses the sentiment I would most like to see condensed on my tombstone.

In 1988, as I surveyed retrospectively, at eighty, the scenes of my earlier government work, I learned to my deep regret that this minority program had fallen into a severe decline in its functioning and in its public image. The basic faults were continued budget cuts from year to year and the declining morale that lack of funds and poor direction made inevitable.

Having retained my strong opinion that this program offered the primary means of remedying the historic inequity of minority under-participation in our economic system, I wrote to presidential candidate George Bush stating that the program needed to be revitalized, and I received an encouraging reply. Immediately after he was elected I volunteered my services in any way he chose, without pay. Eventually, we worked out a plan for the creation of a Minority Enterprise Development Advisory Council (MEDAC), with me as chairman under the secretary of commerce, to evaluate the situation and make its recommendations to achieve desirable reforms.

MEDAC consisted of twenty-four members chosen by the secretary's staff from among especially qualified members of the black, Hispanic, and Asian-American communities, representing various walks of life, and also including five executives of mainstream corporate businesses. I played no part in their original selection, but I was well satisfied that they represented a good cross section of the ethnic groups who needed help and of those in the sectors best able to provide it in conjunction with a government-sponsored long-range plan of action.

In the course of its sixteen-month existence, MEDAC met for eleven full days of discussion, allowing a thorough interplay of ideas from all sides and leading to a consensus as to the underlying nature of the minority dilemma, the essential characteristics of a solution, and the particular steps recommended. Subcommittees of its members had an equal number of meetings.

As chairman, and based on my previous work on minority business years before, which was favorably regarded by the group, I undertook to lead the meetings by preparing position papers in advance to be used as the focus of deliberations. This made rapid progress possible, leaving the meetings for reaching agreement on general principles and the appropriate details to implement them.

There were some major positions that I took at the outset, with the concurrence of the council. One was that any federal program that was adopted should deal with broad fundamentals, aimed at national solutions of long-term impact. A second was that the federal government should participate in future efforts at a "wholesale" level only (with the resolution of problems of individual entrepreneurs occurring at a local level), which meant that it would lead in marshaling resources, financial and technical, for delivery through local organizations in which the communities and business entities would play important roles based on their on-the-ground knowledge, participation, and leadership.

Insofar as I could learn, no studies in the past had ever attempted to measure the magnitude and aggregate cost to the nation of the minority underparticipation in the American economic system. In our determination in 1969 to get a fast-moving agenda under way and produce significant results quickly, that was a type of information we relegated to later research.

Now, we could more readily learn and adopt some basic dimensions. Of the more than fifty million minority Americans in 1969, approximately 30 percent were below the poverty level, and by extrapolation, 50 percent were without the means to make any meaningful investment in improved living standards, education, business, or financial assets, or reserves for health contingencies or retirement years. The underparticipation in the economy was calculable from census data that this 20 percent of the population in 1987, while owning 8.8 percent of the business establishments in the nation, did only about 2 percent of the total sales of goods and services. They had been largely passed by, for example, in the wave of change in retailing brought about by the advent of franchising in the preceding several decades, in which franchised business grew to over 50 percent of retail trade and services; in that period minorities acquired only about 3 percent of the new franchised units, which was much less than we had planned for.

The predominant procedure of our federal, state, and local governments has been to seek improvement of the low living standards of these minorities by the disbursement of welfare funds in a hundred or more categories. The best estimate I could get was that the combined cost of welfare payments at all levels of government was close to $100 billion a year and increasing rapidly. Most analysts seem to agree that this amount is inadequate to achieve more than the continuing status quo of the present welfare society, with no real improvements.

On the other hand, here were many millions of unproductive assets—minds and bodies—that for one or another historic reason were continuing to be untapped.

The discrepancies in comfort, security, and well-being of the persons making up this Third World nation within our borders are of course not measurable. Nor are the physical and emotional losses from poverty, deprivation, lack of opportunity, boredom, despair, growing resentment, breakup of family life, and the helpless retreat to gangs, drugs, and crime.

On the basis of that reasoning, the council suggested seven concurrent avenues of approach to constitute a balanced working formula, adopted step by step by MEDAC. They were:

(1) Indentify and marshal more effectively the financial resources needed to create and sustain minority businesses.

(2) Improve the present delivery system of resources to minority enterprises by restructuring the national network of federally operated Minority Business development Centers; and improve the organization and operation of the Minority Business Development Agency.

(3) Arrange that, upon their creation and continuing thereafter, minority businesses are provided increasingly with contract opportunities to supply goods and services to others.

(4) Stimulate the creation of a nationwide organization of mainstream business to provide strong and continuing support for minority entrepreneurship in a variety of ways.

(5) Improve the starting skills and abilities of would-be minority entrepreneurs through the insertion of business-oriented ingredients in elementary and secondary school education.

(6)  Increase the motivation of minority youth to understand how the American business system works and to want to participate in it.

(7)  Encourage and assist minority entities and minority leadership to organize nationally to consolidate their own power and influence and accept responsibility to support efficiently the types of business development assistance recommended in the report.

One of those projects that I again brought to the starting gate, based upon my own past activity in the industry, was franchising; that idea was adopted at once by the Minority Business Development Agency in Commerce and put into effect in 1991, despite a current recession, with promising early indications of success. To the best of my knowledge, the others are awaiting action.

The MEDAC Report, released in 1990 and unanimously approved by the members present at a meeting called for that purpose, named sixty-three projects for attention. I considered it a highly creditable and potentially very valuable piece of work, and had great hopes for its prompt adoption and full implementation by the secretary of commerce and the president. Unfortunately, it got strangled by budgetary restraints and staffing deficiencies.

That is regrettable. The report deserves exposure and a public hearing, for the possible value of its ideas. Many of the people who have read it, whites, blacks, and the other minorities, have volunteered the opinion that its mere initiation of action in its principles and procedures would have forestalled the climate of antagonism that sprang forth in the Los Angeles riots of April 1992, and those that will undoubtedly follow it. Above all, I believe that the full potential of the nation could be realized and many of its ills eliminated by the enthusiastic adoption of a social and economic development vision such as this, the dream of Richard Nixon for the building of bridges to human dignity. If that were planned and built well, it would be one so sweeping that its benefits would far exceed its cost within a matter of a few decades.

CHAPTER TWELVE

# Growing a
# Government Department

My senior staff and I searched constantly for ways to improve the scope and quality of Commerce's service to the public and the country, thereby to recover some of the department's prestige lost since its high stature in the days when Herbert Hoover was its secretary. Some of these pursuits brought gains rather easily into our hands, and some left us frustrated in failures. Many produced negligible benefits because of the glacial tempo at which bureaucracy permits change, and all taught us much about the vicissitudes of politics in Washington. A good illustration was the birth of the National Oceanographic and Atmospheric Administration (NOAA).

In his desire to reorganize the structure of the executive branch along more practical lines, President Nixon in 1969 appointed an Advisory Council on Executive Organization, headed by Roy L. Ash, president of Litton Industries, to study alternatives and make recommendations. One of its eventual proposals was to create a Department of Natural Resources to replace the Department of the Interior, encompassing within it most of the current units of Interior, plus the Forest Service from Agriculture and scattered other functions elsewhere in the government; it would also include the new

180

NOAA, created to combine some elements of Interior, the Environmental Science Services Administration of Commerce, and several organizational units from other departments. In one sense it was a logical step and I was impelled to say so. I could not feel that the loss of ESSA by Commerce was an event I should seek to prevent if the overall reorganization made sense.

Another concurrent proposal of the Ash council was that what remained in Commerce should then be merged with portions of Agriculture, Labor, and Transportation to form a new Department of Economic Affairs. This I did not believe would possibly be acceptable to the constituencies involved, especially when I recalled the extremes of opposition that President Eisenhower had encountered when he tried a few simple organizational moves in the late 1950s, or President Lyndon Johnson's difficulties when he proposed merging Commerce and Labor in the 1960s. Anyway, I did not want to see Commerce denuded of major units until the entire plan was effective, and I doubted that would ever occur.

So I made a counterproposal to the White House. It was that the units to make up NOAA be brought together in Commerce, where more than two thirds of it already was located, and where they could be more easily integrated. NOAA could then be considered for transfer to the Department of Natural Resources at a later time after that new entity had been created and pulled together effectively. The Ash group opposed my plan and so did most of the White House people, but the president approved it. I believe he felt, rightly or wrongly, that Commerce was better managed at the time than Interior. With strong support in the Senate from senators Hollings of South Carolina and Magnuson of Washington, NOAA was attached to Commerce as I had proposed. In the end, the Ash reorganization plans failed to be adopted by the Congress and NOAA has remained ever since in Commerce, where it has been well administered.

From the time I first entered federal service I have been skeptical of the tendency for every new administrator to start to solve national problems by reorganizing the units and people under him. I opposed many such plans in the departments when I was director of the Bureau of the Budget, because I felt that all that would be accomplished was a loss of time in getting into the problems at hand. For the same reason, I resisted a number of similar suggestions from my aides while I was secretary of commerce. I felt that with good management such reorganizations were usually immaterial. With poor management they would accomplish nothing. It was my honest belief, for example, that the functions of NOAA would be performed as well under Commerce as they would be under Interior or a department of another name. I permitted only one internal reorganization within Commerce and that was to terminate the misoriented Business and Defense Services Administration, which had been created right after World War II, and realign those few of its functions that were worthwhile within the Bureau of Domestic Commerce.

Early in my term of office I found that I was being visited by many ministers of commerce from foreign countries, each with a specific mission concerned with commercial affairs. It was evident that these dealings were important considerations in the lives of the other countries, and I believed that it would be helpful to our relationships if I accepted as many as possible of the reciprocal invitations to visit their lands. During my three years I made ten trips, including those to Europe and the Far East on textiles, to a total of thirty-two countries. One of these was to Portugal, where I represented President Nixon at the funeral of President Antonio de Oliveira Salazar, and then stayed on to talk business. On two ten-day vacations in Africa, at my own expense, I stopped off en route going and coming to make official calls in Kenya, Ethiopia, Yugoslavia, and Spain for discussions on pending commercial topics. I went to Nicaragua at the specific request of Nixon, and also traveled to Canada for a ministerial-level meeting. One official tour took in six countries in Latin America and another visited four countries in southern Europe plus Iran and Ireland. The last was a trip to Sweden, Poland, and the Soviet Union in November 1971.

In each instance, I was warmly greeted by the government officials, who welcomed the idea that, for the first time, a secretary of commerce from the United States had paid them the compliment of meeting on their home ground to review current business topics. My usual schedule in a country called for sessions with the head of state, the foreign minister, the minister of commerce, and the minister of finance, plus others where appropriate. I carried with me personal letters to the heads of state from President Nixon, and was well briefed on current diplomatic matters by the State Department. Upon my return, I wrote reports for the president and State Department with my observations and suggestions, and also usually reported my impressions orally to the Cabinet. To the extent that I had direct authority, or was authorized specifically after my reports, I set in motion in Commerce the steps I deemed appropriate as a result of the talks. The exchanges with these countries were, I believe, healthy and mutually productive.

In one way or another these countries have important and enlarging trade, investment, and tourist relations with the United States. They all seek major growth in their economies, and view United States cooperation as critical. Personal contact at the Cabinet level provides a greater understanding of their needs and concerns and almost always leads to beneficial results for both sides.

My stopover in Yugoslavia in mid-December of 1969 was made at the insistent urging of Yugoslav ambassador Crnobrnja. There were many topics he wanted reviewed with his government in his hope that full discussion would lead to significant increases in communications and trade between the two countries. Yugoslavia was in 1969 classed in the general category of Iron Curtain nations, and he wanted to demonstrate firsthand that it had a distinctive kind of Communism that was not a challenge to the United States but could be welded into a strong alliance.

Things worked out that way, at least as far as trade was concerned. We found it possible after my visit to open up several new avenues of mutual advantage. One was with Sears, Roebuck & Co., whose chairman told me it was not then dealing with Yugoslavia "because it is a Communist country." When I replied with assurances that our government wanted to distinguish the Yugoslavs from the mainline Communists, Sears began importing its products, although handicapped somewhat by the limited production capacity of almost every item; Yugoslavia was just not then accustomed to large-scale production in the quantities Sears needed to put articles into its stores and catalogs. In the subsequent years, the trade grew considerably.

Because he was in residence in Zagreb during my visit, President Tito sent his personal plane to Belgrade to pick up our ambassador, William Leonhart, and me. The flight went bouncingly through severe winter storms with violent turbulence, and was quite terrifying. Zagreb was covered with deep snow. Kathleen accompanied us; Tito's wife, Jovanka, was with him when we met in the Presidential Palace.

After opening greetings and during casual conversation about the unusually severe weather, there came a flood of beverages and food, served so closely together that conversation made little progress for twenty minutes because of the frequent interruptions. Slivovitz was the central theme, but several other drinks were also offered, and there was a procession of holiday cookies, cakes, and breads. Having given up all forms of alcohol more than ten years earlier, I was spared the risks of overindulgence from such generous hospitality.

In the conversation, Tito expressed strong interest in closer relations with the United States, feeling that progress had long been delayed because of incorrect political impressions and beliefs that ought not to be tied to his country. He hoped the new American president would want to join him in seeking a closer rapport.

"Have you ever met President Nixon?" I asked.

"I have not had that pleasure, but I certainly would welcome it," was his answer.

I promised to carry that message back to Washington. Nixon was pleased with the report and included Belgrade as a stop on his next European trip.

Most of Tito's conversation with me centered on the Middle East. He expressed strong feelings that a conflagration in this area must be prevented, and said that he was carrying on his own private diplomacy to cool tempers. He was planning a trip soon to Egypt to convince President Nasser that concession and peace offered the only solution to the Israeli problem. He commented at length on his concerns as to the course of events if no one took the leadership to calm the traditional antagonisms.

As for his own country, he was confident it had found a stable base that would advance the living standards of his people under its special brand of Communism, which offered incentives to workers and citizens not available elsewhere under Marxist principles.

Nixon visited Yugoslavia in 1970, and Tito came to the United States the following year. I did not participate in the diplomatic discussions, but I did host a private dinner meeting at Blair House in his honor, to which I invited eight American industrialists connected with large multinational companies interested in doing business with or in Yugoslavia. There was a strikingly frank exchange, under an advance understanding that no topic was barred. Tito answered all questions directly and fully, with the overall context one of insistence that his country welcomed their participation. Some specific roadblocks or presumed roadblocks built up over a long period of bureaucratic frustration on both sides were shattered on the spot, once he heard about them.

Tito was a man of unlimited energy and a charismatic leader. He left no doubt of his intelligence and determination to build, modernize, and strengthen his country. Yet most people who talked with him wondered, as I did, whether his hold on the country was so personal that the apparent unity of the diverse ethnic groups might not survive his inevitable departure. Despite his advancing age, he had not groomed a strong successor. He died after a lingering illness in 1980. Yugoslavia held together for ten more years, but its ethnic breakup then began in earnest.

Another side of the Tito regime may have been implicit in my press conference at the American ambassador's residence in Belgrade after my return from Zagreb. I made a few opening remarks to local reporters about the objectives of my visit and the gratifying exchanges of views I had enjoyed, and then said I would be glad to answer any questions. I waited for almost two minutes after the translation, without response, and finally a subdued voice broke the silence by saying, "Mr. Minister, would you please tell us what questions we may be permitted to ask?" It was obvious that the press was quite well disciplined at the time.

I visited Ethiopia as a private citizen during the holiday season in December 1969 for two weeks on safari in the Danakil Desert and the Bale Mountains, and then in my role as secretary of commerce spent four more days on official visits with Emperor Haile Selassie and other government leaders.

Accustomed as I was to poverty and primitive living conditions among the native tribes of Africa, I was depressed to see how poor the people of Ethiopia were. With probably the lowest per-capita income in the world, then less than $75 per year, its economy beyond Addis Ababa was almost entirely one of earthen-floor grass huts, meager food for subsistence, and a pathetic battle for survival, with a life expectancy at birth of only about thirty-five years. Its government clearly had failed its citizens. Shifta bandits controlled sections of the dirt roads in the western provinces, and in the Danakil in the northeast victors of tribal battles still collected the testicles of the vanquished.

The emperor lived in the new Jubilee Palace, built to commemorate his fiftieth anniversary on the throne and his seventy-fifth birthday, and still guarded by live lions. Kathleen and our son Ted joined me in our visit to His Majesty in the palace. Once inside the throne room, we faced a long walk of over a hundred feet to the point where he sat. That was not made any easier by his two Chihuahua dogs that barked at our heels as we advanced, while he smiled at our obvious discomfort.

His greeting was warm, and he introduced us to his niece and his grandson (the commander of the Ethiopian navy), whom he had thoughtfully invited to match the members of our party. After a pleasant fifteen minutes over tea, cakes, and light conversation, he suggested that I withdraw with him to an adjoining small room to converse about economic and trade matters. He was sharp and constructive.

"We need capital and industry to develop our country," were his key words, "and we need especially the help of the wealthy companies and people in the United States to provide them." Having been fortified in advance with questions, I asked about the difficulties with government red tape and obstructive tactics of local entrepreneurs.

"There should not be any. Our country is open to anyone, and if there are any obstacles in the way I want to know about them," he retorted strongly.

That was reassuring, until I met some of the Ethiopian ministers and spoke to the commercial staff in the American embassy. It became evident that His Majesty was in a dreamworld, in which he had lost control of the government except for ceremonial occasions. The ministers made it plain to me that they did not welcome foreign business intrusion, that they would be very selective about letting anyone come in, and that the process of getting approvals was sure to be a long and difficult one. Our embassy told me about an American battery manufacturer, successful in Kenya, that wanted to build a plant in Addis Ababa; after two years of red tape, confusion, and delay, the company finally gave up and withdrew the idea.

I also learned about an aid grant from the United States to provide an office and facilities in Addis for the local chamber of commerce in the downtown area where foreign businessmen could meet by appointment with government officials on matters of information, clearances, and approvals of proposed investments and trade. The whole project had been delayed for several years because the government and local interests couldn't or wouldn't even agree on a location for the office.

The powerlessness of the emperor, evinced by the resistance of local businessmen and officials to newcomers in their markets, made it clear that Ethiopia was far from ready for emergence into the twentieth century. They were clearly disregarding the emperor's views and actually impeding foreign contacts. It was impossible for me to get any ground rules from them except for platitudes and generalities that apparently would be and were being discarded whenever specifics came up for action. This hardheaded opposition to reform undoubtedly was one of the causes of the assassinations of these ministers when revolution came. To a certainty, Ethiopia's stagnant economy and its lack of social progress encouraged an atmosphere of revolution. It is possible that revolution may have been inevitable, but its violence may have been averted had the regime been more constructive and more forward-looking.

A year after our meeting in Addis Ababa, Haile Selassie was in Washington and we saw him again at the White House. Kathleen asked about the two Chihuahuas, and he told her they were along on the trip with him. I did not bother to ask him about business conditions. I felt sad that the emperor had not by then realized his own ineptitude and created a succession to the throne.

He was deposed four years later, in 1974, and died in 1975.

Few national leaders in history survived on their thrones as long as Haile Selassie, and few died as little mourned or as little missed by the world community or by his own people. Part of the reason was that time and change had passed him by. He had led his country for more than fifty years, broken only for a time by the disgraceful and unwarranted invasion of his country by Mussolini of Italy, and had all the power and pomp of a caesar, yet when revolution finally came, he was killed by assassins with apparently no defense from his own palace guards.

It was at one of Nixon's White House dinners that I first met Anastasio Somoza Debayle, president of Nicaragua. After the food service in the East Room there was the usual mix of conversation and coffee in the Red and Blue rooms. I was chatting with one of the African potentates about conditions in his country when a Marine aide tapped me with a message that the president wanted to see me.

Nixon was in earnest conversation with Somoza and was obviously relieved when I appeared promptly. He introduced me, said, "Talk to President Somoza and see what we can do to help him," then departed to talk with other waiting guests.

Somoza's immediate problem had to do with difficulties he was having with discipline among the countries in the Central American Common Market (CACM). I knew little about the subject, but promised to look into it pronto. After the entertainment in the East Room, I sought out Nixon to report to him briefly. He responded immediately: "Somoza is a great friend of the United States. Go down to Nicaragua and spend some time with him talking it over. Maybe we can help."

Somoza was delighted. I arrived in Nicaragua two weeks later, in an air force plane, to be greeted with full honors—guns booming in salute, a military band playing the two national anthems, and a review of the assembled troops. My quarters were in a spacious modern apartment in the National Palace. Somoza lived elsewhere, in less ostentation, for greater personal security.

His entertainment was lavish, including a picnic with a hundred important Nicaraguans at his beachside resort on the Pacific Ocean. In the three days I was in the country, we had more than ten hours of formal and informal conversation on a wide range of topics. The talks succeeded in reassuring Somoza and Nicaragua of United States interest in their welfare, but did not accomplish anything in immediate specifics.

On the CACM matter he had originally raised, there was little I could see for the United States to do but sympathize. The individual ambitions of the member countries, and the rivalries among them, offered little opportunity for the United States to rearrange their trade and economic policies. We spent much time talking about sugar. The United States, in order to protect its domestic sugar industry from excessive low-priced foreign imports, fixed quotas for the amounts that could be brought in from each sugar-producing country. Somoza's case was specific: Nicaragua's quota was low and he wanted it increased.

"When Allen Dulles, head of the CIA, needed a base to train men and planes in preparation for the Bay of Pigs invasion, he came to me. He promised that, if we would provide the place, in secrecy, he would see that when it was over and all was quiet we were compensated, among other things, by a substantial increase in our sugar quota. It never came, as though part of the responsibility for the fiasco was assigned to us. That was not fair; it was your president that blew it.

"We are the best friend the United States has in Latin America. We have supported you more often than any other Latin country, in the United Nations and in world opinion. The least you could do in return is keep your word," Somoza told me. I promised to carry the message to Washington. By this time Dulles was dead and neither the CIA nor the State Department would acknowledge that such a commitment had been made. I could not get any concessions for Somoza.

We talked also about the future of Nicaragua. He recognized that he had the burden of advancing the average living standard of his people in a limited amount of time, without the lifting force of either an industrial base or underground natural resources. His conclusion was that he had to develop a modern agricultural nation, using the latest technology on a wide scale and producing a diversity of raw and semiprocessed products that would reduce the national dependence on bananas and a few scant crops. "This is the only way for Nicaragua, and with it we can be the most prosperous nation in Central America. We have the soil to do it." I was impressed by the thoroughness of his planning and the seeming soundness of his concepts.

Somoza lost his race against time in 1979, when the United States supported the local and foreign rebels who turned him out. He was assassinated in South America a year later.

By common definition, Somoza was a dictator. That is not by itself grounds to condemn him, because in the setting of a banana republic the governing question should be how he used his power of position and wealth. It is hard to judge a man's sincerity, because it can sometimes be only words-deep. But Somoza convinced me that he put relieving the plight of his people as a high priority, and that he was willing to offer his record of progress on the line every few years in regularly scheduled elections. I regretted that he did not have the chance to prove his good intentions.

Emperor Hirohito of Japan is another national leader who held his throne for many years, first as a godhead to his people and then after the humiliation of World War II in a human role. I met him in 1969, the year the United States first landed men on the moon. The dramatic feat was watched on television all over this planet. We learned of the reactions of this world figure a few days later.

Under a custom of Japan and the United States to hold a joint meeting of their principal cabinet members every year to discuss matters of mutual interest or disagreement between the two countries, I was among the 1969 group that visited Japan. In between our business meetings we and our wives were scheduled for an audience with the emperor and the empress in the Imperial Palace.

After being escorted through the beautifully manicured grounds, sand gardens, and some of the magnificent reception rooms of the palace, we were taken to a smaller room for the meeting. The royal pair arrived promptly and after introductions all around the empress took our wives to another chamber. Conversation in both rooms was almost all confined to the moon landing that had just occurred. The empress, who wore a Western-style dress, spoke in a whisper. She told the ladies that every television set in Japan had been sold days before the landing was scheduled.

The emperor was also dressed in well-tailored Western-style clothes. Full of excitement and enthusiasm, he greeted us and opened the discussion, "I stayed up all the night to follow the story and pictures of the landing, and was as excited about it as anyone could be. No feat in the entire history of the earth could have been as dramatic or as important."

As the conversation progressed from there, mostly in platitudes, he suddenly stopped and said, "It would be nice if our people could see the rocks that were brought back. Do you suppose the United States would sell us some?"

Secretary of State William Rogers replied that he was sure that some plan would be found whereby some of the moon rocks and moon dust would be made available.

Catching the emperor's word *sell*, I was saucy enough to add, ". . . at cost, Your Majesty?"

Rogers was distracted and missed my remark, but the translator related it to the emperor. His Majesty caught its significance, rolled his eyes to the ceiling, and chuckled.

"That would be beyond our means, I'm afraid," he responded.

A small, wizened man, the emperor was pleasant and cheerful during the audience. None of us saw in him the deity-figure that he was to his people up to the end of World War II, and the conversation proceeded without the awe that a godhead would have inspired. The emperor was a human being, and his admitted admiration for the moon feat showed that, on that subject at least, he was one of us.

His Majesty the Shah of Iran was a tragic figure whose place on the stage ended in disaster for him and his country. On one of his visits to the United States, he was guest of honor at a luncheon given in the elegant State Department dining hall by Secretary of State Rogers. As secretary of commerce, I was ranking guest to sit at his right during the meal, but I had little direct conversation as Rogers, on his left, held his attention with diplomatic matters.

After the dessert course, the group arose for coffee, and I strolled with the shah onto the spacious balcony, where the sun was shining warmly. He had a point to make: "Why can't the United States buy more oil from Iran, its longtime ally, and not so much from some of the less friendly countries?" he asked plaintively. Oil was then selling for under three dollars a barrel.

I told him I was sympathetic. He elaborated on his plea.

"We have just one generation in which to bring the people of Iran into the twentieth century. Our petroleum resources must be used now to create an economy of industry and commerce that will be strong enough to survive the day when they run out. With Communism on our northern border, we can't delay one day or one month. We need to convert all the oil we can into permanent industrial power, to advance the living standards and longtime welfare of our people."

Trying to further the subject, I asked whether the natural gas that was being produced with the oil was still being burned off at the wellhead. He was almost bitter at the thought. "It's an inexcusable waste," he retorted. "I've been trying to get the oil producers to build a pipeline or put the gas back into the ground, or find some way to save it until we can use it, but they say it can't be done at a sensible cost. It's a valuable asset and we're going to force the issue, if it means we have to do the job ourselves. We know it will be expensive, but still very much worthwhile."

He returned to the goal of assuring the country's modernization by building its economy, and urged me to tell American business about the opportunities for free enterprise in Iran. I asked about the infrastructure—the highways, communications, education, health facilities—and wondered how he determined which and how much had to come first in building a nation.

"It's a big problem—a constant problem of evaluation. I get advice from many sources, and there's a lot of disagreement about the rankings in priority. The final decision comes up to me. Bridging a social and economic gap of a thousand years in a few decades is a monumental task, and the only way we can win is to cash in our underground resources for surface wealth that will mean sustained progress. That's why we need to sell more oil."

That was about five years before the OPEC countries began their massive raises in the price of oil. The shah was understandably one of those in the forefront of the advocacy for higher prices. But the clock ran out on him in 1979, before he could really get his act together. There was no way he could advance all the elements of progress with equal speed to keep his people patient, and his communications were inadequate to build a level of confidence in his aims strong enough to survive the thrust of the reactionary religious movement that forced his abdication.

I am aware of the charges of police brutality to dissidents during his reign. I can readily believe that he may have been so imbued with the urgency of his plans that he felt he had to brush aside any resistance that would slow down his gains. Yet in the end he yielded without a fight. In any event, his fall was a tragedy for the United States and seems in the long run to have been a tragedy for Iran. His dreams for his country may have been lost forever, and with them its chances to join the leading nations of this century. He lived only a few years more, in a frustrated search for peace and health, shunted ignominiously from country to country, until he passed away in Egypt in 1980.

The shah was an intense man, almost dour, with sharp, piercing eyes and a firm jaw. He showed no sense of humor, and his conversation was serious to the point of grimness. He had goals, and mental blueprints to reach them, and he was determined to get there in the shortest possible time. The realization that he was attempting to build a modern nation, to go from tribal nomadism to twentieth-century industrial and military technology in a decade or two, something never before done for a nation of thirty-five million people, did not daunt him. Iran was to be one of the world's five great powers, a bulwark of strength against Communism.

He did accomplish much. He implemented land reform, mass education, women's rights and welfare programs, reduced internal migrations, and built steel mills, telecommunication systems, public works, a large industrial base, extensive roads and highways, and a formidable military machine. He was a committed ally of the United States.

Unfortunately, his changes were too far ahead of his people. Resistance to Westernization in some quarters forced his regime to become more and more authoritarian, and he seems to have used his secret police to suppress some of the open opposition. Yet the country was free in the sense that its people could practice the religion of their choice, engage in a business or profession, travel and study abroad, dress as they wished, choose the entertainment they liked, and live according to their individual preferences. The standard of living did rise, but it did not reach everyone uniformly.

The shah was in a hurry, and time was fleeting. To build a secure industrial nation before the oil ran out may have been an impossible dream in the best of circumstances. As it was, his feats outpaced his ability to sell his countrymen on his plans, and the reactionaries among them collected enough power to throw him out. That may turn out to be one of history's worst tragedies, because a backward-looking Iran may now be condemned to a minor role in world history.

Did the shah line his own pockets, and those of his family, during his time on the throne? That is possible, and it certainly is not without precedent in this world of uneven morality. Whatever the case, it is bound to be grossly exaggerated, since it is a sure fate of a fallen leader to be accused of every crime in the books. That's one way that successors justify their revolutions.

Above all, from several talks with him in the United States and in Iran, I was convinced that, however grandiose his goals may have been, and however badly he communicated them to his citizenry, the shah's reign was dedicated to the improvement of life for his people. History will never know what he might have achieved had he been able to marshal and hold full popular support.

Invariably I found that the major subject of my conversations in the less developed countries was that of capital formation. These nations all had enormous ambitions for economic and social growth, and in varying degrees recognized that these results could come only through massive additions of capital, not just in industry and commerce, but also in educational facilities, transportation, and all the other elements of infrastructure. They professed to have a strong belief in free enterprise but often seemed compelled, for political reasons, to pursue policies that moved in an opposite direction. Many created state enterprises when private companies could do better, or suppressed imports to protect small local enterprises.

Almost all of them were ambivalent about their attitude toward foreign investment. While they professed to encourage its inflow, they harnessed it with controls, restrictions, and limitations that discouraged its entry; and they frequently changed the rules of the game after it was in. The competing political demands almost everywhere for nationalism forced countries to adopt slogans like "Colombia for the Colombians," which in turn lead to rejection of foreign investment, to discrimination against it, and sometimes to a confiscation of that which was present.

Recalling to foreign cabinet ministers in the developing countries the history of the United States, which from the beginning welcomed capital from any source and for any purpose, I said I could not understand a contrary practice. I tried to make the point that once foreign money is invested in local plants, equipment, markets, and payrolls, it is no longer foreign capital but domestic capital, at work to produce jobs, income, taxes, exports, and rising living standards. Any other process of accumulating indigenous capital is entirely too slow to meet the expectations of the people. To make that thrust stand out, I sometimes challenged a foreign official in conversation to have his experts put on paper the standard of living his country wanted twenty-five years ahead, with all the accoutrements in education, communication, transportation, housing, welfare, and industry, and then price it out in terms of the total capital required to get there and the operating budgets to sustain it. They would find, I was sure, that they could not even approach their goals without importing a third or a half of the capital needs. If this were understood, they would not be so selective as to the industries in which to allow foreign participation, so discriminatory against foreign capital, or so politically susceptible to anti-foreign sloganism. The best course would be to treat foreign investments no less favorably than domestic. I said all this and more, with honest conviction, but I'm afraid in retrospect that nationalism was an awfully big barrier to be brought down by the logic of economics.* Nonetheless, my views seemed to be gratefully received and noted. One finance minister told me a year or so later that he had run the figures and found I was absolutely correct. He wasn't prepared to say what he would do about it.

My overseas trips were hardworking affairs, and I was always accompanied by a staff party of six or eight persons, sometimes including some from other interested departments. Several times I used one of the president's planes, but most were supplied by the Air

---

*An example of narrow provincialism was the initial radicalism of the Andean Common Market, formed early in the seventies by six western South American countries. It limited any foreign investment to a 49 percent interest in a local venture, put a 14 percent maximum on return on the investment, and had many other restrictions. Investors stayed away in droves, because there were better and safer opportunities elsewhere. Within a few years, enforcement broke down, the restrictions were ignored, and some of the countries broke away. The realities were that national growth was best pursued by welcoming capital on the same terms it received elsewhere in the world, thereby building up the local economies in terms of jobs, income, and taxes. By 1976, these countries had made a startling turnabout in opening their doors wider to foreign private enterprise.

Force. Our local ambassadors invariably welcomed these visits as evidence of interest in the country, and I know of no instance in which they did not feel my presence had been valuable. I did have one negative experience, however, when our ambassador to a South American nation, in the presence of the country's president, said that he did not consider it his responsibility to present the case for any American company to the host government. Later I asked him indignantly what he thought his mission was if it were not to represent American interests, and I complained about him to the State Department upon my return to Washington. Whatever the reason, he left the service six months later and I considered it a good change.

On these travels, the plane became a working office, with the time fully occupied in reading briefing papers, reviewing with staff people the pending issues to be talked about, and working on what to say in arrival statements, in toasts appropriate to each country, and in departure statements. On the way home after the last stop on a trip, reports to the president had to be written and reviewed, and concurrences to them received from accompanying representatives of other departments before landing. There was little time to put our feet up or to enjoy the scenery.

It was usually hectic after arrival in a country. Once greeted, and the arrival statement presented to the local media, we were rushed into the city from the airport to our sleeping quarters, usually our ambassador's residence, and briefed at length by embassy staff. Then we were turned loose for a series of meetings with government officials, normally five during the workday interrupted by a two-hour formal luncheon and toasts. With perhaps thirty minutes to dress and organize one's thoughts on the day, we were off on an evening round, frequently a cocktail reception, followed by a dinner and official entertainment. In later reflection, I realized that with such fully scheduled activity I had gone through many countries without seeing them. There were some stolen moments but not many: a trip to the souk in Shiraz to bargain for Persian rugs, an evening watching flamenco dancers in Madrid, a tour to Isfahan and to the 2,500-year-old ruins at Persepolis, the visit to the hometowns of three grandparents in Belgium, a boat ride out of Athens with friends, a day in Brasilia and a stopover at the mildewed city of Manaus on the Amazon, a football game in Ottawa, a weekend in Leningrad, a stop at an ancient monastery in Baku, and a few others.

I made two particular observations from these trips. First, talking through interpreters, which we had to use in all but the English-speaking countries, is a slow process that doubles the time for each meeting, but it also gives valuable time to think ahead on the words and phrases most appropriate. Japanese is an especially complex language that always takes a third more time to express than its equivalent in English. Giving toasts through an interpreter is a bit clumsy, and using humor is very difficult because of idiomatic differences. Second, our ambassadors were, with but one or two exceptions, impressive representatives of the United States, respected by the officials they dealt with and in harmonious relationships with them. In quality, I found no notable distinction between those who were career diplomats and those who were not. The non-career appointees had been carefully chosen, were knowledgeable, diplomatic, conversant with the country, hardworking and able, and often had the advantage of business backgrounds that made them especially effective in trade development.

The statistics of these trips tell a story. In 32 national visits encompassing a total of 75 days, I met 30 heads of state, had 125 meetings with other officials, made 25 formal speeches, held 30 press conferences, attended 50 formal lunches, dinners, or receptions at which toasts and responses were given, attended 25 ballets, operas, athletic competitions, or other social events, and lost untold hours of sleep.

There were some lows and some highs on the trips, and some quite astonishing occurrences.

My first attempt to visit Spain was almost aborted. I had arranged to stop there early in January 1971, on my way back from a personal African vacation, but this met unexpected difficulties when I caught a severe dysentery while fishing at Lake Rudolf in Kenya. I was too groggy and weak, I concluded when I flew back to Nairobi, that I should go directly home to recover. When I sent a cable to Ambassador Robert Hill in Spain to that effect, he responded instantly with a series of cables that bore strong indignation and insistence. Things were delicate in Spain at the time, he said, as the result of events following the recent trials of some Basque separatists. A planned trip to Spain by Minister of Foreign Affairs Schumann of France had been canceled in response to critical public reaction, several other foreign official visitors had postponed or called off their visits, and if I were not to show up it would be taken as an act of censure by the United States.

Faced with this predicament, my Commerce staff came up with complex arrangements so as not to disappoint the ambassador and the Spanish government. Assistant Secretary McLellan and five staff people who had been scheduled to meet me in Madrid to help make the official rounds and then accompany me back to Washington had already arrived at our Terrejón Air Force Base outside Madrid on an air force plane before they received word of my illness. They added their pleas for my presence. To solve the dilemma, Kathleen and I caught an uncomfortable commercial flight from Nairobi to Athens as soon as I could be adequately medicated and sedated. The air force plane, bearing my secretary and a doctor, then headed from Madrid to Athens in time to bring me early to the Terrejón base hospital for attention to my feverish and weakened condition.

The next morning I was photographed in bed, wan and pale but in conversation with the minister of commerce of Spain, and the story and picture appeared throughout the Spanish press. The Spanish officials were lavish in their expressions of appreciation. So was Ambassador Hill. In the esoteric world of diplomacy, an international misunderstanding had been prevented and our relations were preserved intact. McLellan kept my other appointments in Madrid and effectively delivered my prepared speech to a combined meeting of the American Chamber of Commerce and the American Club.

Despite this stressful effort, my make-up visit to Spain four months later produced a small bit of unexpected flak. One of the pressing concerns at the time was the accelerating level of their shoe exports to us, causing distress to the American industry. We had hopes of working out some voluntary limits in the rate of this growth, which I discussed quietly but with unpromising results with the Spanish government ministers. In a press conference just before leaving for my next destination, I answered a question by acknowledging the shoe talks and said I was confident the Spanish government would find a way to accommodate our needs in the situation. This innocent remark hit the fan in the local press and some of the ministers thought it necessary in their own defense to make critical remarks about my suggestions for restraint. Later, Ambassador Hill and Henry Kissinger assured me that the brief wave of publicity generated by the Spanish officials was merely to demonstrate at home "that they were not in the United States' pocket."

I visited Greece for two days in 1971 during the term of President George Papadopoulos, the leader of the colonels' revolt that had overthrown the liberal government of Panayotis Kanellopoulos in 1967. His administration was essentially a rightist dictatorship, with emphasis on economic development. The stopover turned out to be more eventful than I had intended.

Because of the considered delicacy of the political situation, I was given an especially thorough briefing by the State Department. It was clear that any visit by an American Cabinet official had local overtones that might produce criticism back in the United States, but I had a full agenda of commercial topics and was determined not to go beyond it. I stuck strictly to the program, but not without some misunderstanding nonetheless.

At a luncheon given in my honor by the minister of commerce, I was pleased to see that nine ministers of the government had attended and mentioned the fact in my toast, commenting also on the historic close connections between the people of Greece and those of the United States. I went on to applaud "the welcome given here to American companies and the sense of security the government is imparting to American companies in Greece." Then I remarked on recent economic gains in the country, which were statistically as high as any in Europe, and said that "given continued economic stability and continued political stability, there is no limit to the growth that can take place in Greece." These were truisms, of course, but they ran into strong criticism at home by *The New York Times* and Senator Hubert Humphrey on the grounds that I was giving aid and comfort to an oppressive right-wing regime.

The next day I had a touchy firsthand experience that taught me about the opposition to the Papadopoulos regime. Kathleen and I, and some of the Commerce aides with me on the trip, were taken on a full-day cruise to the island of Hydra by Tom Pappas, an American with sizable business interests in Greece. It was a very relaxed and pleasant interlude, until we returned to port. All around the dock and for a considerable distance along the road were hundreds of armed Greek troops. I found this surprising but gave no further thought to it until we reached the ambassador's residence, when he passed on the word that the government had uncovered a plot by guerrilla opponents of the regime to bomb the yacht the moment it hit the dock. I never learned how serious the danger really was.

In my conversation in his office, Papadopoulos was alert and intense, and expounded at considerable length on the problems of increasing the gross national product of his country. He professed close interest in current events in the United States and in its economic and political systems, commenting that it was regrettable that democratic government had been such a failure in Greece in building living standards. His main objective, he said, was to remedy that situation.

The Papadopoulos regime stayed in power until 1973, when it was overthrown by a coalition led by Dimitros Ionnidis, who in turn lasted only a year until democracy was restored in 1974. Papadopoulos and seven of his regime were sentenced in 1975 to a life term in Athens's Korydallos prison, where he was reported in 1981 to be conducting himself as an Olympic god, treating his former subordinates with condescension, dining in regal solitude, and insisting on being addressed as "President." His quarters were outfitted, it was said, with air conditioners, refrigerators, and television sets, and he was systematically "coddled" in other ways. Dethroned dictators usually fare less well.

A pleasant incident, with some surprises, occurred on one of my vacation days in Kenya when I visited the town of Garissa on the Tana River, several hundred miles northeast of Nairobi in bleak desert country. When it became known that an American Cabinet member had come to visit a friend at the American Catholic mission there, I was invited to attend an outdoor dinner at the Jamhuri Club and address those present. To an all-native audience of over a hundred people, I talked briefly about my interest in Africa through the years, invited them to visit the United States, and then suggested that they might prefer to have me answer questions about my country. The response astonished me. There in the bush country of Africa the meeting took on the quality of a Foreign Affairs Council in an American city, and I was bombarded with sophisticated questions about the trends and problems of migrations to the cities, about the pros and cons of the parliamentary versus the congressional system in government, and about the priorities in economic development plans. Their knowledge was impressive, and their astute reasoning taught me that the people of progressive countries, as Kenya was at the time, could more knowledgeably and with foresight move through the twentieth century. I must have answered the questions well, because I am now an honorary lifetime member of the Jamhuri Club of Garissa.

# CHAPTER THIRTEEN

# The Diversities
# of Commerce

In Washington, our monthly director's meetings held in the quiet of "nonworking" Saturdays reviewed a long agenda of proposals for addition or deletion of functions, or for research into business and economic matters. To implement the ideas that were brought forward, sometimes through brainstorming sessions, I initiated a project-improvement system under which each approved project was assigned to a responsible official who reported monthly on its progress and the percentage of completion attained. At all times there were from three hundred to four hundred major projects going on, covering a range of topics such as computerizing patent searches, reducing the time for examination and issuance of patents, examining the barriers to international transfers of technology, establishing a presidential "E" award for outstanding performance in exporting, establishing a new maritime program, developing an understanding of air-sea weather interaction in the tropics, analyzing growth and trends in the various industries, creating additional franchise opportunities for minorities, phasing out obsolete ships in the National Defense Reserve fleet, and surveying the U.S. position in the commuter airliner market.

Among the innovations we initiated or pursued aggressively were:

• Major improvements in accounting and budget controls, and better financial reporting. With my prodding and encouragement, Assistant Secretary Larry Jobe saw to it that Commerce became the first department in the entire government to have its complete accounting system qualify for approval by the comptroller general.

• A vigorous endorsement of the metric system. In response to a 1968 law of the Congress requesting a study to develop answers to numerous questions regarding metrication, our National Bureau of Standards completed a 188-page report in 1971 on a three-year study of the system, concluding that the United States should get in step with the rest of the world by adopting metric measurements. By then, only Burma, Brunei, Liberia, and Yemen remained with the United States on nonmetric measurements. I reviewed the conclusions in this report and fully endorsed them in a public statement proposing that Congress adopt a target period of ten years for the United States to be "predominantly, but not exclusively" metric. Regrettably, it was one the Congress was unwilling to make. Under pressure from industries reluctant to bear the cost of change and from citizen groups fearful of confusion, it legisla ted weakly, leaving the whole matter to voluntary action. The predictable result was that little was accomplished in the ten years, leaving the United States still in the laggard company of Burma (now Myanmar) and the other three small countries. In 1991 a new drive to complete the job was initiated by the Bush administration.

• A strong push for the proposition of a two-step minimum wage, the first of which would be lower by perhaps 25 percent and would apply to teenagers for a limited period of about two years. The differential would compensate business owners for the costs of training and breaking in such youngsters. The program would take them off the streets and out of crime and drugs at a formative age, and the long-term social and financial benefits to the country would be enormous. To my great disappointment, organized labor resisted the plan on the main ground that it would force the early retirement of an equal number of older persons. Even if that were to be the case, which I doubted, the net gain to the nation would have been very substantial in view of the horrible costs in money and agony of misdirected teenage lives.

• Strong sponsorship beginning in 1970 of the idea of incentives to American business for exports. To encourage business to work more intently for foreign sales, thereby using more labor at home, I enlisted the support of Treasury Secretary Kennedy and his staff in developing a tax break for profits made on export shipments. As a result, the Congress enacted a provision for partial tax relief on export profits reinvested in building more foreign sales, through the mechanism of a Domestic International Sales Corporation (DISC). This move was necessary to allow American exporters to compete in foreign markets with exporters from other countries who all had the advantage of tax credits or other government subsidies. Most notable of these are the border taxes of the principal European countries. Although under constant criticism as a "handout" to business, DISC seemed to have served its purpose well, which means that it did benefit employers and employees in this country. Companies using DISC were able to reduce their export prices to meet competition and still maintain adequate margins. To the extent that DISC aided them in meeting competition, they were able to avoid the building of plants overseas, thereby holding and enlarging employment in the United States.

Several years after my departure from Commerce in 1972, DISC was determined by Congress as being too much of a good thing for business. It was repealed.

• A continuing effort to end our government's controls on American investments overseas. This Johnson administration restriction was detrimental to efforts of our companies to expand in foreign markets, and was contrary to the traditional economic belief in the free flow of capital among nations. I managed to get some relaxation in the controls each year, but complete abandonment of them was resisted by Treasury and the Federal Reserve Board because the freer outward flow of money would have worsened our balance of payments position. The controls were finally removed about a year after I left office.

• A deliberate effort to develop more trade with the Eastern European countries. In Yugoslavia I initiated steps to open several long-closed doors for American imports and exports. In Poland I was tendered a shopping list of $350 million in machines and other products that would be bought if normal export credit terms were available. I recommended to the president that these countries be given access to Export-Import bank credits and nondiscriminatory tariffs. They were eventually granted and the commerce ministers paid return visits.

• The creation of a National Commission on Minerals Policy to study long-range projections of our requirements for and the availabilities of industrial raw materials. The Paley Commission in 1952 had studied and reported on this subject, but changing conditions since then mandated that it be brought up to date. After some months, I secured the approval of Interior and the White House, and announced at the American Mining Congress in the fall of 1970 that a new commission would be created by the president. The United States Congress, however, preferred that the commission be created under its aegis, and that was done with administration concurrence. I served as a member of the commission until I retired from Commerce. Its report was finally issued in 1973.

• The termination of the whaling industry in the United States. When Commerce acquired from Interior the responsibilities for marine resources, I had to deal with a longtime program for the licensing of American ships to harvest whales. This industry, which in the early days of the nation provided fuel, food, and such miscellany as corset stays and baleen, had dwindled through the years to where only one American company remained in the business and they were down to one ship. Many species of whales were endangered and the total population was a tiny fraction of the number that once roamed the seas. The Russians and the Japanese were still harvesting heavily under quotas allowed by the International Whaling Commission. Considering all the circumstances, as an act of conservation and as a moral lead to other countries still killing whales, I announced that no licenses would be issued to an American whaler by the United States government after 1970. That closed this long page of history. (Since then quotas on some other countries to take whales have been significantly reduced.)

• A disposition of the emotion-charged issue of the annual harvesting of seals in the Pribilof Islands. The United States had been in the seal business since it acquired Alaska and the Pribilofs from Russia in 1867. While the seal population had varied considerably in the subsequent years, after about 1921 it had been stabilized by a system of controlled harvesting. As a protection against overkilling offshore by nearby countries, the United States had entered into an international agreement with Canada and the Soviet Union to divide each year's crop. Ecology groups had regularly criticized this operation on the grounds that the killing by clubbing was brutal and that the harvesting was so heavy as to risk the survival of the species. In a calculated and dishonest way, the censure was often tied to stories and pictures of the killing of white-furred baby harp seals in the Canadian Arctic, which had nothing to do with us.

In order to resolve this matter, I met in the Pribilofs in July 1971 with a group of six veterinarians selected by the American Veterinary Medicine Society to study alternative methods of killing. They concluded after a thorough study that the clubbing method was the most humane possible, preferable to any other available. They also established that no baby seals were being killed; only males in the four- to five-year-old bracket, who lived apart from the family groups, were being taken. They confirmed that the annual harvest was limited to a total that would not deplete the population, which had been rebuilt to an ecologically optimum number of around 1,300,000 over a period of years and was being held at that level. These findings, when published, destroyed the arguments of the critics and materially diminished the attacks on our policy.

• A practice of inviting heads of state of other countries visiting Washington to meet with selected American businessmen at lunch or dinner to discuss mutual interests. Many apparently imposing misunderstandings were ironed out quickly in these top-level face-to-face talks.

• A study of the cost of crime against business. This was the first attempt ever made to show how much consumer prices have to carry the costs of shoplifting, retail employee theft, illegal use of credit cards, cargo thievery and hijacking, arson, embezzlement, and other criminal acts. The report of this analysis, issued in February 1972, showed an annual loss of $15.7 billion from these crimes.

• A pioneering study of the cost of labor featherbedding in the United States. Because of the delicate nature of this term to organized labor, and the problems of definition, these costs were hard to pin down. Estimations were made by Commerce researchers from the best available data, however, and summarized in a report initially prepared for the president's National Commission on Productivity. The Department of Labor challenged its premises and its conclusions, and because of that the report never surfaced.

• A study of multinational corporations and their contributions to or detractions from the welfare of other nations. Always a target for attack because they are the ultimate in big business, these companies have meager means of defense to random charges of profiteering, overdomination of markets, and other allegations. There was not much accumulated factual information to go on, and I directed that studies be initiated to pull together the best possible data as to volume of investments, return on investments, taxes paid, jobs created, and other factors upon which government and the public, here and abroad, could make judgments. The work was under way and only partially completed when I retired from the department, but a first-stage report was released on February 11, 1972.

• The naming of an ombudsman, with the responsibility of giving a guiding hand to any businessman needing direction or an answer to a question in Washington. Under Tom Drumm, an old-timer in Commerce, the office handled thousands of requests a year for legitimate assistance from government agencies for people who would not otherwise know where to go. That function served with considerable satisfaction to users for several years, but eventually lost out to budget restraints.

• An increase in identity of the department by requiring the use of a common insignia and a common format in the publications of its constituent units, and by merging the subordinate offices of Commerce in the various cities. Previously four different units of Commerce in a single city might have been housed in four different locations. This is something that would take many years as opportunities arose.

This list is only a small account of the myriad of subjects with which we contended, considering the wide range of the department's responsibilities. It does, however, give an inkling of their scope and our persistent effort to break new ground.

One innovation I undertook with high expectations was getting top men in American business to sit down together and address the basic problems of the environment and consumerism. I believed that business in the main did not want to ignore these issues but was handicapped in dealing with them to the best public advantage because it did not have suitable ways of providing organized input into government decisions, or of joining together to work out coordinated plans and codes of conduct. What was needed were positive-action programs that would dispel some of the erroneous impressions that business did not care a hoot about the consumer or the environment.

As a result of our earlier discussions concerning Commerce during the campaign, Nixon had mentioned in his public introduc-tion of me as his designee for secretary that I had exciting plans for mobilizing business to solve national problems. Furthermore, I had told the Joint Economic Committee of the Congress a month after I took office that "I believe it is possible in many instances to induce American business, in its own self-interest, to contribute time, money, and skills to the redressing of society's imbalances. That will be a major objective." It was a worthy cause. Consumerism and the environment were issues crying to be met rationally and constructively.

My convictions about the rights of consumers were outlined in several speeches. I insisted that the consumers are entitled to full value for their money, that they have the right to expect merchandise to have the quality and characteristics it is represented to have, that warranties and guarantees should mean what they say (and say it clearly), and that consumers should be able to presume the safety of what they buy.

I knew well from my own background that it was not correct to say that business had no real interest in giving full value and service to the consumer, since it is only by repeatedly satisfying its customers that a business survives.

Businessmen generally want to be around to sell to their customers again and again, and that can happen only if they satisfy them in value and service. The biased professional critics who see nothing good in American business are blind to that reality. They would much more deserve credibility if they acknowledged that integrity does prevail generally and shifted their targets to the mischievous and dishonest few. If they did, they would be on a common wavelength with the 99 percent of legitimate businesspeople who suffer from the wrongs done by that 1 percent, and business in general would be truly and properly respected.

The second major aspect of the public attitude toward business is inherent in the problem of air, water, and land pollution. In response to a wave of national emotion, the Congress had passed laws that imposed requirements beyond the technical competence of industry. Business was being pulled and pushed by conflicts between federal and state regulations and regulatory authorities. A company doing its best to reduce effluents in one part of the country could be hammered for inadequate performance in another. Regulations were often issued on the basis of meager knowledge, then amended and sometimes withdrawn as new facts were established. Detergent-makers, for example, were told to reduce and promptly drop phosphates as an ingredient in their product in favor of another component; then, after investing hundreds of millions of dollars in plants to make the new component, they were prevented from using them because new test results questioned the new ingredient's safety. The clamor for instant action was creating chaos. Plants were being forced to close in communities where there was no other employment, thus creating new cadres of unemployed. There was little recognition of the logic of balancing environmental benefits against economic costs and vice versa.*

Despite all this, my impression was that business was attempting to adjust its plans and its budgets to meet the new demands. All it wanted was some order of priorities out of the mess of laws and directives. I felt business could contribute much to solutions of the problems if it were allowed to organize and marshal its top brains to present and prove out ideas, and if it were permitted a greater input of data before decisions were made. I was confident that business would voluntarily work to solve many of the environmental problems if allowed to pursue its own methods of reaching specific objectives that were achievable. In other words, given a chance to do so, business could and would play a major voluntary role in improving the environment, while taking some of the burden off the government.

The businessmen who had wanted to work together for market discipline, environmental improvement, and public credibility were

---

*On one occasion I gave a talk entitled "Wait a Minute," suggesting that we were sweeping ahead too rapidly in environmental judgments, with meager knowledge, at high cost and in a way that invited expensive mistakes and frequent changes in direction. I proposed that a more orderly approach would get the job done more smoothly and at less cost and upset to the economy, and made suggestions to that end. The *Reader's Digest* reprinted a condensed version. Ralph Nader, the self-anointed critic of American business, self-appointed monitor of the nation's conscience, and self-publicized savior of the American environment, demanded that I resign.

inhibited from doing so by their legal advisors, who feared antitrust charges for the mere act of meeting. The government, however, could exempt them from that risk by organizing them, putting the problems before them, and asking for solutions. I did this by getting the president to form a National Industrial Pollution Control Council and a National Business Council on Consumer Affairs, each made up wholly of chief executive officers of important corporations, from General Motors down. NIPCC had 250 executives on its council and thirty subcouncils, and NBCCA had over 150, all carefully chosen to represent the whole gamut of business and industry. They were charged with a responsibility to address themselves to these public concerns, to consider workable alternatives that business and government together or individually might pursue, to publish their conclusions, and to follow them to provable results. NIPCC subcouncils met often, under the chairmanship of Bert Cross of 3M Company and exceptional staff direction and prodding from Walter Hamilton of Commerce; they produced workable conclusions and reports on such matters as acid mine drainage, air pollution by sulfur oxides, animal wastes, deep ocean dumping, detergents, exhaust emissions, junk car disposal, glass containers, mercury, paper, plastics, industrial wastewater, wood products, and many other technical subjects.

Each paper was a reasoned result of hundreds of hours of discussion and deliberation by top executives, backed by their own technical experts. Each presented a balanced analysis of the problem, the stage of progress in meeting it, and the possible means of solution. Each paper identified how environmental pollution was manifest in the production processes, in products, and in disposal of by-products and containers. Each contained a catalog of what industry had done, was doing, and would do to improve the environment. Each described the state of the art in pollution control and the breakthroughs still required to resolve identifiable barriers. None was written to express negative bias or self-serving conclusions; they were all addressed to finding ways in which industry, government, and the public could work together to clean up the environment. The council itself also issued periodic reports of pollution-control accomplishments, one type listing cases of antipollution actions completed by business, and one enumerating cleanup actions in progress and future commitments to that end.

NBCCA groups headed by Robert E. Brooker of Marcor, Inc. and Donald S. Perkins of Jewel Companies Inc., and effectively staffed by Bill Lee and Paul O'Day of Commerce, concerned themselves with meeting problems of the consumer by stimulation of voluntary, responsible corporate action. This council was asked to identify and examine current and potential concerns of consumers and evaluate alternative solutions. It also was requested to encourage action by the business community to redress legitimate consumer dissatisfactions and to cooperate with federal, state, and local agencies in evolving and effecting consumer affairs policies. Federal government agencies with consumer interests and responsibilities participated in the meetings. Subcouncils were created on packaging and labeling, advertising and promotion, warranties and guarantees, credit and terms of sale, performance and service, product safety, and complaints and remedies. Each of the subcouncils worked diligently to identify current issues and to develop solutions. They produced reports on all these topics, including recommended codes of conduct.

I attended some of the meetings of these councils and subcouncils. There was, in my mind, no doubt of the sincerity and directness with which the participants viewed these sessions and their reports as ways by which business could earn its way back to respectable public opinion by showing what it was willing to do and could do if it were allowed to work together. Had the process been permitted to continue for a period of years with the same interest and enthusiasm demonstrated in the time the councils existed, the benefits to society would have been immeasurable. Instead of being put in the position of merely reacting to pressures, the business community had volunteered to address the pollution and consumer problems in good faith and with determination. It was a unique dedication to the public interest, but it was brought to an end by unreasoning outside forces.

What happened? Almost immediately after the two councils were formed, so-called public-interest groups antagonistic to business disparaged them as "putting the goat in charge of the cabbage patch" or "putting the fox in charge of the chicken coop." Senator Lee Metcalf of Montana said it was "sending the rabbit to fetch the lettuce." All this was a knee-jerk reaction that displayed an obvious unwillingness to believe any good motivation on the part of business by those who had dedicated themselves to attacking the corporate world, rightly or wrongly. I almost wept at the asininity of the rebuttals by these critics every time a sincere proposition was offered by one of the Councils, and I resented the obvious "attack force" implications of the deprecatory allegations that were their only responses to worthwhile proposals. The climax came when these critical groups insisted on participating in the meetings. I refused to allow this, certain that it was designed not to be helpful but to harass and impede. Senator Metcalf echoed the demand by alleging that "not one member of the council represents conservation groups, consumers, universities, or other public-interest groups." That was exactly correct for a purposeful reason. I felt that the conclusions of the business deliberations should be allowed to stand or fall on their own merits, without interference. It was the conclusions that had to be judged, not the process of argument or reasoning by which they were reached, and at the time and place of those judgments the other groups would have their say. These distrusting, narrow-minded opponents, sad to say, forced the issue in Congress and got a law passed making all meetings of government advisory groups open to the public. They also managed to get the small amount of staff expense for these Councils removed from the federal budget by the Congress. It was the death knell of constructive participation in solving public problems by those most knowledgeable, all because of overweening suspicions by self-named public guardians that no one but themselves could be trusted. Their victory was a severe loss to the common good.

Early in 1969 the president appointed a Cabinet committee to study issues that had arisen in connection with controls over oil imports. For some years, our government had in effect a system of quotas to limit imports of oil and refinery products. They were designed to prevent undue price competition to American producers and to ensure the continuation of a domestic industry and the constant search for new reserves. Secretary of Labor Shultz was chairman of the seven-man committee, of which I was a member. The staff collected by him conducted extensive research over a period of almost a year, digging into our domestic reserve data, foreign reserves, alternative fuels, market risks, possible actions to protect the country from a cutoff of outside supplies, and many other facets of the problem. It was a thorough study that produced a large mass of pertinent information.

By a vote of 5 to 2, with Interior Secretary Walter Hickel joining me in dissent (supported by Federal Power Commission chairman John Nassikas), the committee recommended that the quotas be phased out and that a tariff be imposed at a varying level that would hold down the price of domestic oil to three dollars or less while raising a half-billion dollars in revenue. Our disagreement was so sharp that Hickel, Nassikas, and I joined in a "separate report" pointing out the unworkability of the kind of moving tariff that would be required in markets that were constantly changing, and insisting on the retention of the quota system with some refinements. We questioned the premise of the study in basing its conclusions on projections to 1980 when it was evident that declining domestic production and increasing demand made 1985 a much more critical date. We challenged as an overstatement the majority's estimate of our ability to increase domestic production. In our dissenting report we contended that a changing tariff would introduce or magnify instability, generate serious international problems, introduce inequities greater than those of the quota system, eliminate the pass-through of lower prices to the consumer, and seriously impair the position of small independent refiners. We believed that national security would be jeopardized, American producers would suffer major investment losses, the economies of a number of states would be damaged, and the available supply of natural gas would be reduced and/or its price increased. These conditions would put the petroleum industry continuously at the mercy of government price controls, a policy incompatible with free enterprise. Finally, we felt that the majority understated the probabilities, severity, and consequences of oil supply interruptions in the United States.

The reports were followed by heated controversy in Washington. The Congress became aroused, and the House Ways and Means Committee voted 17 to 7 to freeze the quota system into law. Faced with a tough choice, the president appointed an Oil Policy Committee early in 1970 chaired by George C. Lincoln, head of the Office of Emergency Preparedness, to monitor the quota system until a conclusion was reached on what to do next. A few months later, upon Lincoln's recommendation, Nixon gave the tariff plan a quiet burial.*

Only a few years later, the United States had to face an Arab boycott, an increase of 500 percent or more in the price of imported oil, and the expenditure of many billions of dollars a year to devise alternative means of ensuring that the nation's energy requirements would be met. Under such conditions, neither the tariff plan nor the quota system could have survived, and the reports became academic.

---

*George Bush, then a congressman from Texas, wrote congratulating me on the courage and judgment of our dissenting report.

The most significant surviving reservation I have about the whole exercise is that the study bared to the world all the long-term strengths, weaknesses, and concerns about our energy requirements, our reserves and projected demands, and our fears of short supplies and possible plans for dealing with such predicaments. While portions of the information may have been publicly available, our putting it together and releasing it for everyone to know may well have invited some of the moves that followed by supplying nations, and perhaps increased their severity. This is the kind of subject that a government ought to deal with in privacy.

It was in the aftermath of the debate on this report and its implications that I became the first member of the Cabinet to endorse the building of the Alaska pipeline. I wrote Secretary Morton of Interior in April 1971 that I found nothing in the environmental impact studies on the project that would override the urgent economic and national security requirements for early availability of the oil on the North Slope, estimated to be recoverable at two million barrels a day. After long delays caused by objectors, it finally went ahead, and the oil it delivered turned out to be a valuable asset for the country, especially in coping with pricing policies of the oil-exporting nations.

An unresolved interagency difference that got bogged down in bureaucratic rivalry and the absence of a White House decision was in the field of foreign commerce. Shortly after entering Commerce, I picked up the pieces of what had been almost a historic conflict of opinion with the State Department as to the conduct of our government's commercial activities in foreign countries. It was an important element in our international trade and investment that the government take an active interest in the commercial relationships with each foreign country. This concerned not only the serious international confrontations like nationalization or confiscation of property, but the day-to-day and year-to-year differences over taxation, trade policy, investment restrictions, and treatment of foreign corporations. It also included helpful actions such as the development of trade leads for American business on the forthcoming construction of major public works like airports and harbors, on the development of natural resources like oil or iron, and on local interest in new manufacturing industries. Such leads, furnished at the earliest stages, could be invaluable information to American companies and could provide very important avenues for investment, sales, jobs, and profits. Other countries, such as Japan, Canada, Britain, and Germany, had developed superior systems of collecting and disseminating such data. According to businessmen with whom I talked, the United States was very far behind.

While the basic responsibility for overseas commercial matters was theoretically with our ambassadors, many of whom had little practical experience in the subject, in reality it was performed by the commercial attaché in each embassy. About twenty years earlier the control of the commercial attachés had been transferred from Commerce to State, and Commerce had been unsuccessful in several attempts to get them back. This was a battle that I hesitated to undertake, as I saw no profit in empire building. The national stake lay in upgrading the function and the service, not in who ran it. The advisability of upgrading it was bolstered by complaints I had received from many American businessmen about the poor attitudes and service received from our embassies. A number even said that when they were in a foreign country to resolve a business matter or to get information they went to the Canadian or British embassy for real help. Be that as it may, the problem was that the commercial attaché, about four echelons below the ambassador, was too far down the totem pole to have access to high-level officials in the local government or have any influence with them. My point was that if the world is going to live in a generation or more of peace, the competition between the nations will be on the economic and commercial front, and in this respect our foreign service was in no way directed or geared to compete with the other great trading nations. We needed to plan for an era of "economic diplomacy."

The British had found a way to meet their goal of maximum effective commercial services as the result of a report in the late 1960s of their Duncan Commission, which had studied the question for several years. The fundamental conclusion was that the "commercial work is the most urgent task of (British) overseas representatives," and "should absorb more of the Foreign Service resources than any other function." Business experience would be an important element in the selection of ambassadors, and traditional "striped-pants" diplomacy would be secondary to representing the interests of trade. The United States was well behind the parade, and in my opinion was living in a nineteenth-century concept of political representation and espionage.

On September 8, 1970, I wrote Secretary of State Rogers offering a fourteen-point plan to settle the argument. It was not a grab for power but a carefully reasoned proposal to help business meet the competition of other countries in overseas commerce, by matching our embassy support to theirs.

Despite continuing discussions between Rogers and me and other meetings between lower-level officials of the two departments, the plan was ultimately rejected by State. There was obvioiusly no basis on which it was willing to give up the territory.

Time went on. I made several attempts, personally and through then Under Secretary Lynn, to get the subject off dead center but never succeeded. More than a year later, on November 22, 1972, Rogers finally responded to my letter in a very friendly manner but without agreement on the heart of the matter. He would not move without his staff's approval and clearly his staff resented any intrusion by Commerce into its domain. In typical bureaucratic manner, State suggested more study, research, and consultation; thereby it won by a stalemate, and nothing of real significance had been done by the time I resigned. Still later in 1972, a study team headed by former ambassador John Pritzlaff reviewed specifically the personnel and functioning of the commercial staff in European embassies and came up with a list of recommendations quite similar in scope to mine.

Not until 1980, however, was the major issue resolved. President Carter transferred the commercial attachés from the State Department to the Department of Commerce. Although I was curious to learn what magic he used, I never did find out.

A favorable media account can add much to the satisfaction of completing a difficult job, and can cancel much of the memory of its difficulties, as I learned in 1975 from an unexpected source. It was quite some time after my departure from Commerce when I found a media evaluation of my services in that position that I consider both significant and satisfactory. *The New York Times*, occasionally one of my severest critics, in a news analysis on the Commerce Department, gracefully said three years after my departure:

> Within the Department, the Secretary most talked about is Maurice H. Stans, who served in the first Nixon administration. Commerce traditionally has been an institution without political clout. . . . It mattered under Secretary Stans. Mr. Stans gave the department much more influence at the White House than anyone could remember, and morale perked up. . . . Under [his successors] the department's traditional lassitude took over.

# CHAPTER FOURTEEN

# Life in the Nixon Cabinet

Looking back, I think it was a major miracle that so many things went right and so few went wrong while I served as secretary of commerce; I'm grateful that my health and state of mind survived such a tension-filled and almost overwhelming responsibility. Every one of my Cabinet colleagues felt the same pressures, and some of them found the strain too much. Living with bureaucracy is not simple.

Rivalries between government departments sometimes waste an unreasonable amount of time of Cabinet officials. A typical example occurred during preparation for an international meeting on patents, in 1971, over who should head the United States delegation. A State Department bureaucrat insisted that, this being an international affair, the delegates should be headed by an assistant secretary of state. The commissioner of patents, within the Department of Commerce, contended that other nations regularly entrusted their delegations to their chief patent official and that we should do the same, making him the spokesman for our group. After the debate had gone on for some weeks within the organizations, with the two warring factions heatedly unwilling to yield, Secretary Rogers and I had to get into the matter and come up with the only decision possible: to designate the two as cochairmen, with one speaking on diplomatic understandings and the other on patent arrangements and procedures. At that, it was considered a victory by the Commerce team, because it was the first time State had ever yielded to a principle of equality with Commerce in this field.

The relations between Commerce and the White House during my years were pleasant and satisfactory, though not always as fruitful as I wanted them to be. Those with most frequent need of such contact, besides myself, were the successive under secretaries, Siciliano and Lynn, and the successive general counsels, Lynn and Letson. Every day one or more of us was in communication with the White House at its staff level on one matter or another, ranging from legislation to patronage, to public relations, politics, and matters overlapping with other departments. Few of these subjects needed the attention of the president; if one did, we could always trust the White House staff to get Commerce's views to him before he took action.

Once, on a bill in Congress involving so-called failing newspapers, which would have permitted two papers in a city to combine the use of plant and delivery facilities if the resulting savings in expense were necessary to keep them both in business, I found myself in a directly opposite position from Richard McLaren, the head of the antitrust division of the Department of Justice. I wanted to see such mergers permitted; he wanted them prohibited. It was necessary to get an immediate presidential ruling, because McLaren had publicly committed himself, and his position was assumed by Congress to be that of the administration. Through a telephone call to John Ehrlichman, who was knowledgeable on the subject, I got an immediate response from the president that sustained my view and killed the opposition. The bill passed readily. This procedure saved time all around.

The White House staff had a well-known hierarchy, which I believe is best described as being in concentric circles. The inner-inner orbit was viewed as consisting of H. R. Haldeman, John Ehrlichman, Charles Colson, and Henry Kissinger, all of whom had instant access to the president, as did Attorney General John Mitchell.* Bob Haldeman was the housekeeper, with him and his staff arranging the president's meetings, travel, and necessities of office, and looking after the rest of the White House internal management. I considered

*From time to time Nixon named individuals as counselors to the president, most notably Arthur Burns (who later moved to the chair of the Federal Reserve Board), Donald Rumsfeld (previously head of the Office of Economic Opportunity [OEO] who later became secretary of defense), and Robert Finch (previously secretary of HEW). These men appeared to have direct links with the president, working on matters directly assigned by him, but did not seem to be fully integrated into the White House power center.

him exceptionally capable, a good manager of time, and able to carry an astounding workload of detail. His working pace was very much like that of Sherman Adams under Eisenhower, quick to understand, quick to agree or disagree, and quick to act, all without flourishes and almost invariably in harmony with the will of the president.

Most of Commerce's dealings were with John Ehrlichman, a bright, incisive lawyer who had the faculty of demonstrating patience even when he was sorely pressed. As director of the Domestic Council and as the White House lawman, he found us at his doorstep frequently to present our cases, most commonly on proposed legislation or regulations of other agencies with which we had an unresolved conflict, less often on proposals of our own.

Ehrlichman was congenial, had time for byplay, was perceptive of nuances, and was eminently fair in his judgments, even though we sometimes thought he decided the wrong way. We had infrequent dealings with Ronald Ziegler (the president's press secretary) or Colson. Our contacts with Kissinger were most frequent during the textile negotiations, but I cleared all of my foreign travels with him and got his suggestions on conduct. In the case of my visit to the USSR, his remarkably painstaking but progressive development of a working relationship with the Soviets set the stage for a warm welcome and for the constructive results that followed.

In the outer-inner orbit, as we saw it, were Peter Flanigan, Herb Klein, Len Garment, Ron Ziegler, and later Ken Cole. Our public relations people took advice from Klein, but we had little in the way of business with Garment except for his supporting interest in minority enterprise. Flanigan was a main point of association; most matters affecting the business community, business legislation or regulation, and sometimes patronage, were worked out with him. He called frequently for suggestions as to persons qualified for positions on commissions or committees or to fill vacancies in independent agencies. Sometimes, but only sometimes, he adopted our recommendations and sent them to the president; most often he did not. To assure a free flow of information as to what was desired and what was going on, we eventually set up a regular Wednesday breakfast meeting in the White House mess, attended by the two of us and several key members of our staffs, to go over an ever-changing agenda.

The inner-outer circle was comprised of all the members of the Cabinet except Mitchell, who was inner-inner. George Shultz worked himself into the inner-inner orbit after a time and so did

John Connally. The rest of us were generally at arm's length, envious but not resentful at the closeness of these few to the throne. I had excellent relations with all members of the Cabinet, based on mutual respect and team spirit, and except for one or two frustrating moments, there were no occasions of less than complete smoothness and mutuality.

I did originate some topics with the president by written memos when I thought that procedure was most suitable. For example, on July 1, 1970, I wrote to him complaining that fourteen members of his Cabinet had flown in a single helicopter to a meeting at Camp David; I felt that it was in his interest and in the interest of the nation that a risk of losing an entire administration in one accident be avoided. I received no direct reply but I did not observe such a grouping again.

On July 21, 1969, I proposed in a memo that he schedule a private meeting with each member of his Cabinet at regular intervals. At that point I was not sure what arrangements he wanted us to use for periodic reviews of our departments, our problems, and our projects under way. I learned later that Hickel had sent him a similar memo at about the same time. When I did not get an answer I worked out my own schedule with him to meet for a broad review of pending matters every three or four months, with only a few urgent meetings in between, and that worked well.

The public scrutiny to which a government official is subjected can give him some moments of embarrassment and requires a constant alertness to avoid more of them. Within the first year of my term, as part of a thorough modernization of the Commerce building, a private kitchen and dining room were installed across the hall from my office. This brought down on me the wrath and condemnation of columnist Jack Anderson, even though he acknowledged that the improvements had been contracted for by my predecessor. Before this story appeared I had arranged for the installation of a sauna and exercise room for use of the department's executives; although I felt the cost of $2,000 could be justified as a legitimate government expense, I had paid for the installation with my own check. It was fortunate that I had or I would have had to run Anderson's gauntlet again.

One of the embarrassments in office was the custom of foreign government officials presenting generous gifts. United States rules prevented its government officers from accepting anything given by a foreign nation that had a value in excess of fifty dollars. To refuse gifts obviously could offend a well-intended foreigner who was merely following his country's custom. The Saudi Arabians were the most notorious givers of valuable gifts, including diamond-studded jewelry and similar items. I did not receive any such pieces, but did get two gifts that clearly exceeded the limit.

In June 1970, Kathleen and I were invited, along with a dozen other government men and their wives, to a dinner given by the Japanese ambassador in honor of a visiting Japanese business executive. Several weeks after the pleasant affair, each of the wives received a gift of a pearl necklace from the honored guest's wife. I took one look at Kathleen's and called a conference. Whether or not the gifts had been given with improper motives, it was obvious that they exceeded the limit. Kathleen's string of pearls was appraised at $2,600 by our jeweler, the others at somewhat less. Diplomatic steps had to be taken, both with the donor and the recipients.

I checked with officials of the State Department, who were concerned about embarrassing the donor if the gifts were returned. However, it was our joint conclusion that there was no other proper course. Some of the wives were far from happy at giving up their lovely necklaces, but we collected the pearls right away and I made a special trip to the ambassador to ask him to explain to the benefactor that no offense was intended by the return of the jewelry. The custom of gift giving is common in Japan.

As I traveled to other countries and met government officials, I fell into the practice of exchanging gifts, but to discourage items of high value, I made the first move by presenting tokens such as presidential medals or Department of Commerce medals, or souvenirs of nominal worth, to those I called on. As a result, while I received many gifts in my travels, most were of relatively small value. Nevertheless, I was delighted to get them, as pleasant mementos of these experiences. In 1971, however, at the end of my visit to the Soviet Union I was presented with a 12-gauge over-and-under Baikal shotgun, hand-engraved and with gold and silver inlays. Its value was at least $1,000 and the circumstances were such that I did not feel I could smoothly refuse it. To meet the law, I turned it over to the State Department, who gave it to the Minnesota Historical Society, who in turn gave it to the Scott County Historical Society for its museum. Here it could someday be displayed as part of my collection of memorabilia from public office. This was done, but I continued to regret not being able to use the attractive weapon on the big honkers in Chesapeake Bay.

One day in Chicago in 1971 I found out how transient fame is. Kathleen and I were staying at a North Side hotel and decided one Sunday morning to walk a few blocks to a service of the Church of Religious Science. The preacher's subject had to do with respect for authority, and he was eloquent. By way of illustration, he pointed out the importance of believing that our public officials were qualified and dedicated to doing their best, and deplored some unfair criticisms he had just read and heard about the president of the United States. I was so pleased that I went through the departure line and thanked him. To introduce myself I said I was a member of President Nixon's Cabinet.

"What department do you head?" he asked.

"Commerce," I replied.

"Oh, Mr. Weeks!" he exclaimed. It was such a blow that I didn't even attempt to correct him. Weeks had preceded me by twenty years.

I was spared one unexpected cost that precedent might have exacted. At a Cabinet meeting, the president announced that he thought it was time to replace the worn Cabinet table and chairs with some that would be more modern and attractive. Looking directly at me, he then said, "There is a plate on this table that says it came as a gift to the White House from Jesse Jones when he was secretary of commerce. Perhaps the present secretary would like to carry on the tradition." I gulped but took the bait and said I would. However, when I pursued the subject a few weeks later I got word from Haldeman that the president had decided to pay for the new furniture himself.

One jarring note came along in 1971, when Senator Vance Hartke of Indiana demanded an investigation of whether I had been in a conflict of interest position in June 1970 during the government's consideration of ways to save the Penn-Central Railroad from bankruptcy. The charge was that as secretary of commerce I had taken part in negotiations for a government loan to keep the company out of bankruptcy at a time when I held some stock in a subsidiary. There were immediate enlargements of this theme in news stories and editorials while I held off answering for several days to search my records to gather precise data as to the facts and publish them in a press release, following which the whole case evaporated. In its urgent desire to see that the full story came forth, the White House had provided me with the assistance of John Dean, head of the president's legal staff. I was able to demonstrate that my only participation in the loan matter had consisted of a brief initial meeting with some of the company's bankers in the office of the secretary of the Treasury, and another of government agency officials in the White House, and that upon learning of the possibility of government financing I had disclosed my meager holding of stock in the subsidiary and disqualified myself from any further meetings.

In July 1971 another frustrating incident occurred. I stopped over in Minneapolis at the annual meeting of the National Association for the Advancement of Colored People, for the purpose of presenting a plaque in appreciation of its organized support and help in connection with the 1970 national census. It seemed an appropriate time to add a few words about our work in the field of minority enterprise, but when I said in opening, "No one before President Nixon had really tackled the fundamental question of how to create more opportunities in business for minorities," I was overwhelmed with a roar of boos and catcalls. The name of Nixon was anathema. I tried two or three other approaches, with the same results, and finally subsided in frustration. Senator Hubert Humphrey, who was on the speakers' dais at the same time, was clearly amused at my discomfiture but was gentleman enough not to mention it in his own speech. I came away with my first realization of how deep the feelings of resentment against Nixon ran among blacks and how hard it would be to erase them, no matter how well we performed. At that stage, they did not want to believe.

There are some moments of physical danger, too, in being a Cabinet officer. While that is certainly more likely to be true for such persons as the secretary of state, the secretary of defense, or perhaps the attorney general, I found some occasions when even a secretary of commerce should be fearful. There were several telephone or mail threats on my life, all of which checked out to be from harmless fanatics. There was one burglary of my office, when a few keepsakes were stolen; after it was discovered the next morning, I was barred from entering for half a day by the FBI, who checked everything out fully to see that no bomb had been planted. In Rio de Janeiro, visiting only a few months after the kidnapping of our ambassador there, I found that everything and everyone was under close scrutiny; I was assigned seven bodyguards in three cars to look after me whenever I left the building, even during a brief shopping trip to get a gift to bring home to Kathleen. In Montevideo, Uruguay, I was given special protection by the local police for fear of a possible attack or kidnapping by the militant antigovernment Tupemaros. On my first trip to Japan I was greeted at the airport in Tokyo by a crowd of pro-textile demonstrators bearing unfriendly signs and placards, but the police had erected barriers keeping them fifty yards away from my line of exit and I felt secure. Much more serious, in retrospect, was the experience in Athens in 1971, already related, when it was learned by authorities that a revolutionary party intended to ambush and bomb the yacht on which my party was returning from a one-day excursion to a nearby island.

In New York one day in 1970, I was engaged in the taping of a one-hour television interview with William F. Buckley before an audience of about a hundred young students. The proceedings went well for nearly thirty minutes, when he was interrupted by a messenger with a note saying that there was a bomb planted in the studio. Buckley and I were both prepared to doubt the threat and go ahead, but when we considered our responsibility for all the young people in the studio and to Kathleen sitting in the control room, it was too much risk to assume. We agreed to vacate and endured a two-hour delay while the premises were searched, spending the time at Sardi's over coffee. When we were finally allowed to return and resume where we left off, neither of us found it easy to get back in stride. I never did learn whether the threateners were aiming at me or at Buckley.

The frequent hijacking of airplanes during this period was troublesome. It was often necessary for Cabinet members to travel around the country on official business, visiting offices, making speeches, and attending ceremonies. The president said in a meeting one day that he did not relish the idea of having to ransom one of his Cabinet officers from Castro in Cuba and suggested we avoid commercial planes on our trips by using government aircraft. I did so for a while, but the billed price by the military of such charters to my department was so high that I took the chance of going back to the regular airlines at more reasonable prices. No trip thereafter was without some apprehension.

Though the responsibilities and risks are many, there are numerous gratifying consequences of being the secretary of a Cabinet department. As secretary of commerce, I had a much more active part in Washington social life than as budget director, especially because of the relationships with foreign countries. This put us in line for many dinner invitations to foreign embassies, almost all of which were delightful and many of which presented tasteful selections of their national dishes. In turn, we entertained many visitors from other countries, mainly ministers of commerce.

The president generously made available to his Cabinet members the use of some of his special facilities when he was not occupying them. I was able to charter his yacht, *Sequoia,* on the Potomac for evening cruises with important guests, or for staff discussions in relaxed circumstances. Camp David was also accessible from time to time, and I held a number of staff meetings there or used it to entertain VIPs.

At the White House, Cabinet officers were invited to all of the president's Sunday church services and to many of the elaborate dinners and concerts for visiting heads of state; generally, the social secretary followed a rotation system, so that other secretaries and I were invited to every third or fourth dinner. Kathleen and I attended fifty or more such affairs. We also had the fairly frequent use of the president's boxes at Kennedy Center for official entertaining. I had the right of access to the executive dining room in the White House mess, at which I could join members of the White House staff I wanted to see or bring official guests. While the price of the meals was low, the main attraction was the instant service, making it possible to eat, do business, and leave in less than half an hour.

We did miss one prestigious social occasion at the White House, to our deep disappointment. We were probably the only couple in the country to decline the invitation to attend the wedding of the Nixons' daughter Tricia to Edward Cox in June 1971. Our reason was that our son Ted was being married on the same day to Diane Richter, in New York City.

Another very valuable perk was the regular use of a chauffeured car with a telephone at any time of the day or night.* I also had a direct White House telephone line in my apartment, and its operators were unbelievably efficient at locating anyone anywhere in the world when official business required it. The other side of this was

---

*A demagogic senator a few years later took after this practice, alleging it was wasteful and inappropriate, and forced Cabinet officials into small cars. This penny-pinching did save a few dollars, but it was demeaning to Cabinet members, and it lost more time than it saved by making impractical the use of traveling time to carry on the office work of reviewing documents and communications. It also forced them into disgracefully embarrassing situations when called upon to entertain and transport visiting foreign counterparts exposed to such niggardly treatment.

that I was always on call, available to the White House and Cabinet colleagues, and the phone rang often.

There were some less frequent privileges, too. Each year the Cabinet sat in the front row at the joint session of the Congress to hear the president's State of the Union message, and I had the distinction six times of being among them. Members of the Cabinet rode in style in the inaugural parade after the president's swearing-in and sat in his reserved stand on the White House lawn to watch the parade. Government helicopters were available for trips to Camp David or nearby government installations, and planes could be had for out-of-town trips where security or mutual convenience was involved. The western White House at San Clemente could be used for meetings on government business when in that part of the country.

These special rewards may seem in the aggregate to represent a more than opulent lifestyle, but they were not that. They were the only means by which a Cabinet officer could handle the requirements of his job. The minutes and hours they saved cut down the time required for many chores, often contributed to needed relaxation, and helped to relieve the excessive burdens of office. Even a White House party or church service gave opportunities for brief exchanges of official business before and after the ceremonies, with associates, the president, members of Congress, or other important guests.

In the Eisenhower term, Kathleen and I had considerably less access to such presidential perquisites, and Kennedy Center was not yet in existence. We did, however, receive occasional invitations to White House dinners and receptions and almost invariably accepted them, enjoying most those given for the heads of state of countries like Nepal or Yugoslavia or Ireland, and one at which Soviet leader Khrushchev was the honored guest. Kathleen also appreciated having regular daily use of the White House swimming pool, originally built for therapeutic use by Franklin D. Roosevelt from pennies contributed by the children of America. Originally set at 86 degrees, it was regularly held at that level, even though Eisenhower and subsequent presidents almost never used the pool. (Nixon later had it boarded over to provide a room for the White House press corps.) We also were permitted to use the *Susie E.*, one of the smaller boats available to the president, for Potomac dinner cruises with Budget Bureau staff, members of Congress, or other government officials.

Kathleen's fondest memory of all the White House events was the night Eisenhower entertained Field Marshall Montgomery of Britain at dinner and a movie showing. As the new director of the budget, I happened to be next ranking guest, since almost all of those present were high military officers who placed lower on the protocol totem pole, so Kathleen sat at the president's left. The protocol office briefed her very carefully in advance, instructing her to be sure not to attempt to talk serious government business or politics. Montgomery was not so well briefed on his side, because he kept leaning over to bring up to Eisenhower topics of current world affairs. Kathleen decided to confine herself to asking the president questions about his interest in art and he, obviously pleased, gave her a long dissertation on each of the paintings in the room. Years later, long after he had left the White House, we were together with the Eisenhowers at their home in Gettysburg for an afternoon visit, and Kathleen recalled the occasion. When he heard about the instructions she had received not to talk about anything serious, Eisenhower slapped his thigh and laughed heartily. "I never gave such directions," he said. "That just goes to show how everyone on the staff decides what's good for the president without even consulting him."

A pleasurable benefit of secretaryship was the opportunity to meet in Washington and around the world with important figures in history: people like emperors Hirohito of Japan and Haile Selassie of Ethiopia; presidents Tito of Yugoslavia, Kenyatta of Kenya, Ceauşescu of Romania, Franco of Spain, and Mobutu of Zaire; prime ministers Wilson of Britain, Trudeau of Canada, Park of Korea, Papadopoulos of Greece, and Adenauer of Germany; the shah of Iran; and the heads of state of many other nations. Of the countries I visited, I missed only presidents de Gaulle of France and Chiang Kai-Shek of the Republic of China. Probably the most impressive event that Kathleen and I ever attended was the White House dinner in 1970 in honor of all the heads of state who had come to the United States for the twenty-fifth anniversary meeting of the United Nations. I don't remember exactly how many were present, but we were able to converse with at least twenty, from the prime minister of Great Britain to the president of Chad. Each of these contacts was a stimulating experience, and each added to my impressions that powerful people can be earnest and humble, that there are many good leaders in government but few geniuses, that political power is fragile and temporary, and that few of the problems besetting heads of state are unique to their own countries. The temporary tenure of political power was dramatically evidenced to

me in the fact that within a decade of my visits, four of the leaders
that I had met died at the hands of adversaries within their government: Haile Selassie, Ceaușescu, Park of Korea, and Somoza of
Nicaragua; the shah of Iran was ousted from office and died in exile,
and Papadopoulos of Greece was routed from his office and jailed
indefinitely in palatial style. What price glory!

Equally entrancing was the opportunity to rub shoulders with the
greats of my era in the United States. Beyond the presidents, these
included such luminaries as Senator Everett Dirksen, the mellifluent
orator who could hold any audience spellbound by the rhythm and
inflections he gave his words; Senator Howard Baker, the brilliant
son-in-law of Dirksen, who followed in his tracks some years later
as Senate majority leader; Gerald Ford, the sometimes bland but
able Republican House leader who moved into the vice presidency
when Spiro Agnew resigned and into the presidency when Nixon
resigned; Frank Sinatra, the unparalleled vocalist and friend of several presidents; Bob Hope, as funny in casual conversation as on
the stage; George Meany, the longtime powerful leader of the AFL-
CIO; Billy Graham, the best-known evangelist of the era; Norman
Vincent Peale, whose sermons were superb lessons in humanity and
logic as well as dogma; Clare Boothe Luce, one of the most accomplished women of her day, author, congresswoman, and ambassador; Hubert Humphrey, the amiable, lovable, political, loquacious
fellow Minnesotan who became vice president but failed to move
up to the next notch he so desperately sought; Foster Dulles, a brilliant analyst and strategist in cold war diplomacy, who served as
Eisenhower's secretary of state; Nelson Rockefeller, a man of
charm and suavity who served New York as a multiterm governor
and in Washington in many capacities up to vice president; Bob
Dole, war hero, senator from Kansas, and Republican leader of the
Senate; Henry Kissinger, whose perceptive reading of world events
made him one of the all-time best practitioners of this discipline;
and the first Senator Harry Byrd, the principled symbol of government economy in his era, who fought a delaying action for decades
to hold down the size of the federal budget, but found victories difficult against the forces of big bureaucracy and big spending. They
were some of the towering figures of the several decades in which I
was in public life.

Finally, there was the stimulation of participating in deliberation
of many national policies. The secretary of commerce was a member
of numerous official active committees, councils, and commissions

dealing with a wide array of problems, some ad hoc and some long-range. These included Cabinet committees on economic policy, environmental quality, the cost of living, oil import policy, domestic affairs, productivity, international economic policy, and many more—each of them dealing conscientiously and at length with pressing or emerging national concerns. Their meetings and discussions could be very demanding of time, certainly in the aggregate. A subcommittee of the House Committee on Government Operations reported in 1970 that the secretary of commerce was a member of forty-eight committees, more than any other member of the Cabinet. Only an impressively high quality of staff work made such a load possible. Every meeting was preceded by a detailed briefing on the subjects to arise and their pros and cons; this was essential because to go unprepared might be to allow an important issue to be lost by default.

Offsetting all those special prerogatives were many definite disadvantages. To avoid possible charges of conflict of interest, I was required to give up control of all of my investments in securities for my term of office; this was done by putting them in a "blind trust" with a New York bank, which had the authority to sell and buy as though it were all its own property, without telling me what was going on. The bank even saw to it that my income tax returns were prepared without my knowledge of their contents except the few figures I supplied as to salary earned and the deductibles I had personally paid. Not until I left office did I learn what had occurred in the meantime. I was distressed at the result, but helpless.

Most disconcerting of all were the demands on time. There were always at least four ways to spend a given hour, and choosing the most valuable application of time was hard. Members of the Congress often came in to talk about problems of their constituencies, businessmen with government difficulties wanted to discuss them, office heads within the department desired to consult on current matters in their hands, reporters wanted interviews, fires had to be put out, the White House had emergency meetings, and of course there was a full schedule of attendances at councils and committees. Every luncheon, and a great many breakfasts, were given over to such demands. Testimony had to be prepared and presented to the Congress, and every word had to be carefully chosen so it would be defensible. Speeches had to be readied, and the best efforts of my able speechwriters often had to be edited and revised. Public appearances were frequent. Altogether, I gave more than 650 speeches, interviews, press conferences, and congressional testimonies in three years in Commerce, moving from one subject to another, all requiring advance briefing and preparation. I submitted myself frequently to public questioning in many forums, including business conventions and on nationwide television on *Face the Nation*, *Meet the Press*, and the *Today* show. In all, I traveled to a hundred cities.

Visitors were frequent, usually scheduled but some unscheduled. There was correspondence to read, replies to be written, mail to be signed, and every day an unbelievable pile of papers and reports to be perused, digested, and decided upon. Screening all this fully occupied two personal secretaries, two administrative assistants, and a support staff of several more persons. My able, loyal, and hardworking secretaries, oblivious of the clock, Arden Chambers and Jean McRae, and my principal assistants, Joseph Casson and Paul O'Day, were invaluable in multiplying my production tenfold. Each day presented a nerve-racking problem of scheduling, of farming out responsibilities, of splitting minutes to cope with the demands of the job. Life was a typed sheet of paper, given to me by my secretary as I left the office each evening, telling me who I was scheduled to see and where to go and what to do the next day, with few blank spaces for thinking or for doing other chores that always stacked up. And each night meant carrying home a huge briefcase of documents needing attention, taking advantage of the quiet to concentrate on the most urgent among them.

Most exacting of all was the avoidance of jumping the gun by hasty decisions or actions, especially those that might run crosswise to the views of another department or someone in the White House. Very few matters that I dealt with involved exclusively the interests of Commerce, and just as I had to be alert to actions of other agencies that affected my constituencies, so also I had to be sure that I recognized the views of others in the government with respect to things Commerce did or wanted done. Often this put me in a delicate position with my former associates in the Bureau of the Budget, which had the right of oversight and approval or disapproval of any remark made publicly on budgetary or legislative matters.

I made it a point to understand every issue on which I had to rule and to send the file back for further information I thought necessary. To be safe, I scrutinized every paper presented on a vital issue, to avoid missing an obscure but important fact. Bureaucracy is merciless. A head of a department can lose face with his own subordinates if he does not respect their work; he can lose the respect of his

Cabinet peers if he makes casual decisions that they can appeal; and he can fall from grace with the White House staff and the Congress if he cannot defend every judgment on every meaningful issue. Many Cabinet secretaries and agency heads fail to survive this exacting gauntlet and its punishing wear and tear. All in all, I was blessed with stamina and good fortune in this respect.

# CHAPTER FIFTEEN

# Engaging in Détente

Unquestionably the acme of my Commerce experiences came toward the end, in November 1971, when the president sent me to the Soviet Union on an official trip as his representative six months prior to his own détente-building visit there in 1972. My mission, while not of itself historic, turned out to be a prelude to history. I had asked him in 1969 and 1970 to allow me to go to Moscow to stimulate trade matters. He told me the time was not ripe and suggested I keep in touch with Henry Kissinger. I saw Kissinger on this idea about once every four months, urging that an opening to increased trade and travel between the two countries would lead in time to improved understanding and could set the stage for détente and peace. He agreed, but said such a move had to wait for the right set of political circumstances. Although he didn't say so, I was sure he was referring to the early SALT talks, which had run into temporary difficulties.

In September 1971, when I broached the subject for perhaps the fifth time, Kissinger surprised me by saying I would shortly be invited to the Soviet Union as its guest and should be prepared to leave. The invitation came soon after that; I then met with Soviet ambassador Dobrynin in my office for lunch, and we worked out the dates of a general itinerary. Up to the time my plane left I did not have a detailed schedule of appointments in the Soviet Union or a clear idea of what the Soviets would be willing to talk about, but I had spent many hours in briefings by Kissinger's people and with the State Department and knew well what items we wanted to bring up. It was to be an economic mission exclusively, and I was to steer clear of diplomatic or military issues.

I had no acquaintance with the Russian language so I took along an interpreter from the State Department. Just for fun, however, I spent about four hours being tutored in the Cyrillic alphabet and found it most helpful to me, and impressive to my hosts, that I could look at a sign PECTOPAH and say "restaurant," and at MOPPNC CTAHC and recognize the phonetics of my own name. Sometimes they gave evidence that they suspected I knew more about their language than I admitted to.

Along with me on the trip, in addition to Kathleen, were Assistant Secretary Harold Scott, my secretary and six others from Commerce, Helmut Sonnenfeldt of Kissinger's office, and Jean Tarttar of State. We were ready for anything, assured of a friendly reception but uncertain whether we were likely to get down to serious business or just have a good time being entertained.

We found out quickly when we reached Moscow. On the way, in one of the president's planes, we had stopped in Stockholm for an official two-day visit and to overcome jet lag. There we picked up a Soviet pilot to guide our plane to the Moscow airport. As soon as we landed, taxied up to the gate, and disembarked to be greeted by American ambassador Jacob Beam, we were told that Chairman Aleksei Kosygin of the Council of Ministers was awaiting me in his office. I sent Kathleen in one of the Zis automobiles directly to the guesthouse where we were to stay, and left for the Kremlin with Beam, Scott, Sonnenfeldt, and our interpreter.

The Kremlin is a great walled fortress-within-a-city, perched on a summit overlooking the Moskva River in the heart of Moscow. It is bounded by a mile of red-brick walls that are topped by twenty medieval towers and enclose a seventy-acre complex of palaces and cathedrals built by the czars over the centuries, and various dull yellow-and-white structures built to house the offices of the men who were ruling the Communist empire of 250 million people.

The sun was shining brightly as we raced the twenty miles from the airport in a Zil 114 limousine, accompanied by police escorts. Arriving at the Kremlin, we cruised through the Borovitskaya Tower gate and up the paved driveway. The sunlight gleamed on the magnificent gilded onion domes of the medieval churches—the Cathedral of the Assumption, the Cathedral of the Annunciation, the Cathedral of the Archangel Michael, and the bell tower of Ivan the Great. These fantastic domes, their gold shining as if freshly applied, caught the day's bright light and glowed like the towers of dream palaces in fairyland. The late November air was chilly, and many of the structures were old and dark, but the welcoming atmosphere was one of warmth and cheer.

Kosygin was in a friendly, pleasant mood, quite in contrast with the dour impression he made in published photographs. He greeted me with outward charm, expressed his delight at my visit, and said he and his government wanted to do everything possible to make the stay enjoyable and fruitful. He told me it was the first time a United States secretary of commerce had ever come to his country, a fact my own briefing books had not mentioned, and he said, "We have looked to your visit with high hopes. We hope it will be constructive and will help to develop economic and commercial ties between our two countries." I took all this to be normal protocol talk, and I responded in kind. Then Kosygin got right down to business in a long statement that clearly demonstrated his intention to talk about serious matters in depth. I responded in equal terms, and the discussion went back and forth for three hours and twenty minutes before it came to an end long after the normal lunch hour.

Kosygin said he thought the time was long overdue for the two countries to establish normal economic relations worthy of their status as the two largest economies in the world. He disparaged the small amount of trade, quoting exact figures for the previous year, a total of only $179 million in the two directions. He went down a long list of items he said the Soviets wanted to buy from the United States and mentioned the products that they could offer to sell. They were interested in acquiring a wide range of machine tools and factory equipment, feed grains, the technology to produce consumer products, and even some types of consumer goods. He referred specifically to the Kama River truck plant, then in the early stages of construction, mentioned some orders already placed in the United States, and said much more of the equipment required was still to be contracted for.

When he came to farm products, he pointed out that the new Five-Year Plan called for a 25 percent increase in protein consumption, which in turn meant a heavy importation of feed grains to produce beef. He said that corn could not be grown in much of the Soviet Union, and they would be willing to buy substantial quantities from the United States.

"In fact," he offered, "I'll give you an order right now for three million tons of corn a year for five years, if you'll give me the right terms."

It was beyond my authority to enter into such a negotiation, but rather than parry or ignore his direct offer, I asked him what he meant by the "right terms."

"Oh, about seven or eight years' credit," he returned.

I laughed, because I knew he was not serious. "Seven or eight years might be possible for long-lived machinery or equipment, but not for a consumable," I said.

"All right," he came back. "What do you have in mind?"

By this time I was afraid of getting in too deep, but I did have an answer.

"Back in 1962, I believe you bought some wheat from us on six-month terms."

"That's no credit," he said, with a smile, apparently willing to see how far I would go, and perhaps testing my authority.

I retreated. "Mr. Chairman, that's a matter for another department of our government. I'm not prepared to get into credit terms and such details, but I'm sure our Agriculture people would be willing to, and I'll tell them about your offer when I return."

After an hour or so, Kosygin broke the businesslike mood by inquiring solicitously whether I was tired and wished to discontinue the conversation for the present. He noted that it took two or three days to become accustomed to the time difference and he would not want to take advantage of my fatigue. On the other hand, he said, it was unusual to have an opportunity to meet with a Cabinet officer from the United States, and he considered the economic and commercial opportunities for the two countries of great importance. He was hopeful the meeting could continue. Pointing out that I had rested during the two-day stop in Stockholm, I urged him to go ahead, and he did.

He went on again into the subject of what they could sell us, and mentioned oil, gas, timber, pulp, diamonds, rare earths, copper, nickel, platinum, chromium, titanium, and zinc. When he spoke of diamonds he said, "I'll bet you didn't know that we now produce more diamonds than South Africa." I didn't. Then he proceeded to display a sense of humor I had not expected. Running again down the possible sales of goods to the United States, he paused and smiled and said, "And I understand you Americans like to buy old bridges. We've got hundreds of old bridges we'll sell you." I laughed, taken completely by surprise that he should have noted that an American had recently bought the fabled London Bridge and moved it into the Arizona desert.

Finally, he came to his key position. All these possibilities depended upon the Soviet Union being treated in nondiscriminatory fashion as compared to other countries. A "normalizing of relations," he said, meant equal credit terms on its purchases, equal tariffs on its exports to us, and the elimination of our export controls on nonmilitary goods. He boasted that his country had never defaulted on a commercial obligation. I had been briefed to expect these points to be raised—especially Export-Import bank credits and "most favored nation" rates of import duties—and agreed that they were proper subjects to be included in an overall package of arrangements for trade normalization. On the matter of our export restrictions, he was disarmingly direct. "You may as well sell us the things we can buy in other countries. And as for military hardware, we don't expect you to sell us any of yours and we won't sell you any of ours," he said with a broad smile. "All we ask is that you don't humiliate us with rejections. Just tell us what things you don't want to sell us, and we won't try to buy them."

He then turned the floor over to me and I replied in kind, reviewing the various trade possibilities from our side. I suggested, for example, that imports of our consumer goods ought to be given more consideration. I pointed out the opportunities for earnings from tourism, if they made it easier and more comfortable for Americans to visit the many geographic and historic points of interest in his country; this might well suggest franchising some American hotel chains. I asked for broader travel rights in the USSR for Americans, access by American businessmen to the industrial plants in which their equipment might be useful, the opportunity for them to establish sales offices in Moscow, and the elimination of discrimination against our products. I suggested a foreign trade center in the Soviet Union similar to the one we were building in New York. None of these items seemed to give him pause, and he agreed that all of them would be given consideration and could probably be worked out to mutual satisfaction.

I then came to the $64 question, the one most likely to stand in the way of rapid progress along the lines we had been talking. "All of this should be workable," I said, "but I am afraid there is one precondition. I don't believe the American people would support the president in extending credit to the Soviet Union unless the slate is first wiped clean, and there is still outstanding the matter of the lend-lease debt from the last war. There hasn't even been a negotiation on this since the last one broke down eleven years ago."

He was less disconcerted than I expected. "Well, that's a new subject, but we'll consider it positively and give you our answer. In fact," he said, after pausing a moment, "let's address it now. You name five people and we'll name five, and we'll tell them to get together anyplace in the world and not come back until they've worked it out." It was a big step forward, and I accepted it in principle, and within a few later months an agreement was reached.*

As our current discussion went on, we were seated at one end of a long table covered with green baize, five of us on one side and Kosygin, Nikolai Patolichev (his minister of foreign trade), and an interpreter and an aide on the other. On the table between us were assorted bottles of vodka and wines, and at one juncture Kosygin interrupted his own exposition to offer me a drink. Since I had been well warned about Russian drinking capacity, and in fact had been on the wagon for fifteen years, I had to decline, thinking it best to explain that I did not drink alcohol. This seemed to please him.

"You see, we already have something in common," he said. "I don't drink either. I take tea. Would you like some tea?" I accepted, and tea was brought to the table in sturdy twelve-ounce glass tumblers. He took his and drank from it freely, but when I reached for mine it was so hot I couldn't even hold the cup in my hand.

He laughed. "We drink our tea hot in Russia. We make it in a samovar. Have you ever had tea made in a samovar?"

"No."

He turned to Patolichev. "I want you to go out and buy a samovar for Secretary Stans and send me the bill." Then he looked at me and said, "That's the only way to make tea." The samovar—copper-plated, with a central cylinder to hold hot coals for heating the water, and unpretentious but sturdy—is one of the treasured mementos of this trip.

---

*There was much misunderstanding in the United States about the lend-lease debt of the Soviets, and the figure of $11 billion was sometimes tossed around. However, what was actually involved was the value of our equipment still in existence in the Soviet Union and usable at the time the war ended, and this was less than a billion dollars. The negotiations produced a settlement of $800 million, on a formula similar to that we had agreed upon with other countries.

Kosygin also talked at length about what was translated as "joint ventures" between Soviet institutions and American companies. He offered arrangements to the United States for sharing in the production of Soviet oil, natural gas, and selected minerals and, at my question, spelled out more specifically what he meant. The Soviet Union had such resources beyond its requirement for many years, he said, and was willing to make them available as a means of paying for goods it would import. There could be no foreign ownership of property in his country, but if foreign companies would advance the money, for instance, for gas pipelines, freezing plants, and cryogenic ships, the Soviets would supply all the labor in the fields and produce the gas. The American investment would then be returned through a contract for a fixed portion of the output for a term of years. Kosygin volunteered that such an arrangement need not jeopardize our national security, because he was not thinking of more than 5 percent or so of our energy requirements, whereupon he quoted from memory statistics as to our energy production, consumption, and imports. He suggested the same principle could be applied in other deals, even in manufactured goods, with capital advances and technology by us paid for by a percentage of production in kind. It was all a forthright proposition that I thought might have appeal to American companies, and I said so, also pointing out that there were of course many considerations of national policy and economics to be resolved before such ventures could proceed. He agreed.

As the meeting drew to a close we both summarized our positions. He then said my visit could end up as merely a pleasant exchange or could produce real results, and he hoped it would be the latter. He urged that some agreements be reached quickly so that they could be announced during the president's visit the following May and proposed that the two countries name negotiating groups to proceed rapidly in that direction. This was beyond my authority, so I replied that I would give him an answer on the suggestion before I left the country. Several days later, I proposed instead to Patolichev the formation of a joint fact-finding group of second-level members of his ministry and my department to meet within a month in Washington, to assist in moving things along. This was accepted and proved to be workable and useful. The Soviet delegation came to Washington on January 6, 1972, after just five weeks. Unfortunately, I left the department two months following my mission to Moscow and could no longer play a part in what I felt could be a historic change in the relationships between the two nations.

As the meeting concluded and we were exchanging light comments, Kosygin told me a story which should delight bureaucrats of the middle and higher levels. I remarked to him that while in the USSR I hoped to learn what it was that allowed some persons in Soviet Georgia to live to 130 or 150 years. "I'll tell you about that," he said. "There's one man in Georgia who just reached 165, and we thought our government ought to find out his secret of long life so we could pass it on. So we sent a committee of doctors to his hometown to study his diet, his habits, his sex life, and anything else they could find that might have aided longevity. They learned nothing unusual. Next, we sent a committee of mental experts, psychologists and psychiatrists, to probe whether his life attitude would teach us anything. Again, no results. We politicians weren't ready to give up so we brought him to Moscow before a committee of officials. Again, nothing was learned, until after hours of questioning one commissioner said, in frustration, 'All right, you tell us the secret of your long life.' 'Well,' the old man replied with dignity, 'until a few months ago I never attended a committee meeting!'"

As we parted, I remarked to Kosygin that I was gratified with our meeting, "even though it is eleven years late," reminding him that in 1960, during Eisenhower's term, he and I were to have exchanged official visits. "It's more late than that," he countered. "For the two greatest countries on earth not to have been talking and working together for the last twenty years is a cosmic crime."

During the meeting Kosygin spent quite a bit of time telling me about the new Soviet Five-Year Plan. He stressed an intended shift from capital goods to consumer goods and quoted a number of statistics as to how the standard of living would be raised. After a considerable bit of this, he paused. "By the way, I'm going to present the Five-Year Plan to the Supreme Soviet on Wednesday at eleven, and I think it would be nice if you could be there."

"I accept, Mr. Chairman," I said, not quite sure of what was involved.

On the following Wednesday, Scott, Sonnenfeldt, an interpreter, and I arrived at the auditorium of the Palace of Congresses a few minutes early. I expected to be given a place somewhere in a balcony, but we were escorted to four reserved seats in the center of the floor between the delegates from Georgia and Kazakhstan; we were greeted on all sides with friendly but curious smiles from the members who were already seated and orderly, engaged in hushed conversations.

The Palace of Congresses is an elaborate modern building in the Kremlin, and the auditorium's normal capacity of 5,000 was more than ample for the 1,500 members of the Supreme Soviet, all seated on the main floor in rows fifty-six seats wide. The balconies were apparently filled with favored bureaucrats and party members. The stage was angled so that those in the audience could see everyone on the multilayered dais.

Party Secretary Leonid Brezhnev opened the meeting on the minute, spoke briefly, and introduced Kosygin to present the Five-Year Plan, while we listened in on headphones with simultaneous translation into English. Kosygin mentioned that since all the delegates had had an opportunity to review the plan in advance he would merely summarize the most important parts. Most of it sounded exactly like someone quoting dull statistics from the United States budget. He dwelt on the shift to consumer goods and ended with several comments on international affairs and particularly on the hope for a better economic relationship with the United States. It was implied to me later that some of these words had been inserted specifically because of my presence in the country and at the session. Kosygin concluded after about an hour and fifteen minutes, there was some discussion and then a unanimous vote and adjournment. I was told that it was highly unusual for a Western official to be on the floor for a meeting of the Supreme Soviet and certainly a rare courtesy to an American. I have claimed, facetiously, that I am the first and probably the only American who ever voted *Da* on a Soviet Five-Year Plan!

After the first gratifying pace-setting meeting with Kosygin, the rest of the visit to the USSR was almost anticlimactic. I saw him once more, shortly before leaving, and we had a warm interchange about the potentials of my trip and our mutual desire for progress. He expressed satisfaction with the reports he had received concerning my discussions. I had several long meetings totaling more than ten hours with Patolichev, in the course of which I developed an affection for him and a respect for his direct manner of dealing.

I had cordial and businesslike meetings with the ministers of the Natural Gas Industry, the Maritime Fleet, Petroleum Refining and Petrochemicals, and the Automobile Industry, the head of the Soviet Foreign Trade Bank, principal officials of Intourist, and the chairman of the State Committee for Science and Technology. In all of these there was the very evident desire on the part of my hosts to be open and forthcoming. I met no evasiveness or hesitation to give me any information I requested, or to discuss any subject. Some of the things I proposed, like opening the country to American hotel chains or joining the Geneva Copyright Convention, were obviously difficult matters of policy, but in every case the issue was discussed pro and con, and I was promised that further consideration would follow. There was no doubt in my mind that the official word throughout the government was to make my visit the first step of a workable détente, and to be sure that I carried back that precise impression. I did, and so reported to the president and to Kissinger, both of whom were pleased.

In my meeting with the minister of the Natural Gas Industry, I probed more into the concept of "joint ventures." He pointed out that the Soviets have large proven natural gas reserves, both in the northern and the southern sectors of the western part of the country, and in the northern areas of Siberia, the sum of which was more than enough to take care of their needs for 150 years. It was their proposal that, depending upon the selection of the source, American companies build a pipeline either to an Arctic or a Baltic port, construct there a liquification plant, and build in the United States fifteen to twenty cryogenic tankers at an estimated cost of $70 million each. Our total investment might be as much as $3 billion. The Soviets would propose to buy half of the tanker fleet. This enormous investment would, of course, require a high percentage of Export-Import Bank financing.

The initial deliveries of gas under the proposed arrangement would be applied largely in repayment of the American investment. Thereafter, our investors would have the right to purchase on prearranged terms continuing quantities of gas for a long period of time. The estimated value of such deliveries would be approximately $800 million per year. The Soviets would agree to utilize the proceeds from such sales for the purchase of American goods and technology, the contract in both directions to cover up to thirty years. I cite this specific project in some detail in order to indicate the Soviet definition of joint collaboration; the magnitude of projects that they had in mind; and the potential advantage to the United States of access to needed raw materials in such quantities. The Soviets described analogous projects in copper and forest products.

In my other meetings, we talked in detail about such topics as scientific and technological exchanges, joint operations in outer space, the protection of copyrights, and arrangements for the mutual use of each country's ports by ships of the other. Assistant Secretary of Commerce Andrew Gibson joined me in Moscow for meetings with the minister of the Maritime Fleet that led to a formal agreement a few months later on a number of shipping matters.

There was some minor byplay in my Moscow discussions that would not be noteworthy except for its evidence of accommodation on the part of my hosts. While at Intourist, I delivered a complaint from the American Express Company to the effect that it had been requesting the installation of telex equipment in its Moscow office for ten years without results. The telex was made available within the next thirty days. In a meeting with Patolichev, while we were discussing the improvement of the climate between the two countries, I told him I had observed a billboard cartoon, on the way into Moscow from the airport, that was severely critical of the United States and its capitalism. I suggested that this must be a carryover from earlier times and that it would not be a desirable greeting for President Nixon when he arrived in May. The billboard was changed before I left Moscow.

All in all it was a whirlwind experience, physically taxing. In the eleven days I had fifty-four official meetings, ceremonies, visits to plants, press interviews, and other business events. The social schedule was heavy, too, even for one who did not do any drinking. Kathleen and I were feted at nine official lunches and dinners, and entertained at five ballet performances, one opera, the Moscow circus, and a performance of the Georgian State Dancers. A seventy-passenger TU-134 plane was put at our disposal; on one weekend we spent two days in Leningrad and on the next weekend we visited Baku in the Azerbaijan Republic and Tbilisi in Georgia. In all three cities we were dined and toasted by state and city officials. I was permitted to go through the huge Electrosila generator factory near Leningrad, the Rustavi steelworks in Georgia, and the oil fields of Baku. In each case I was allowed to ask questions and talk to workers at their machines or during their rest periods playing dominoes, and I felt that I received open and unguarded answers.

The general manager of the GUM department store in Moscow showed me his departmental sales and expense figures. I met with and talked to service industry employees, shopkeepers, and school officials. In the factories, the bulletin-board pictures of winners of suggestion awards, and the descriptions of incentive pay plans, left me with a feeling that their motivation systems for employees were perhaps moving closer to ours. In Tbilisi, the Georgian dance troupe of 120 members put on an entire performance in the new opera house exclusively for our group of twelve and our twelve Soviet escorts. Throughout, Kathleen was kept pleasantly but energetically busy visiting day-care centers, museums, and schools.

There were many other personal impressions of this trip that did not go into official reports. The guesthouse in the Lenin Hills of Moscow was commodious and the service elaborate, with our every desire met immediately. In flashbacks of scenes I recall the bowls of caviar and plates of smoked sturgeon at every meal, a profuse flow of vodka for those who wanted it, repeated toasts across the table, the magnificent ballets, and the pleasantly intimate one-ring circus. I remember in Tbilisi drinking from a ram's horn, eating from a whole roasted lamb, dancing with beautiful Georgian girls who had been added to grace our party, being complimented by an organ grinder with a gift of his hat, altogether the most fun and relaxing part of the trip. I recall, in Baku, the equally warm hospitality, the rough boat ride on the turbulent Caspian, and the roomy guesthouse on a high hill.

I'll never forget, in Leningrad, the treasures of the Hermitage, for which our tight schedule allowed less than two hours where art lovers spend weeks, a luncheon by the mayor in a magnificent guest hall, and on the serious side, a visit to the immense Piskariovskoye Memorial Cemetery near Leningrad where a half-million people are buried in mass graves, all victims of starvation during the nine-hundred-day siege of the city by Hitler's Nazi armies from 1941 to 1944. At the cemetery I stood prayerfully before the eternal flame, and then stopped to read the pathetic story left behind by one little girl, twelve-year-old Tanya Savicheva, who recorded one by one the deaths of six members of her family until she herself was the last one left to die. I could feel sure in my heart that no one as seriously touched by the stark tragedy of war at firsthand as were the Soviet people could ever want to see its ravages again. Surely they would do all they could to prevent another.

As our plane taxied down the runway in Moscow for the return trip, I reflected back on the feelings I had acquired about the way of life of these universally friendly people. I had gained strong convictions about the Soviet Union, which I have continued to hold through subsequent events. First, the Soviets, meaning both the government and the people, did not want another war; they had not forgotten that the last one cost them twenty million lives. They wanted peace, they wanted détente with the United States, and they wanted a mutual reduction of armaments. Second, through the years they had been as suspicious of our diplomatic, military, and economic motives as we had been of theirs; it would take a long while for full understanding and trust to be generated on both sides, even in commercial transactions. Third, their leaders realized that the time had come to make major moves toward providing more consumer goods to their people; that necessarily meant producing proportionately more capital equipment and less military hardware. Finally, the Soviet Union, on the average, was several generations behind us in economic and living standards, as it probably was when the Communists first came to power, and would not catch up unless we defaulted. While there were no visible shortages of basic living necessities, there was an obvious lack of the major items like automobiles and roomy housing. I saw nothing to convince me that their system could produce nearly as well as ours. As I told the Nixon Cabinet upon my return, it was just too clumsy.

It is probable that for many years our trade with the USSR would be especially advantageous to us because we would be buying raw materials and selling finished factory products with a high labor component, plus farm crops. Thus every billion dollars of business back and forth could net tens of thousands of jobs in the United States. Their sales to us would not displace labor as do our imports from many other countries. I estimated to the president that, on reciprocal terms and without diplomatic setbacks, our exports could increase to $2 billion by 1975 and more than double that by 1980.

I tried to calculate mentally the vast sums of capital the Soviet Union would need to catch up with where we were then in the infrastructures of modern society, and the amounts are beyond imagination, as would be the time frame to achieve that goal (while we would still be moving ahead). The diversion of so much of its productive capacity to satisfy its military and space objectives had forced its people to suffer great societal deprivation, and that contest showed no sign of changing.

The Soviet system, however dysfunctional its internal workings, had one relative advantage over ours: consistency in direction. Its leaders stayed in power many years, sometimes decades; ours tended to turn over every four years. Its policies were consistent; ours fluctuated. Minister Patolichev made that point to me in one of our meetings: "How can your government operate? I've been minister of foreign trade for twelve years. I know what's expected of me and what policies to follow, and so does my organization. In that same time, you've had six secretaries of commerce under three presidents with different philosophic directions." Ten years later Patolichev was still in the same office; the United States had had six more secretaries of commerce under three more presidents with varying attitudes toward international relationships and toward the Soviet state.

A surprising incident on the fourth day of my trip to Moscow gave me a bit of striking evidence of the desire of Kosygin to move in the direction of accommodation. It had happened that my visit there coincided with a group trip by about a hundred American business leaders conducted by a trade organization. Among them was my close friend Don Kendall, the chairman of Pepsico. Responding to an invitation from the group, I addressed their lunch on my second day, telling them of the purpose of my trip and expressing considerable optimism that the timing was right for some real progress toward economic détente, although I conceded that it was too early in my experiences in Moscow to be certain of the outcome. Kendall told me in an aside after I concluded that he thought I was too optimistic and he doubted that any positive results were possible at the time.

In the course of events, on the evening of the fourth day my party and I were entertained by Ambassador Beam at a dinner at his residence, at which Patolichev and several other ministers of the Soviet government were also present. Shortly after the serving of the main course, Patolichev received a quiet message from one of his aides that caused him to leave his seat at the table, whisper to our host, and take his departure. Beam promptly told me that the message was that Kosygin was on his way to a reception given by the group of American business executives that I had addressed. The ambassador and I agreed that under the circumstances it was desirable that I also leave the dinner and show up at the reception, to which I had earlier been invited but had pleaded the unlikelihood that I could attend.

When I arrived I found the Americans scattered around a large unfurnished room, with Kosygin at the center of the main group of thirty or so in conversation. When I moved in, the group parted to allow me to greet him, and he in turn responded warmly. Noting that he was then talking to Kendall, I remarked facetiously, "What's Kendall trying to do, sell you his Pepsi-Cola?" to which Kosygin promptly responded, "I've tasted your Pepsi-Cola and I like it," and then added teasingly, "I'll buy your Pepsi-Cola if you'll buy my vodka and wines," to which they immediately shook hands. Then turning to me he said, "Your country does not like monopolies, but I am ready right now to make that a monopoly contract. Will you approve it?" I said in immediate response that it would be no problem. I did not follow the course of subsequent moves by Kendall, but it soon was clear that this chance conversation had provided an unexpected door opening, because it was only a short time later that Pepsi announced an exclusive franchise to make and sell its product in the entire Soviet Union for many years.

The Soviet policy mechanism, however, was sluggish, as demonstrated when I proposed to Minister Patolichev after our talks that we exchange letters before I left the country, describing our mutual understandings of the economic problems we had reviewed that needed resolution and how they might be resolved. I presented my letter (with embassy approval) the next day, and Patolichev promised a reply within the two days remaining before I left for Washington. To his embarrassment, he could not get the clearances from his government until after I had arrived back home, even though there were no significant differences of opinion as to the issues or the approach to be taken to find solutions for them.

This 1971 trip to Moscow afforded the first series of Cabinet-level meetings between the United States and the Soviet Union under the Nixon-Kissinger plan to negotiate a détente between the world's two most powerful nations. All definitional and tactical arguments aside, détente was a vaguely described term for a broad recognition by both sides that their common interests would be served by a thaw in tensions that would result from mutually advantageous economic steps toward increasing trade, travel, and investment. Nixon believed it was a fortuitous time for developing and understanding longtime peaceful relations.

In Senate testimony in 1974, Henry Kissinger spelled out the logic of this principle: "Over time, trade and investment may leaven the autarkic tendencies of the Soviet system, invite gradual association of the Soviet economy with the world economy, and foster a degree of interdependence that adds an element of stability to the political relationship. . . . By acquiring a stake in this network of relationships with the West, the Soviet Union may become more conscious of what it would lose by a return to confrontation. Indeed, it is our expectation that it will develop a self-interest in fostering the entire process of relaxation of tensions."

I was very pleased to have been given this initial role in creating the groundwork for such forward movement by what appeared to have been a successful mission. Certainly Kissinger, Patolichev, and others I worked with gave every indication that they believed the time was ripe for such a relationship, and they went far out of the way to make my trip pleasant and productive.*

Peter Peterson, my successor, in 1973 concluded a trade agreement with the Soviets containing many provisions that I had worked out on my visit to Moscow.

All of this rationale, and its optimism, blew up on us suddenly soon thereafter as the result of a politically planned move by the Democratic opposition in the Congress. In one calculated action, they wiped out all that we had accomplished.

By then a bill ratifying the trade agreement was pending in Congress. The deal-breaker came in the form of an amendment sponsored by Senator Henry M. "Scoop" Jackson of Washington and Congressman Charles A. Vanik of Ohio challenging a Soviet decision of 1972 to impose a tax on émigrés with high academic degrees. The Jackson-Vanik amendment provided that the terms in the agreement granting the Soviets tariff rates at the same level as "most favored nations," and also extending trade credits, be postponed until they abandoned their émigré tax and gave assurances that emigration would be considerably increased. The ostensible reason for the amendment was that the tax discriminated against Jews wanting to leave Soviet repression.

The Soviet government resented this action as an attempt to interfere in its internal affairs and in early 1975 responded by canceling the trade agreement. This brought all progress to an end. Later, any hope of reviving détente was destroyed by ruthless military adventures of the Soviets in other independent nations. This was the final blow to the demise of the dreams of détente.

---

*Media comment on my Soviet trip was generally favorable. For once I seemed to be on the side the liberals could support. Columnist Jerry Greene in the New York *Daily News* called it "an expedition of the utmost magnitude on the way to peace in our time. The implications are dramatic and staggering."

Nevertheless, television commentator Eric Sevareid had his fun with my trade effort in the broadcast made on the day I left Moscow: "When it comes to the religion of capitalist private enterprise, Mr. Stans is an old-time fundamentalist. With him, what is good for General Motors, General Electric, and General Dynamics is not only good for America, it's so good it may even help the heathen Communists reach the promised land." That, I observed to myself, was a consummation devoutly to be wished.

The collapse of the Soviet government and the death of Communism occurred just twenty years after my trip to Moscow. There was no thought around Washington that, however confident our leadership may have been about the ultimate fall of Communism, it could have happened as soon or as dramatically as it did in 1990 and 1991. And there is little sense in pondering, except argumentatively, whether a full development and growth of the détente initiated by Nixon and Kosygin would have increased or decreased the probabilities and scope of that collapse.

Peace across the world can be gained, one way or another, only when a plane of understanding arises among the major nations that they never again want to suffer the costs and terrors of intermittent mutual destruction that postpones mutual progress. Granted, it will take all the genius of man to find the path that erases the historic tribal rivalries and hatreds in our "civilization," but the circumstances of today clearly identify it as the dawn of a new era in which peace and freedom are attainable with vigor and good faith.

# CHAPTER SIXTEEN

# Watergate and the American System of Injustice

On Sunday, June 17, 1972, I awoke as usual at about seven-thirty and walked out of the apartment to pick up *The Washington Post* at the front door. Glancing at the headlines, I paused to read an article that at once attracted my attention: FIVE ARRESTED IN BREAK-IN AT DEMOCRATIC HEADQUARTERS. That subject interested me considerably, not because of who was likely to have been involved in it, but because of the more threatening thought that the same thing could happen to us at Nixon campaign headquarters. My mind went at once up and down a hypothetical list of the valuables that might be endangered and what we should do to protect them.

I had been serving as chairman of the Finance Committee for the Reelection of the President for four months, since February 15. It was not a position I sought, because I had been enjoying my work as secretary of commerce and had a number of very interesting and fruitful projects under way that promised significant public benefits if I could have carried them further for a few more years. My game plan thereafter called for a consideration of retirement or other options to fill my remaining days. The White House, however, had different ideas and I felt obligated to consider them. Because I had been successful at raising the campaign funds in the 1968 Nixon election, Nixon thought I was the ideal person to do it again. While I was not enamored with the idea, I had to concede that it would be practical for me to begin early in 1972, and that my knowledge of fund-raising and of potential contributors constituted assets that could not be replaced easily. In politics it is a good rule that you either serve where your boss wants you to or you withdraw, and I was not about to withdraw.

It was several days after the newspaper article came out that I learned, through the press, that the burglars were suspected of being in the employ of Nixon's campaign committee. It took a few more days to learn that there was no apparent damage to the targeted Democratic National Committee, located in the Watergate building, and no loss of money or other assets. The five burglars, who included four Cubans, had been apprehended on the premises without any resistance. I was not given any information as to the inside facts of the situation by any of the members of our campaign committee organization; they weren't talking to me on this subject. I continued in my work of fund-raising, depending on the media for the rapidly breaking news of what had gone on and where it was leading.

Nothing that I learned during the week of the break-in led me to even consider the possibility that this "third-rate burglary" would have such a profound effect on me that it would become a watershed in my life, and that I would be dragged through a horrifying sequence of events that threatened my physical, mental, and financial resources. These events are worth recounting, because my experiences might help educate the American public about what really goes on behind the scenes in Washington. There is often more than merely a few grossly guilty public figures involved in special prosecutions, investigations, and news reporting.

What happened in the next three years added up to a ghastly nightmare. But after that period of ensuing investigations, accusations, threatened indictments, numerous civil suits, $1 million in personal legal expenses, and a trial in New York federal court for imagined breaches of law, I finally walked away from Watergate with all doubts removed as to my innocence of any willful violations of any law, and with the air cleared for me to rebuild a future. At least that's what I thought. I did not estimate the residual effects of our system of Washington injustice.

Like all presidential campaigns, Nixon's was conducted under the principal aegis of two wholly separate committees: the campaign committee, chaired by former attorney general John Mitchell, that managed the operation of convincing citizens to come out and vote for Nixon; and a finance committee, chaired by me, that handled the business of generating and collecting the funds needed to cover all the costs of the campaign, banking them, and disbursing them as directed by the campaign committee. This distinction was especially emphasized in the 1972 Nixon campaign, along with other conditions I imposed on the president at the time I accepted the assignment, in order to avoid some of the confusions that had occurred in the 1968 election. In my pre-acceptance meetings separately with Bob Haldeman, his chief of staff, and then with the president, I said that I felt I could not perform my best unless these conditions were present:

1.     There should be no other committee authorized to receive funds except my committee.

2.     The expenses of the campaign committee and its sub-committees should be controlled under a carefully prepared budget, administered by a budget committee of two members from each of the two major committees, with Mitchell and me acting as co-chairs.

3.     No funds of any amount should be accepted from contributors in return for a quid pro quo in government favors or appointments.

4.     All transactions of the finance committee, inbound or outbound, should be closely accounted for with fully modern computer equipment.

5.     The budget committee should prepare a budget for the entire campaign, broken down into its expense subcategories and no increase in any category should be allowed unless it was matched by an equal decrease in another.

6.     None of the funds left over from the 1968 campaign, which were originally in excess of about $1 million and had been sequestered by Chief of Staff Haldeman and delivered to Herbert Kalmbach, personal counsel to the president, for use from time to time for polling or other White House purposes, would be intermingled with the funds of the 1972 campaign, and I would exercise no jurisdiction over them.

I was determined that the raising and spending of money for the campaign, and the accounting for it, should be the best of any presidential campaign up to this time.

All of these conditions were acceptable to the president, Haldeman, and Mitchell, and were carried out to the best of my ability and

knowledge, except for one, and that related to the periodic adjustments of the budget. The campaign staff people were sometimes just
too busy to carry out the formalities of budget increases and decreases.
They found it easier to rely on their confidence in the finance committee to raise any amount required. Ever has it been so.

At the time of the break-in, the election was almost five months
away. Our committee had raised about $25 million up to this time
and was still going to need much more, so I carried on the money-
raising at full pace despite the multiple interruptions by reporters
and investigators seeking information from our records.

My staff had come under heavily increasing tension in accomplish-
ing its work as Watergate investigations proceeded. The earliest one
was a very irritating attempt by Common Cause, a public-interest
organization headed by John Gardner, to force the disclosure of all
of Nixon's contributors from the beginning of the campaign in
1971. That this was planned only as a harassment and publicity
maker seemed to be evident from the fact that the Congress had just
a few months before passed a bill making a change in the election
laws to provide for public disclosure of contributions received only
on or after the law's effective date, April 7, 1972. The demand by
Common Cause for total disclosure, and my refusal to comply, led
to a spate of published rumors that we were concealing large contributions from such corporations as Lockheed and ITT.

Common Cause's legal maneuvers continued off and on in considerable volume and force until well after the election. Thereupon,
after clearing it with all our early contributors, we disclosed all the
amounts they had given. There were no surprises and no illegalities.
The issue was dead, but Common Cause had created enough smoke
to fuel a substantial increase in its membership. Their actions included such extremes as suing me and threatening me with contempt of
court, but while they had the effect of diverting some of my attention, they ultimately resulted in nothing whatsoever.

Only a short time elapsed before the subject of the Watergate
break-in was expanded by then special Watergate prosecutor
Archibald Cox to include investigations by the General Accounting
Office, the FBI, the IRS, and other interested agencies to cover the
entire fund-raising and disbursing operation of my finance committee. This opened the floodgates of intrusions into our work and created heavy demands on us for information. The GAO investigations
alone involved a considerable portion of our staff time, but produced several reports of no significant findings. Interwoven with the

other matters of inquiry was one headed by Democratic congressman Wright Patman of Texas, chairman of the House Banking and
Currency Committee. The issue at stake was the derivation of a size-
able contribution that had been routed by a contributor to Robert
Allen, chairman of our Texas committee, through a bank in Mexico
to our bank in Washington. After one appearance of their staff investigators at my office (which they aborted after an abusive, profane
attack on our general counsel for being present) and a hearing of
Patman's committee, there were no findings that challenged the pro-
priety of the contribution or our acceptance of it. Upon the issuance
of two staff reports on their investigations, I found both so inaccurate, confusing, and meaningless that I publicly characterized them
as a "mess of garbage." After gauche efforts by Patman to publicize
unfounded allegations, which continued almost to the time of the
election, he quietly gave up. That's politics.

The campaign had meanwhile moved on smoothly despite continuing "disclosures" by the media, daily releases of information from
one source or another, opposing party accusations, and leaks from
politicians and prosecutors. Our efforts were bolstered by the fact
that the finance groups across the country were successful in raising
more and more funds until the totals of contributions and expenditures both were almost double the original budgets. When the bal-
lots were counted in November, Nixon had received a resounding 61
percent of the vote and forty-nine states! The Nixon strategy of
applying all the resources of the White House and the campaign
committee to produce a maximum vote had paid off and the
Watergate issue had been kept quiescent. To his great disappointment, he had not succeeded in changing the Democratic hold on
either house of Congress. There was no doubt that a second term
would bring with it much more overt opposition in the Congress
than ever before, even though the arithmetic proved that Nixon had
sufficient support of the voters to submerge any negative effect that
Watergate may have produced upon them at the polls.

There still remained, of course, the obvious difficulty of deter-
mining a continuing strategy, while it was still possible, to dispose
of the case once and for all. Nixon has been criticized for his failure
to stop the cover-up at an early stage. However, that would have
tangled him in lengthy discussions at a time when he was highly
involved in foreign affairs with Henry Kissinger and others, including the war in Vietnam, the normal run of domestic affairs, and also
the physical and emotional stress of the continuous travel of his

campaign for reelection. It seems clear that he looked initially for strategy to Haldeman, Dean, and Ehrlichman of his staff, but none had the depth of experience for dealing with such a crisis and all of them in fact looked back at Nixon for the way out. Mitchell, who may or may not have been one of the original planners of the break-in, was also preoccupied with the campaign, and similarly failed to urge Nixon to hold court in his own organization and dismiss the guilty ones. All had their minds transfixed on their part of winning the vote.

Meanwhile, the White House had found no way to stop the Watergate steamroller, and the heat on Nixon and his associates continued to grow.

When Senator Sam Ervin's Senate Watergate committee convened in February 1973, John Dean confessed to his participation in the affair and the cover-up and named others of the campaign committee and White House staff as having participated. However, the main factor which converted Watergate into a cause célèbre was the disclosure by a witness before the committee that Nixon had a taping system within his offices to automatically record the conversations taking place within them. The more Nixon contended that they were protected as his property by precedent and under executive privelege, the more vociferous became the media and public demands for their revelation. Eventually, Nixon lost this battle in the Supreme Court and turned over the tape recordings. Up to this point there was no implication of criminal activity in Nixon's claim of exclusive right to them or in the negotiations concerning the release of them, although there were a few gaps in the tapes that were revealed. Much more meaningful was the contents of the taping system, of which three or four items received the mass of media attention.

Strangely, one of the earliest disclosures of the contents of the tapes was one that related to me personally. This startling discovery of the White House strategy for frustrating the investigations was presented to Nixon by John Dean near the end of February. It proposed that I be named an ambassador with the objective that the hearings on my nomination would develop into a Watergate inquiry and thus defuse any later hearings. The nuances of this discussion are such that the exact quotation of the heart of the conversation is worth reviewing.

DEAN:    I think it was my idea, in fact. I think it could defuse, be one defusing factor in the hearings. Stans would like to get his side of the story out. He is not in any serious problem ultimately. It could be rough and tumble, but Maury is ready to take it. It would be a mini-hearing, there is no doubt about it, but his would further detract from the other committee.

PRESIDENT:    So you sort of lean to having Stans starting out there?

DEAN:    I think it would take a lot of the teeth out of it—you know—the stardom the people are trying to build up to. If Stans has already gone to a hearing in another committee, obviously they will use everything they have at the time and it won't be a hell of a lot. It confuses the public. The public is bored with this thing already.

PRESIDENT:    Stans is very clean. Unless I make a mistake on this thing, the way I analyze it, and I have stayed deliberately away from it, but I think I can sense what it is. The way I analyze the thing, Stans would have been horrified at any such thing. And, what happened was he is honestly outraged . . .

DEAN:    He does, and he is a victim of circumstances, of innuendo, of false charges . . .

While my initial reaction to this potential ambassadorship was one of surprise that Nixon would even consider my being drawn into such a plight, I soon decided to consider it in a better light as a vote of confidence in me and my integrity. After discussing the subject with Kathleen, I promptly declined the offer, despite Dean's very obvious show of disappointment. Read as a whole, this was a splendid tribute, but a lousy trick to try to play on me.

Another tape dated March 26, 1973, which attracted much public attention, was one in which Nixon and Haldeman discussed trying to influence the government investigators by shifting their responsibility from the FBI to the CIA, based on the assumption of Nixon's staff that the FBI would be much more zealous in its work than the CIA because of their respective leaderships. This obviously absurd idea sprang from a piece of information that a campaign contributor from Texas solicited by a state finance chairman had offered to make a contribution of approximately $100,000 out of funds he had on deposit in a bank in Mexico. After it had been determined that such a contribution could legally be accepted under the limited reporting requirements at the time, it was delivered by check from the Texas state finance chairman to the treasurer of the National Finance Committee in Washington. To the best of my knowledge, there was no illegality in this but the unusual internal characteristics of the transaction gave Nixon's conspirators a reason to believe that the

CIA ought to undertake the investigation. When this taped conversation was disclosed, it was identified and spoken of in the media and among prosecutors as the "smoking gun." It was hard to see that there was anything to that term. The smoking gun was actually never loaded.

There were many other Nixon tapes that received public attention as and when they were released, including some in which he and staff members dicussed how to provide subsistence money for the burglary group during the time they were awaiting trial and thereafter. So far as I know, there has been no public accounting for the sources and funds that may have been used for this purpose.

Also covered by the tapes were a series of conferences and meetings between Nixon and his legal counsel regarding Nixon's determination at a certain point in the proceedings to have Archibald Cox discharged or forced to resign as Watergate special prosecutor. This matter finally came to a head with the resignations of Attorney General Elliot Richardson and his deputy, William Ruchelshaus, both of whom individually refused to fire Cox, who was then discharged by Solicitor General Robert Bork, the next person in line in the Department of Justice. These transactions, which occupied only a short time in hours, became known in the media as the Saturday Night Massacre, and did much to tarnish Nixon's reputation for cool-headed deliberation. His motivation was that Cox, being a Democrat, should not have been appointed special prosecutor, and was using that position to do intense harm to Nixon and his administration. Again there was apparently no criminal action by Nixon in this shocking handling of the matter, because it was in the scope of his authority.

Without doubt, the blaring use by the media of the terms "smoking gun," "money for the burglars," and "Saturday Night Massacre," as disclosed in the tapes to an aroused public, was an overwhelming force in convincing Nixon that he had no course except to resign the presidency, which he did on August 9, 1974, thereby avoiding an impeachment trial.

While the Watergate investigations were going on, John Mitchell and I were indicted by a federal grand jury in New York on May 10, 1973. We were each charged with ten felony counts alleging conspiracy and perjury in connection with a campaign contribution by one Robert Vesco. Mitchell professed ignorance about the charges, and I knew nothing about them or the circumstances leading up to them. It seems Vesco was a financial freebooter, although we didn't know it at the time, who headed a group of foreign mutual investment funds. At a meeting with Mitchell and me, he suggested he would contribute $250,000. Part of this went to New Jersey Nixon committees and the balance to our national committees. About the time we first met Vesco, and unbeknownst to me, he was in the early stages of an investigation by the Securities and Exchange Commission. Mitchell apparently learned about it soon thereafter.

Our trial did not take place until almost a year after our indictment, during which time the media headlined a growing conclusion that we were both guilty as hell. When it did start on February 20, 1974, it continued for twenty-eight days as the federal district attorney and his staff introduced numerous witnesses who had known one or the other of us at some time in the past, and produced voluminous telephone records and other documents. Our counsel objected on the ground that the testimony and evidence were totally irrelevant to the case, but the judge agreed to allow them on the record subject to future connection. No such connection was ever made.

One of the witnesses, however, was John Dean, whose testimony seemed to be directed more at Mitchell than at me, but still had no substance. Mitchell and I each testified in our own defense and were each cross-examined for the better part of a day. There was one significant point in my testimony, which related to a telephone conversation I had had with Dean during the fund-raising period in which I asked whether or not we should return Vesco's contribution. He advised against it at the time. When I of course denied all of the allegations in the ten counts against me and did my best to point out that there was no evidence of any kind supporting them, Dean was called to the stand and testified on the same subject, denying that he had ever had such a conversation with me.

To challenge Dean's credibility, my attorneys then read to the jury excerpts from the February 1973 tape in which Dean proposed to Nixon my appointment to an ambassadorship. The point we were trying to make was that Dean was not a trustworthy witness, and it seemed to work. When the ordeal came to an end, the jury's verdict was to acquit both of us on all counts. The foreman said that the jury believed both Mitchell and I were extremely busy taking care of matters of the campaign and would not have had the time to conspire in the manner alleged by the prosecution.

Only then could we find comfort in the opinions of the press about the case. The general consensus shifted from the early assumption of guilt to an acceptance of the idea that the charges were so thin and lacking in evidence that they should not have been brought. The most precise of those opinions was that of author

George V. Higgins in his book *The Friends of Richard Nixon*, who wrote that in the indictment "[t]here was at least as much of Whitney North Seymour's egotistical desire to leave office as United States Attorney for the Southern District of New York with a couple of big scalps up for the scissoring, as there was no solid evidence against the two men."*

And indeed there had been no want of effort on the part of the district attorney's staff. I learned later, for example, that they had brought Ed Nixon, brother of the president, from the West Coast to New York eleven times. They tried to induce him by implied threats to change his testimony to contradict his recounting of my statement to him that I had not asked Vesco that his contribution be in cash, but had said we would accept it in any form he chose. Ed Nixon's lawyer confirmed in writing that he viewed this entirely as a continuing effort to coerce him.

The frightening thought that surrounds this exposure is that if the unproven charges had, by such tactics or other turn of fate, seduced the jury into a guilty verdict, we could each have been sentenced to up to forty-five years of imprisonment.

In the meantime, I was under heavy threat from the Watergate special prosecutor. After I was fully acquitted of the wild and unfounded charges of the Vesco trial in New York, I was allowed one day's surcease and exhilaration before his office, then headed by Leon Jaworski, called my lawyer to say that I was wanted at once in Washington for questioning in connection with campaign money illegalities in 1972. The office had unlimited powers to investigate improprieties in connection with the Watergate break-in and the 1972 election.

What followed was another yearlong wonderland of discoveries about the processes of justice and injustice.

First, I was denied a request for a respite of a few days. Nor was I allowed a plea for a delay of a few weeks to tend to Kathleen who was then quite ill in Florida and unable to travel home. I was required to return from there every five days or so for questioning.

At our initial meeting, before I had an opportunity to answer a single question, Jaworski told my lawyers that his staff had evidence against me of over a hundred campaign finance violations. He made constant, frightening references to a big loose-leaf book supposedly

---

*George V. Higgins, *The Friends of Richard Nixon* (Boston: Atlantic Monthly Press, Little Brown & Co. 1974).

containing the details of these charges, but at no time did he acqui-
esce to my lawyer's request to let him see it or copy it. And he
would not tell us what the details were.

I was questioned principally by a team of two, headed by Tom
McBride, for a total of 120 hours, covering over three hundred subjects of agenda, and I was required to produce innumerable specific
documents, even though investigators for the special prosecutor had
spent weeks examining every document carefully preserved in my
finance committee files. This search occupied more than a hundred
additional hours of my time, but all such demands were ultimately met.

The questioning was cynical and caustic, especially by eager young
staff members. These inquiries were embellished several times by
challenges that my statements were not believable. On one occasion
McBride himself, stating that a document was missing, said bluntly
and with prejudgment, "You destroyed it, didn't you?" Being unfamiliar with the document, I asked my staff to look for it, and within
an hour it was found properly located in a file cabinet. When I produced it, McBride was gracious enough to apologize.

My loyal secretary, Arden Chambers, was accused by younger
members of the staff of lying to protect me. The allegation was
unfounded, but she was greatly shaken upon being told that unless
she changed her story she would be in the dock with me. True to her
nature, she refused to be intimidated, and ultimately no such thing
happened to her.

Finally, when the questions ended, and I had answered every one of
them with every allegation demolished, I believed I had fully erased
all doubt about my integrity, but we had a foretaste of McBride's attitude that cast doubt on the outcome. He had already refused to grant
a request by my attorneys for a letter clearly confirming what his staff
had stated, that *there was no evidence connecting me with the
Watergate break-in or cover-up* and that their continuing inquiry related only to fund-raising transactions.

This was a normal and reasonable request. However, bloodthirsty
reporters were insisting with impunity that I was deeply involved in
improper financial transactions, and the prosecutors insisted on a
plea of guilty on some charges. My attorneys told me that the prosecution considered me a figure so well publicized that my guilt was
generally assumed; therefore, I could not be allowed to go free.

My lawyers fought back bitterly, insisting that the evidence did
not support a single count of impropriety. The prosecutors, nonetheless, finally said that they had six charges that they intended to sub-

mit to the court, but they would waive one of them if I would plead guilty to five. The absurdity of these petty misdemeanors to which I was pressured to plead guilty easily demonstrates the lengths to which the prosecution went to find charges to file. Here they are:

1.     *Non-willful* receipt of an illegal contribution of corporate funds from 3M Company. A cash contribution of $30,000 was handed to me by an official of the company. I asked him to give me the names of the contributors for our records and he did it, sending me twenty-nine names with amounts for each. Another company official later acknowledged to me that this money had come from corporate funds and that it had improperly been reported as having come from employees; I returned the money the next day. He also confirmed by affidavit that there was no possible method by which I could have initially known that the funds were illegal.

2.     *Non-willful* receipt of an illegal contribution of corporate funds of $40,000 from Goodyear Tire and Rubber Company. The circumstances being almost identical to those in the 3M charge, I received from an officer of Goodyear a similar affidavit indicating there was no way I could have known the funds were illegal. That money was also returned.

3.     Late reporting of a contribution from Ernesto Lagdameo, a Philippine businessman, who visited my office to offer cash in the amount of $30,000. Hesitating to accept it because I had just been told there was some doubt about the legality of receiving contributions from foreigners, I told the man I could not accept it until I could be sure it was legal to do so, but that if he agreed, I would hold the money until the point was researched; if it were found improper, I would return the funds. When the advice I got was not to accept the contribution, I returned the money within the same reporting month. Under the circumstances, I concluded that this nullified the transaction and no report was required. Ironically, *I learned later that the legal advice had been incorrect and the contribution could have been accepted.*

4.     Late reporting of $81,000 transferred to Fred LaRue for return to an inactive committee from which it had originated and was not to be used for campaign purposes.

5.     The $39,000 received from Tim Babcock as contributions from various individuals whose names he did not provide to our committee until after the date they were due to be reported. We reported them at once, as soon as we received the names.

Do you consider these significant as evidence of either a deliberate breach of the law or a failure of character on my part?

I considered the options: to fight on at a cost in time of many months and in money of hundreds of thousands of dollars, while facing a threatened six or more charges—or to give up and pay a fine that my lawyers believed would be small; in other words, to accept the opprobrium of guilty pleas and the fine or endure another year or more of stress and caustic publicity. In the balance was Kathleen's tenuous health, my own exhaustion, and our dwindling finances. I finally surrendered to the ultimatum to plead guilty to the five technical counts, all the while knowing they involved insignificant lapses. I gave up with a heavy reluctance, suspecting that I might regret not having fought to a showdown, and I was right in my trepidation.

At the time the papers on my plea were to be filed in the federal court in Washington, McBride asked the district attorney's office in New York if it would state in writing that, following my acquittal in the Vesco trial, there were no further matters pending against me in that office. That could have had mitigating value for me in Washington, but New York refused to give it on the grounds that something new might still be dug up.

In the meantime, I was assured by the special prosecutor's office that they would not make recommendations to the court or to the probation officer as to the sentence to be imposed. I learned several years later that that commitment had been violated, and that the probation officer had received and adopted a recommendation from the prosecution that I be given a sentence of six months to two years in prison. Considering the nature of the charges it is certainly not unreasonable to think of them as no more serious than traffic violations. The opinion of the judge who ruled on this case was clearly stated as indicating that there were no willful violations in any of the five transactions. In any event, as the charges were merely misdemeanors and not felonies, he imposed a fine of only $1,000 on each of the five counts.

There is one package of mitigating evidence that I gave the special prosecutor's staff that they ignored completely. It documented that in the same period of time in which I was raising funds, that my staff and I had returned or refused contributions from individuals that totaled somewhere between $4 million and $5 (the difference in totals due to variations in amounts offered by several persons) million simply because we mistrusted the motives of the giver, his or her reputation, or the manner in approaching the transaction. One such contribution was from a New York banker, Michele Sindona, who offered me immediate delivery of $1 million in cash on the sole condition that it not be made public. I explained to him that the law required all contributions of a hundred dollars or more to be published, and the next day I wrote him a letter saying it would not be in his interest or mine to circumvent the law; the letter ended up several years later as an item of evidence against him at a trial for financial misdeeds at his bank.

There were also individuals who offered contributions in return for commitments of appointment as ambassador, one of whom opened the conversation with the question, "How much for Luxembourg?," and several expecting help in connection with government contracts. In one case the head of a California bank gave us a $200,000 contribution, which we accepted, only to return it a month later when we read an article in a popular magazine to the effect that he had become the target of an income tax investigation.

The extreme tactics and judgments of the special prosecutor's staff in this case fully exemplify the prejudgment and unfairness of the treatment often accorded to me and others in Washington. If there were any scale of justice in the building at the time of this inquisition, it would have recognized that these actions by me far outweighed my supposed guilt on the five petty incidents.

It probably cost the government several million dollars to bring me to so-called justice. My lawyers and I never lost our confidence that a jury would have acquitted me of all charges if I had been able to take another year of stress and expense for a trial.

What did my prosecutors accomplish? A balance sheet of Watergate would show some very interesting statistics, some of which are precise and some of which are necessarily estimates. But it seems logical that the dimensions and costs of the Watergate inquisition of me were far in excess of any realistic requirement of the situation.

All told, fourteen people were tried and found guilty of illegal participation in the Watergate burglary and cover-up: the four Cubans (Bernard L. Barker, Virgilio R. Gonzalez, Eugenio R. Martinez, and Frank A. Sturgis); former CIA agents E. Howard Hunt and James W. McCord, Jr.; former FBI agent G. Gordon Liddy; former attorney general John M. Mitchell; former presidential aides Harry R. Haldeman, John D. Ehrlichman, and John W. Dean, III; and campaign staffers Jeb S. Magruder, Fred C. LaRue, and Herbert L. Porter. Fifteen large and five small corporations were found guilty of campaign law violations.

Arithmetically then, there were thirty-four persons and companies found guilty in these two orbits. With undoubtedly many more individuals harassed in one way or another, it seems perfectly fair to pose a few questions. Why was it necessary to involve and endanger the lives of so many hundreds of innocent people in order to bring to justice fourteen guilty of being a party to the Watergate affair (five of whom were arrested on the spot, several of whom told their stories voluntarily, and the rest of whom were available through the White House)? Why was it necessary to harass thousands of contributors to bring to justice fifteen sizable corporations and five small businesses for contributing corporate funds, in order to dole out fines none of which exceeded $15,000? The only conclusion can be that the "forces of justice" were bolstered by the extraordinarily competitive interplay of rumors, suspicions, suppositions, and information feeding between the prosecution, and the media, and politicians.

In contrast to the thirty-four guilty, the number of innocent persons who were investigated to the point of personal damage to their lives as a result of the emotions, stresses, and other psychological injury is in the hundreds. First were persons who, after having been indicted, and at great emotional and financial costs, succeeded in proving their innocence in court, including John Connally, Edwin Reinecke, Robert Mardian, and Kenneth Parkinson. Second were innocent bystanders who were drawn into the web of suspicion and subjected to extraordinary inquisitions and ignominy, including: Bebe Rebozo, Ed Nixon, Donald Nixon, Ron Ziegler, William J. Casey, Ray Kroc, Rose Mary Woods, Kenneth Dahlberg, Robert Allen, Peter Flanigan, Congressman Louis Wyman, and at least fifty others. Third were targeted groups of individuals, the victims totaling an estimated five hundred. All others, including officials of corporations, number over a thousand.

If anything, these estimates are very much understated in numbers. Even if they exaggerate slightly in one category or another, any revision of the totals produces the same composite of an inconceivable number of innocents who were swept up into a legal Roman Coliseum and forced to fight their way out.

Final accounting: The total funds received and fully accounted for in reports filed by Nixon's national committees added up to about $60.2 million, the largest amount ever raised by a presidential candidate. Actual campaign expenses similarly reported and accounted for amounted to $56.1 million, leaving a temporary balance of about

$4.1 million, which might have been available to the Republican party if it had not been for the large number of closing-up costs. To contend with these outlays, including the committee's final legal fees and the legal expenses of employees who were investigated and ultimately dismissed as innocent, these final funds were turned over to a liquidating committee headed by former senator Charles Potter and used to pay all such items. In the end, John Mitchell and I received only about half of the reimbursements due to us for legal fees of our successful defense in the Vesco case.

I have publicly called the national Watergate extravaganza a witch-hunt. It was worse than that. For anyone around who had been close to Nixon, it became a calculated character assassination planned less to punish any target for misbehavior than to add another nail to Nixon's coffin.

The extremes to which the pursuers went were seldom publicly known by anyone but the victims. From my own experience and vantage point of knowing firsthand the ordeals of others, I can catalogue a list of instances in which injustice, impropriety, and harassment were deliberately dominant. Consider these.

One of the ancillary expeditions of the sleuths during the Watergate era was directed toward supporting the common theory that no one makes a sizable contribution to a political campaign without expecting something illegal in return, and inversely that campaign fund-raisers engage regularly in offering such beneficences. Charges of improprieties in 1972 were rampant, even though I had held a steady rein on all of our solicitors with repeated instructions that no such transactions were permissible. The range of accusations was as broad as the imagination of the accusers, and it took a long while before the dust settled and the truth emerged. In the excitement of the hunt, it was impossible for campaign finance officials to take time to answer each aberrant insinuation, and denials that were made did not get the prominence of the original attacks.

The charges did not always imply actions that would have been illegal. Many were designed to insinuate a sleaziness of conduct on the part of the money-raisers. Thus the stories ranged from reports, stated with varying degrees of certainty, that the Nixon campaign had received stratospheric gifts (usually stated in millions of dollars) from the shah of Iran, or from unnamed Arabs, or from unidentified sources in South America, or from wealthy Frenchmen; that its solicitors had secured lists of companies in trouble with the IRS, the

SEC, regulatory commissions, or other government agencies, and by extortion or promises of relief exacted large sums from them; that money was received in return for promised government contracts or favorable rulings on pending contract disputes; that income tax or antitrust or claim settlements were fixed; that government jobs, particularly ambassadorships, were sold (one report even presumed to name the specific prices being asked for various countries); that word was passed that contributions should be made in currency to cover up any quid pro quo dealings; that money was illegally accepted from foreign citizens; that improper contributions were laundered by money-raisers in foreign countries; that contributions were solicited improperly by government officials or on government property; that an "enemies list" was kept of persons refusing to contribute, so that retaliation by the administration could come later; and on to accusations that the laws on illicit dealings had been willfully circumvented and violated in a host of other ways.

*Every bit of this turned out to be pure fiction, absolute hogwash. The Watergate special prosecutor, in his final report, concluded that he had investigated "several hundred" such accusations through thousands of interviews and subpoenas for thousands of documents using his own organization, the IRS, the FBI, the computerized records of data gathered by the Senate Watergate Committee, and information from members of Congress. After two years of ferreting out facts, he acknowledged that he could not find evidence adequate to take to court a single instance within this entire range of alleged corrupt practices.*

One additional annoyance that arose from all this turmoil was in the form of civil suits against the Nixon committees and me for the return of campaign contributions. Some were relatively small claims asking for the return of the claimant's money; several were filed as class actions demanding the return of every dollar collected during the campaign; and others were for varying reasons and amounts. Altogether, I calculated that in the unlikely event we lost all of the suits, I could have been held liable personally for as much as $90 million, an amount somewhat larger than the funds in my checkbook. Nevertheless, the suits had to be defended, however fickle they were, and that took many hours and many dollars in legal costs. Our lawyers succeeded, case by case, in knocking out these specious actions in places as far-flung as Cleveland and New Orleans, some by lawyers using fictitious names of plaintiffs, or plaintiffs who had made no contributions, *until every one was dismissed without trial and without a dollar of liability.* The final case was not over until 1975. What a travesty!

Early in the game it had become certain to me that I had to respond to two central allegations to prove my innocence: first, that I had had no knowing part in the Watergate burglary or cover-up; and, second, that there had been no skulduggery in the handling of the campaign finances. As for Watergate, I knew, of course, that no one could say that I was involved. No one did. My confidence in being able to stand up to questions on campaign transactions had not been so strong, because thousands of people under me had been raising or spending money and could have tried to pin on me the blame for a transgression to save his or her own skin. Yet it turned out that I had nothing to fear in that respect. No one did.

Only a handful of non-willful technical violations was the surviving sum and substance of all the alleged campaign finance corruption in the 1972 Nixon campaign. *Not a single proven case of corrupt action. No favors granted. No contracts awarded. No cases fixed. No ambassadorships sold. No illegal contributions from foreigners. No overseas money laundering. No illegal solicitations. No list of companies in trouble with the government. No enemies lists. No fund-raising by government officials. No extortion or coercion. No intentional circumvention of the law in a single instance. That is precisely what the Department of Justice, the Special Prosecutor, and the courts found.*

Interestingly, while this picayune slicing of jurisprudence was taking place, the GAO found apparent violations in the financial offices of five of the other 1972 presidential candidates and many in other campaigns. The GAO referred to the attorney general more than forty such situations of illegality by Democratic presidential candidates, almost all more significant than the few misdemeanors charged against me, but not one of them was prosecuted and they were allowed to die, without attention, by the statute of limitations.

It seems strange in retrospect that so many 1972 Democratic transgressions were unpunished, especially those that were identified as major violations. The only plausible conclusion is that after the 1972 presidential race, I was singled out for prosecutorial attention, despite the peanut characteristics of the only ones they could find to assert against me. The sympathetic understanding and toleration by law enforcement officials that forgave or neglected violations by other candidate committees in 1972—because of the complexities and confusions of a new law introduced while the campaign was under way, or because they were unintentional—were not applicable to unwitting technical violations by anyone that supported Richard Nixon.

How did Watergate get so big? At first the focus of Watergate was entirely on the break-in itself. As the developing scenarios warmed up the public interest, the territory of the Watergate pursuit multiplied under the collective chase of the facts by three forces that combined, not by design but by opportunity, to build the Watergate matter to gargantuan size. They were the opposing political party, the investigative journalists, and the ambitious prosecutors, not necessarily in that order of importance.

The Democrats and liberals had generally regarded Nixon as an enemy ever since his time as a lowly congressman when he brought Alger Hiss to justice and then as his stature grew by his service in the Senate and as vice president to Eisenhower. They saw Watergate as the opportunity to get even and perhaps to destroy Nixon.

The investigative journalists found their heyday for the maturing of their profession in the obvious conflict between Nixon and his political opponents. They honed their pens on the public's eagerness to peek into the back rooms of national politics—and their own willingness to open every door, whether or not it proved fruitful and unmindful of who was damaged.

The ambitious prosecutors set about selecting possible criminal actions out of the chaos and applying freehand justice to their punishment, with the apparent and indiscriminate goal of tallying as many convictions as possible. After all, they had spent months of time and reputation, hadn't they? Human nature was at work.

Instead of exercising any control over the others, each of these three groups contributed to the increased frenzy of the situation. This is not said by way of criticism; the people involved in these three categories of participation all believed they were merely doing their job. Put in perspective, are there important lessons to be learned about Washington and about public service? What should the reader gain from my sometimes horrible and unfair experiences? And what about the full legacy of Nixon? Is Watergate all there was to his presidency?

# CHAPTER SEVENTEEN

# Reflections

While there have been many volumes written about Richard Nixon and various aspects of his presidency, his final place in history is still being studied. Will he forever remain a tragic embodiment of one political blunder, or will he be granted the memory of his good, often positive deeds on behalf of his country? Not until all his actions are evaluated and reconciled will the people have a full understanding of Nixon's contributions to the world.

As a friend and associate of his for twenty-five years, I too have had to balance the man I knew and admired against the Watergate image of Nixon. Initially, I had no idea what his role had been in the conspiracy or what it was likely to be. All information about the participants in the Watergate crimes and their relationship to each other was carefully screened from me by Dean, Haldeman, Liddy, Mitchell, and all of the other perpetrators. That data came to me slowly only from the media, but as it eventually reached the point of disclosure, it uncovered two solid facts.

The first was that Nixon had no prior knowledge of the burglary and learned about it only as it was disclosed to him in the following days by Haldeman, Dean, and others on the White House staff. There is no evidence in the record of all the subsequent disclosures that anyone ever tipped him off in advance that such an invasion of the property of the opposing political party was going to happen.

But as soon as he heard the story of the break-in, Nixon made what was probably the biggest mistake of his life. He injected himself into the planning of strategies to minimize the damage to the White House and to the reelection results. That objective originated with a broader concern of his and his staff's about how to win the election, not just by a majority but by the widest possible margin in order to bolster his power in his second term.

Nixon was a man who had adapted his political mind to looking at problems with a desire to evaluate them and their potentials over long periods of time and to develop solutions accordingly. He did not like to find short-range answers to governmental needs and have to deal with them over and over again. But in his much lauded efforts in foreign affairs, as with some domestic matters that he undertook to resolve for the country, he had often been frustrated by the Democrat-controlled Congress.

It did not take much knowledge of history for him to conclude that the same conditions would prevail in his second term if he did not win the pending election with a campaign sufficiently powerful to carry almost all the states and to bring with him a majority of at least one house of the Congress. That became his goal. His thinking on this subject permeated the White House and the campaign organization. There is not much doubt either that that led the campaign people into a series of "dirty tricks" and to the dumb actions that included breaking into the Democratic offices in the Watergate.

Observers of the Watergate era, including the citizenry, have made tentative evaluations of Richard Nixon and his career. In such debates, Watergate is often counted as a sinisterly discreditable action. Nixon himself in public statements did admit, "We blew it." Critics and enemies accept that statement as proof that history will give him its lowest possible rating. There are other sides of this picture, however, which seriously challenge the soundness of that reasoning.

How does one understand the action by Nixon in entering into cover-up strategy sessions, and how much weight should that carry in a total evaluation of his record as president? In trying to answer that question, which has been put to me many times, I have discovered the formula that dominated his action and the actions of his staff. Based upon my observations, I believe the Watergate affair was the result of an excess of loyalty in two respects. First, Nixon's staff was determined to deliver to him the largest conceivable electoral majority while also winning one or both houses of the Congress, regardless of cost. This led to the first excess by the campaign managers and experts when they went beyond the bounds of acceptable campaign strategy into illegalities. The second excess was the hastily and ill-considered participation by the president in the cover-up to protect his staff and to prevent early disclosure from costing him large numbers of votes. What he overlooked was the truism that the only successful conspiracy is one in which there is only a single conspirator. What he overlooked was that presidents should not enter self-serving conspiracies.

Through his political life theretofore and thereafter, many people meeting Nixon for the first time were surprised at his apparent nervousness and unease in greeting them and the frequently inappropriate course of his conversation. It was said he did not look people in the eyes when shaking their hands, and was diffident and uncomfortable in small groups. To me this was not hard to understand. His background in a Quaker family in a small town in southern California and his fast climb up the political ladder seemed to be inconsistent with each other and left me with the conclusion that he was an introvert who had chosen the life of an extrovert. That circumstance was enough to explain his sometimes erratic behavior under pressure and outbursts of anger (which later became public knowledge with the disclosure of his presidential taping system).

In many respects, Nixon was a man of high character. Married over fifty years to the same woman and with two devoted daughters, he proved himself to be a high-quality family man with no evidence of the well-publicized misbehavior of a number of other recent presidents. His respect for his religious background was reflected by his action in arranging Sunday church services in the White House when he was not scheduled to be out of town. Each such service had a selected religious leader from a different faith, and similarly, a chosen choir of wide reputation, and accommodated approximately four hundred invited guests.

He was well educated, intellectual, and extremely knowledgeable of subjects fitting to his life, such as history, politics, geography, world affairs, and many others. He was a long-term thinker with horizons and goals for individuals, nations, and the world, many generations ahead. He was a man who, setting aside his errors in Watergate, would rate very highly in competence, judgment, long-range planning, compassion, and determination.

Nixon's first twenty-five years or so of political life exemplified his tendency to deal with current problems with long-range challenges. He demonstrated his capabilities in the House and Senate, and in his solid backing of Eisenhower as president. His discerning ability and determination were proven during his first term in the House of Representatives, by his singlehanded pursuit of Alger Hiss for the Committee on Unamerican Activities, which resulted in trial and conviction of that high government official for purgery. In his remaining terms in the House and Senate, he was an active student and advocate in various legislative proposals, and in his eight years as vice president under Eisenhower he was a politically unobtrusive force in promoting the president's legislative concepts, resisting many suggestions that he intrude when Eisenhower's medical emergencies limited his attention to presidential duties.

He contributed much to America and the world with his long list of accomplishments, both domestic and foreign: the handling of the entry into relations with China; the encouragement of détente with the Soviet Union; the beginning of true international arms control; the negotiated ending of the Vietnam War; the creation of the Environmental Protection Agency; the initiation of the federal government's first continuing program for the benefit of minority business; the effort to establish a modern welfare plan; the elimination of the military draft, and many other achievements. Biased as I necessarily am, I still believe these heavily outweigh the single mark on his judgment for allowing the Watergate matter to develop as it did on his blind side. He also paid a high price in resigning the presidency, but saved the nation from further agony.

Among his largely unheralded accomplishments was the progress made in the reorientation of the functions of the federal government among the departments. Although they did not get as far as was recommended by the Ash commission on government reorganization, he did create a pattern for the shifting of agencies within the government that was partially accomplished in the creation of the National Oceanographic and Atmospheric Administration within Commerce and a number of lesser moves, as well as leaving behind blueprints for other similar changes that ought to have been made. In the 1990s, government is being reinvented, and Richard Nixon would understand.

His activities since his resignation should also be added to the scale of value. Few presidents in history have worked as hard as Nixon for twenty years after his retirement to present the nation and the world a visionary panorama of the international, interracial, and interhuman problems the people of the world must face and successfully resolve before we can achieve a common level of behavior toward each other that can be described as civilized.

Every one of his ten books was a bestseller and his speeches brought on waves of support for his analysis and concepts of future national policies. His announcement of the formation of a center for peace and freedom and its statement of principles, was a cumulative benefit of his unpaid efforts over a score of years and adds up to a value credit that again wipes out a very large portion of the negative significance of Watergate. It was his last meaningful public effort before his untimely death a few months later. This leaves him very far ahead on the scoreboard of history, even discounting any personal significance of my respect and devotion for him. If carried on for two full terms, Nixon's record would likely have marked him as the most constructive president of the century. There is not much doubt that among the nations of the world at the date of his death, April 22, 1994, he was almost universally recognized as the public figure most knowledgeable of international affairs. Who is there among the leaders of the nations today capable of taking Nixon's place in understanding the world?

The chief victim of Watergate was Richard Nixon, and certainly it is clear that he contributed in a major part to his own downfall. The saddest result is that, despite his twenty-year devotion to the cause of improving foreign relations, as a contribution to the future of the United States and the world, and his public service during his entire life, he is still regarded negatively by a segment of the population. The scales of justice for him are viewed from the Watergate side by his critics and inadequate credit is given to him as an offset for his outstanding values. But I don't believe this will be the final judgment of history.

Now that I am eighty-seven years old and Watergate will in a few years become twenty-five, this is the right time and place to bring this narrative up to date with the advantage of retrospection. This gives me the opportunity to say something about the total cost of an experience such as mine, which necessitated extraordinary measures to prove my innocence, and also to recount some of the Watergate aftereffects that have continued to permeate my life. Perhaps these insights will help the true course of justice in the future.

I want particularly to bring up to date my inner feelings toward the newspeople, prosecutors, and politicians who comprised the three Watergate forces that made the course so rough for me and many of its other innocent victims. For me, Watergate was certainly expensive financially. My income in Washington ceased when the work of the finance committee was concluded in June 1974, but I had to remain unemployed and unpaid for several more years to wrap up all the tangles of litigation that carried over. When that was finished, we headed for Phoenix, at Kathleen's suggestion, to spend a year in decompression. During that time, she became an artist and I wrote a book on Watergate that concentrated on the tales of the innocent victims.* Thereafter, I became a business consultant in Los Angeles, but I had a number of disappointments when I found that companies I had served as a member of their board of directors before I went to Washington had filled my place, including several who explained, "We couldn't take you on the board now, guilt by association, you know."

I kept fairly busy, but the level of my income was far below that which I would have earned had I returned from Washington without the false stain of Watergate following me like a black cloud. However, I did well enough for us to resume our earlier lifestyle in California and still engage in exploration in Africa at frequent intervals.

During this time, I felt that my first need was rebuilding my earlier reputation as a person of integrity. My initial move in that respect, however, failed badly, which I regretted, because it would have been the ideal step to clear the air. The best plan, I thought, would be to requalify my image by receiving a presidential appointment to an important post, such as an ambassadorship. That would have had the added advantage of requiring the "advice and consent" of the Senate after a public hearing. The process would have given me my first real opportunity to tell my story fully and without equivocation. Confirmation by the Senate would have been the blessing I needed to convince the public I had been falsely accused and mistreated.

It backfired and I lost ground. When Ronald Reagan took office, it offered an excellent staging for a presidential appointment, and I had strong support among his White House staff from the outset. After all, we were longtime friends and I had been helpful to his financial people in several ways in his campaign for president. My advocates specifically identified the post of ambassador to Sweden as one for which I could well qualify. I did all I could to encourage the idea, pointing out that my maternal grandmother had been born there. Within a few months I understood from the White House grapevine that Reagan concurred in the nomination and it would be made in May 1981.

---

*The Terrors of Justice (New York: Everest House, 1978).

Nothing happened then or for months after.

Finally, in October, I received a call from a White House personnel official saying simply, "The Sweden thing won't fly. There is opposition in the Senate and from Sweden. We'll give you a much smaller appointment now, and if that is confirmed without delay, we can improve on it later."

There was no argument I could present in reply. Within a week I was nominated by Reagan to be a member of the board of directors of the Overseas Public Investment Corporation (OPIC), a federal agency within the foreign aid program. This, too, would require Senate confirmation, but if the hearings were quick and routine, as was expected, I could be sworn in before January.

That was not to be. Three Democratic members of the Senate Foreign Relations Committee expressed opposition to the appointment, stating that when it came before them they would insist on a long hearing to explore fully my actions in Watergate and see what new facts might be disclosed about me or any other person.

That didn't bother me; I was prepared. But it did bother the White House and other members of the Senate when the battle lines were drawn. Two prominent Senate Democrats, Alan Cranston of California and Patrick Moynihan of New York, on the other hand, assured me of their support. At that point, the proceedings were canceled because there was not enough time left in the session for the hearings and action by the full Senate.

In effect, that bounced the nomination back to the White House to resubmit at the next session in 1982. Early in that year, Howard Baker, Republican Senate leader, assured me he had enough votes in the committee to endorse the nomination and would not thereafter expect any serious difficulty on the Senate floor. In my presence, he told that to a member of the White House staff, who said she would pass it on to the personnel office right away so the nomination would be resubmitted promptly.

Again, nothing happened. Months later I was told by a friend in close contact with the White House that it was to be delayed until after the tenth anniversary of Watergate on June 17, 1982, to avoid dragging the Reagan administration into that matter before and during the wave of publicity that would surely occur around the date. Instead, I was assured that later in the year I would receive a presidential appointment that did not require confirmation by the Senate. I waited that out, too, with no action.

Around that time, I was told by several sources that the person blocking my path was the chief presidential aide Mike Deaver, who was concerned that the president might be hurt by the outcry over any appointment for me. Deaver was right, of course. The president should not be asked to bear the brunt of defending an appointment likely to come under heavy political attack. It was my job to clear my name, not the president's. However, I regretted that Deaver had not at least been considerate enough to let me know what was going on at the time.

Late in 1988, I received a phone call from the White House assistant for personnel, who said in substance, "The president would like to appoint you his representative to Tokyo next week at funeral services for former prime minister Kishi." It wasn't Sweden, and it wasn't even OPIC, but it was surely the only nod that I could expect to receive from the Reagan organization in its remaining weeks of office, so I accepted gratefully and carried out the mission on a four-day trip. I was thankful for the small favor, but I never lost the feeling that I had earned more tangible support from the Republican party.

In 1982, as the tenth anniversary of Watergate approached, I contacted the editors or political writers of twenty major newspapers, three news magazines, and two wire services requesting an opportunity for an individual taped interview on my actions in the 1972 election campaign, in order to ensure that any of them writing on Watergate would have my side of the story and my evidence. I wanted it to be clear that what I was seeking was stated exoneration or, failing that, at least no mention of me at all as a participant in Watergate. Almost all chose the latter course and ignored me, but I had the satisfaction that very few of the old untrue statements about me seemed to be surviving. Included among those I talked with was Bob Woodward of *The Washington Post*, my early nemesis; after a pleasant breakfast at his invitation, he agreed that he was satisfied I had had no hand in the Watergate shenanigans and that I didn't even know they were going on.

When we returned to California, we carried with us a continuing concern about Kathleen's health. In 1969, on an official government visit with me to Venezuela, she had been stricken with a mysterious painful affliction and had to return to Washington alone while I continued the formal two-week trip to five other countries. Over a period of months in and out of Walter Reed Hospital, she made little progress and then in November 1972 went into a frightening decline with a disease diagnosed as idiopathic thrombocytosis, an affliction involving an overproduction of platelets in the blood, with a constant high risk of a blood clot. Medications being given her were not bringing down the platelet count, and her situation became so critical and the doctors so pessimistic that in desperation I enlisted the services of the top hematologist of the Mayo Clinic, Dr. Murray Silverstein. After only a couple of days of his immediate attention on the spot in Washington and changes in her medication, she began to recover miraculously, and in less than a month her blood was back to normal. The experience, however, left her in fragile health, although her charm and Irish zest for life didn't change. Kathleen passed away in 1984 after an invasion of her bone marrow by zillions of aggressive cancer cells. She died graciously and at peace, with no bitterness toward the political enemies who had hurt us both so much. Her passing left a great void in my life, one that I have never been able to fill.

However hard it might be to prove, I earnestly believe that Kathleen's life was considerably reduced in comfort and shortened in years by the sharing of my abrasive experiences from mid-1972 to late 1975. At no time, however, did she evince any doubt of my integrity or lack of confidence in my innocence of the horribly exhausting accusations against me. Nor did she ever ask me any questions about anything she read or heard concerning my alleged escapades. All she ever said, in response to blaring headlines or noisy radio and TV blasts was, "When will it ever end?"

Most disturbing of all the post-Watergate occurrences was an unending series of inaccurate stories written by reporters who relied on earlier accounts of that era that a modicum of research would have shown to have been discredited in the subsequent flow of news. Unfortunately, there is no worthwhile procedure in the media to assist a person harmed, intentionally or not, by repeated stories that turn out to be false, and to absolve him or her of guilt.

So I decided that I had to undertake to answer every misstatement of fact about me in the media or literature that came to my attention whenever my side of the story would likely reach the same audience. That left out any practical attempt to answer the many scurrilous books and statements already published, so I had to content myself with trying to get quick withdrawals of inaccuracies only in current publications. With the help of my close friend and attorney, Robert H. Finch, I did just that, with almost total satisfaction in each case. When errors of fact were forcefully called to their attention, the newspapers and magazines apologized graciously and said so in subsequent issues, or at least published Finch's letters of complaint and correction. About twenty-five periodicals (including the *Los Angeles Times, Atlantic Monthly, Forbes* magazine, and the *National Inquirer*) published statements repairing the damage. However, there was no way I could induce the national news services to do the same.

About six years after Watergate, for the purpose of writing about my experiences, I requested my Washington attorney to get from the National Archives copies of all the documents relating to the Watergate special prosecutor's investigations of John Connally, Bebe Rebozo, and me. When I searched them, I found that those relating to me contained many critical statements challenging my actions, *but not a single piece of the voluminous exculpatory evidence I had submitted.* I found the same to be true of the Connally and Rebozo files. No wonder many of the media's stories were often incomplete and inaccurate.

Among the events along the way was a very embarrassing experience for me in the form of a nationwide Associated Press release on December 5, 1981, concerning the announced Democratic opposition to my appointment to OPIC. It was worded as if to invite attack. Its first two paragraphs began as follows:

> Stans, who pleaded guilty to campaign law violation arising from the Watergate scandal, . . .
> Stans is believed to be the first person with a criminal record from the Watergate scandal to be named to a federal post . . .

Other provoking words followed, many with meager explanation. The content of the piece led unsurprisingly to headlines by various AP outlets that expounded on the damaging theme, such as, CONVICTED WATERGATER STANS EYED FOR REAGAN POST.

The headlines and articles were followed almost immediately by a King Features Syndicate cartoon by Marlette of the *Charlotte Observer* portraying a military squad in a battle wagon with a caricature of Ronald Reagan calling by bullhorn, "Give up, Stans. We know you're a convicted Watergate criminal. Come out with your hands up or we're coming in and appointing you to a high government position." This, too, was reprinted from border to border. The disturbing flood of venom was followed by a long list of ever more destructive editorials across the nation that elaborated upon the "get-Stans" theme: "Stans is an insult, a major Watergate figure, the only major one to escape a jail sentence" (*Progress*, Scottsdale, Ariz.); "Stans was convicted of . . . charges stemming from the gov-

ernment's investigation of the notorious Watergate offense"
(*Monitor*, Concord, N.H.); "Stans convicted in the Watergate scan-
dal . . ." (*Eagle*, Dothan, Ala.); "Stans implicated in Watergate;
stained by Watergate . . ." (*Gazette*, Alexandria, Va.).

Finch wrote to as many of the newspapers as we could identify as
having published similar material, and many of them did print his
letter of complaint about this treatment. Nevertheless, none of them
offered a kind word or a mitigating phrase in response.

Looking back at these and hundreds of similar skirmishes, I had to
conclude that my attempts to restore my good name did not seem to
have been very effective, although perhaps there was some value in
correcting the historical record and in dousing the flames of misin-
formation about me.

I kept at it. In 1992, anticipating another flurry of retrospective
Watergate tales for the twentieth anniversary, I again wrote the editors of thirty-five major news outlets a month ahead, pleading for
absolution or at least fair treatment. Again, in almost all cases, my
name was merely omitted from their accounts. Exoneration comes
hard.

Yet out of this last mailing came in one gracious gesture from *The
Washington Post*, instigated by Bob Woodward, my original tormentor
and most intensive accuser from 1972 to 1975. In a two-page spread
in its "Style" section on Sunday, June 14, 1992, under a heading,
"He's 84; He Wants His Good Name Back; Shouldn't We Give It To
Him?" was a thoughtful piece answering the question in a very positive way. It unequivocally said, "Stans . . . in three years of exhaus-
tive investigations and excruciating trials about Watergate was repeatedly found *innocent* of *any* knowing violation of *any* law . . . the
record shows he knew nothing of the conspiracies and cover-up his
money-raising underwrote, and that all of the charges against him
were false."

The invigoration I enjoyed from reading and rereading the *Post*
article and parsing out its words was sharply diminished only three
days later. On June 17, the CBS network ran a long retrospective
piece on Watergate, featuring comments by many of the guilty and
some prosecutors and bystanders. I watched it carefully, expecting
immunity, but that dream was shattered when I found myself named
in several places, in indirect and obscure ways, that might well have
left viewers believing I was one of the culprits. Mentions of me were
wholly irrelevant to the theme of the program.

Incensed, I sent a fax the next morning to Mike Wallace, the commentator on the show. Within an hour I received a telephone call from him, and in a friendly voice he said he understood my objection and would see what could be done about it. I wrote three more times suggesting actions by CBS that could balance the scales, and received repeated assurances from him in reply, but nothing ever happened. I was not surprised.

The lesson was clear: the damages of Watergate can never be undone, because careless writers and careless media will still present distorted, and even wrong, information. And there is no sure way to get a shattered reputation back.

There were some other experiences that saddened me considerably in this period. In 1970 I had caused the Stans Foundation to fund an annual Stans Award for Excellence in Federal Financial Management. My own sense of the importance of accounting and financial controls in management was grossly violated by the knowledge that, twenty years after Congress passed a law in 1950 providing that all the accounting systems of the government had to be approved by the GAO, not a single department or major independent agency had yet qualified. Even though the award had little monetary significance, I hoped that the recognition and respect it would carry would motivate government personnel to vie for it. The responsibility for selection of the recipient was in the hands of a committee consisting of the secretary of the Treasury, the comptroller general, and the director of the Bureau of the Budget.

When my name became regularly associated with Watergate, the award was suspended for a while. Then, after a few years' wait, and without advance notice to me, the remaining endowment money was returned to the Stans Foundation, the committee disbanded, and the award came to an end. Another blow.

There have been other frustrating disappointments. Some of my friends several times nominated me for a Horatio Alger award, only to have it rejected out of hand on Watergate grounds before it even reached the selection committee for consideration. It was an honor I would have cherished highly because of my debt to the principles of the Alger stories that I read so avidly in my early teens.

Also, I was informally nominated at the instigation of some Belgian officials to meet with King Baudouin in Belgium and receive the honors of the Belgian government. The citation was for my having held two of the highest positions in the United States government ever occupied by a person of Belgian descent. It was a recognition I would have received with high gratification and pride, and I so told the Belgian ambassador in Washington when he met with me to discuss the date and arrangements. It did not happen, without explanation, and I can only assume that I was disqualified because of unfavorable and untrue outdated Watergate clippings in someone's files here or in Belgium, without giving me an opportunity to set the record straight.

But there were a few incidents that constituted cheerful recognition by organizations able to act upon solid information about my integrity. In 1982 I was awarded an honorary LLD degree by National University of San Diego, and in 1983 I received the same degree from Pepperdine University in Los Angeles.

In 1984, after considerable urging by friends of Nixon, and some by Nixon himself, I consented to take on the job of raising $27.5 million to build his presidential library. I knew it would be difficult, but he convinced me by using the most persuasive weapon, flattery: "Maury, you're the only person in the country who can do it. Without you, there'll be no Nixon Library." My ego told me he was right; there was some support for the conviction in the fact that I had previously directed the raising of over $100 million as his finance chairman in one California and two national campaigns. The Nixon Library and Birthplace was subsequently completed and is open to the public in his hometown in Yorba Linda, California.

It had to be largely a one-man job, in which I would be phoning or seeing each of the prospects personally and soliciting them to make contributions comparable in size to their past relationships with Nixon and their continuing respect and devotion to him. I did it just that way, and it took most of my time for the next four years.

A special task I undertook in 1990 for the Eisenhower World Affairs Institute was one that gave me an opportunity to evince my high esteem for President Eisenhower, grown out of the eight years I had spent in his administration, and in particular measure the rapport that we had during the three years of that period when I served as his director of the Bureau of the Budget.

Organized in 1983, the institute's objective was to educate Americans on Eisenhower's principles of government and his qualities of leadership in public affairs and thereby to strengthen our democratic institutions. Upon nomination by Susan Eisenhower, I joined its board of directors in 1988. In 1990, following an extensive, nationwide celebration of Eisenhower's hundredth birthday, a disagreement arose among the institute's directors as to whether or not the conclusion of that event would be a suitable time for the termination of the organization. To resolve the question, the board named me chairman of a special committee to consider alternatives. Within thirty days, and after several meetings, my committee recommended that the institute affiliate with Gettysburg University and continue in its work along mutually agreed lines. That action was approved by the boards of both institutions and carried out by May 1991. Concurrently, I was elected chairman of the board of the institute.

My story condenses the struggles of a man trying to redeem the moral principles of his life after they had been crushed in the melee following Watergate.

I spent some of my spare time and committed some of the funds of the Stans Foundation to a joint project with the Scott County Historical Society in my hometown of Shakopee, Minnesota, to the building of a historical museum immediately adjacent to our family homestead and park. It was dedicated to the youth of the county in the hope that my goals, successes, and travails would provide valuable lessons from one who had gone before.

After all these years of retrospection, I need to summarize my feelings toward the three external powers that ballooned the size of Watergate and entangles many victims' lives in its wake. I have few ill feelings toward the media for its exaggerated and often untrue statements about me, or toward the calculated and untrue political attacks by opposing politicians, or toward the overeager prosecutors who pursued me so diligently. I'm satisfied with the thought that they all did what they were conditioned to do by education and training and that the fast-paced nature of their professions pushed many of them into unreasoning excesses. It remains unfortunate, however, that this may be the price one pays in public service.

There have been and will be other "Watergates" of various sizes in the future. Here is my plea to the media to consider when such things happen. The harm the media can inflict on the reputations of innocent people should be balanced by uniform reporting procedures. The injuries done, especially when they occur over a period of time, should be remedied, as soon as they are evident, by a full retrospective presentation of absolving information. This would be an appropriate demonstration of fair play and ethical treatment.

As for my own future:

Through several deliberate measures I have managed to pass without too many untoward incidents into old age, although I prefer the recently rephrased and more euphonious expression of being "chronologically gifted." I have never forgotten that as a twelve-year-old boy in Shakopee, I resolved that I would live to ninety-six to collect on my $1,000 insurance policy; when that happens I'll invest it in medical coverage and change my goal to a hundred.

Finally, looking ahead, I am sustained by my longtime belief that life is a grand adventure made up of thousands of subadventures, some pleasant and some not. What one must do is dismiss the unpleasant without concern and savor to the fullest the happy events. This philosophy has supported me through some very difficult times and helped me enjoy the good ones. I strongly recommend it to my readers.

# Index